"Perhaps the theoretically-richest and conceptually-clearest examination of de facto states yet written. Klich's book is also based on extensive fieldwork in his novel and interesting case study selection of Iraqi Kurdistan, Nagorno-Karabakh and Somaliland. A fresh, original and insightful contribution to de facto state studies."

Scott Pegg, *Department of Political Science, Indiana University Purdue University Indianapolis, USA; and author of* International Society and the De Facto State.

"Our understanding of the place of de facto states in the international system is usually framed in terms of international law and high politics. In this book, Klich goes beyond this. He argues that there are fundamental normative issues at play. Informed by three excellent case studies, this is a valuable and thought-provoking addition to the literature on de facto states."

James Ker-Lindsay, *London School of Economics and Political Science, UK.*

De Facto State Identity and International Legitimation

Examining the state identity formation and international legitimation of de facto states, this book provides a deeper understanding of the relationship between de facto states, the international state system and international society.

The book integrates International Relations theories to construct a framework of normative standing for de facto states in order to better understand the social system they inhabit and the stasis in their relationship with international society, which is demonstrated through detailed case study analysis. Klich appraises the recognition narrative of de facto states in order to analyse their state identities, and constructs a framework for normative standing in an original synthesis of English School, constructivism and legitimacy scholarship. The explanatory utility of that framework is then applied and analysed through detailed fieldwork conducted across an original set of case studies – Nagorno Karabakh, Somaliland and the Kurdistan Region of Iraq – that have varying degrees of international engagement and parent-state relationships.

It will be of interest to scholars and students of International Relations, International Relations Theory, Peace and Conflict Studies, Comparative Politics, as well as Middle Eastern Studies, East African Studies and Post-Soviet Studies.

Sebastian Klich holds a PhD in Political Science and International Relations from the Australian National University (ANU) in Canberra. He is an alumnus and research affiliate of the ANU's Centre for Arab and Islamic Studies, specialising in de facto states, International Relations Theory and the politics of the Middle East. Sebastian also works as a political and corporate strategy consultant in the not-for-profit and private sectors.

Routledge Advances in International Relations and Global Politics

Social Media Impacts on Conflict and Democracy
The Techtonic Shift
Edited by Lisa Schirch

Changing Arms Control Norms in International Society
Kenki Adachi

The Frontiers of Public Diplomacy
Hegemony, Morality and Power in the International Sphere
Colin R. Alexander

Security and Safety in the Era of Global Risks
Edited by Radomir Compel and Rosalie Arcala Hall

Laws of Politics
Their Operations in Democracies and Dictatorships
Alfred G. Cuzán

Climate Change and Biodiversity Governance in the Amazon
At the Edge of Ecological Collapse?
Joana Castro Pereira and Eduardo Viola

Mega-regionalism and Great Power Geo-economic Competition
Xianbai Ji

De Facto State Identity and International Legitimation
Sebastian Klich

For information about the series: https://www.routledge.com/Routledge-Advances-in-International-Relations-and-Global-Politics/book-series/IRGP

De Facto State Identity and International Legitimation

Sebastian Klich

LONDON AND NEW YORK

First published 2022
by Routledge
2 Park Square, Milton Park, Abingdon, Oxon OX14 4RN

and by Routledge
605 Third Avenue, New York, NY 10158

Routledge is an imprint of the Taylor & Francis Group, an informa business

© 2022 Sebastian Klich

The right of Sebastian Klich to be identified as author of this work has been asserted by him in accordance with sections 77 and 78 of the Copyright, Designs and Patents Act 1988.

All rights reserved. No part of this book may be reprinted or reproduced or utilised in any form or by any electronic, mechanical, or other means, now known or hereafter invented, including photocopying and recording, or in any information storage or retrieval system, without permission in writing from the publishers.

Trademark notice: Product or corporate names may be trademarks or registered trademarks, and are used only for identification and explanation without intent to infringe.

British Library Cataloguing-in-Publication Data
A catalogue record for this book is available from the British Library

Library of Congress Cataloging-in-Publication Data
A catalog record has been requested for this book

ISBN: 978-1-032-01414-2 (hbk)
ISBN: 978-1-032-01415-9 (pbk)
ISBN: 978-1-003-17852-1 (ebk)

DOI: 10.4324/9781003178521

Typeset in Times New Roman
by Taylor & Francis Books

Contents

Acknowledgements		viii
	Introduction	1
1	De Facto States and the International System	20
2	International Legitimacy and the Normative Standing of De Facto States	49
3	The Nagorno Karabakh Republic	78
4	The Republic of Somaliland	113
5	The Kurdistan Region of Iraq	142
	Conclusion	175
Index		184

Acknowledgements

This book grew out of my doctoral research at the Centre for Arab and Islamic Studies at the Australian National University. I am grateful for the institutional support provided and the vibrant intellectual environment which greatly stimulated my growth as an aspiring scholar.

I owe an unrepayable debt to my two supervisors. Matthew Gray's resolute support, often irrespective of time and physical location, has been invaluable. His belief in me and the research project were humbling, and I am a far stronger scholar for his judicious, incisive guidance. Kirill Nourzhanov has been a thoughtful and stalwart bastion of scholarly standards with humour and grace in the collegial den.

I am greatly indebted to several other distinguished academics, who provided key advice and guidance at crucial stages. Nina Caspersen, Jacinta O'Hagan and Mathew Davies were generous with their time and challenging with their insights, providing me with valued feedback along the journey of research development. I am grateful to Scott Pegg and James Ker-Lindsay for their rigorous examination, comprehensive and thoughtful feedback, and supportive encouragement, which helped me to sculpt the research into a book. I would also like to thank the anonymous reviewers, as well as Robert Sorsby, Claire Maloney, and the team at Routledge for their confidence and support.

My sincere gratitude goes to all my formal interviewees and to many other individuals in Nagorno Karabakh, Somaliland and Kurdistan who selflessly contributed their time and expertise to help this research (some in challenging circumstances) and made me welcome in their countries. I am especially grateful to Armine Alexanyan, Nanar Alexanyan, Saro Saryan, Nafisa Yusuf, Mohammed Rafiq, and Omar (never have I been so glad that I jumped into a stranger's car). I hope you feel that I have tried to do scholarly justice in difficult terrains with honesty, fairness and cultural respect. I am also grateful for the guidance and rich debate with the many practitioners whom I was fortunate enough to engage with on the ground and who chose to remain unnamed.

A special thank you goes out to Raihan Ismail, April Biccum, and Jessie Moritz at ANU, who provided friendship and encouragement, occasional sanity checks and reliable reference points for scholarly values when it really mattered. I would also like to pay tribute to the work and support of Jacky

Sutton, fellow student, whose untimely and tragic death deprived us all of a valued colleague and friend at the Centre. Jacky's presence and assistance in facilitating meetings in Kurdistan, her willingness to share her knowledge and her concern for my personal safety will always be remembered.

My family's support has been unwavering. My parents instilled a love of learning and a passion for thought and creative work from the cradle; my two sisters, Rosie and Jess, illustrate the fact that families exist to ensure you never take yourself too seriously; and their love has been my constant.

I sincerely thank Alix Biggs for reminding me of the importance of staying true to what we set out to achieve. She was a welcome force of purpose and direction that contributed to bringing this work to fruition, and she continues to inspire me.

My research and living costs while undertaking the research were covered by an Australian Postgraduate Award. I also received other grants for fieldwork and travel from the Australian National University, and I consider myself fortunate to have studied there.

Finally, I cannot express how lucky I am to have Andrea by my side. Her undying support and endless patience never cease to amaze me. I thank her for coming on our lifelong adventure.

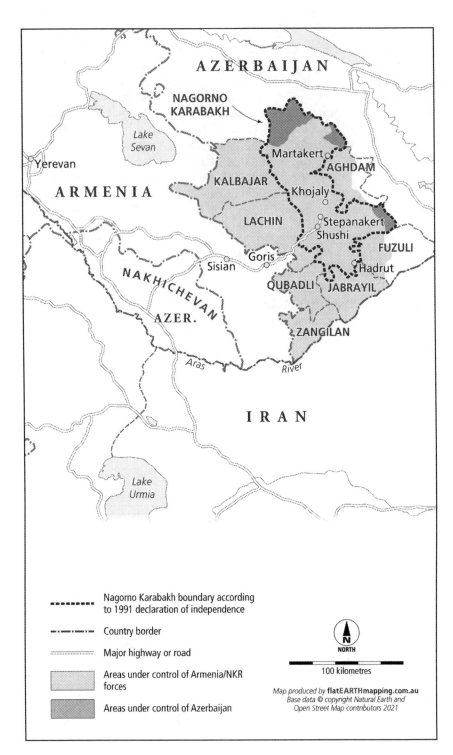

Map 1

Map 2

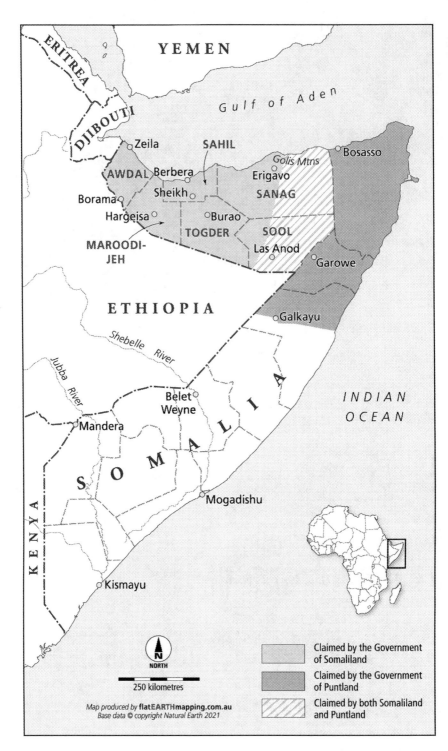

Map 3

Map 4

Introduction

The Perceived Limbo of De Facto Statehood

Notions of nations and states interspersed with concepts of language, culture, race, religion, heritage, identity and allegiance create an intricate kaleidoscope of international relations. A stable state is often considered prerequisite for individual security and economic prosperity, yet across the globe today myriads of people live in states of uncertain status with precarious safety, erratic economies and capricious futures.

At an abstract level, the idea of self-determination may conjure up images of tribes and clans putting aside local differences for a common cause, communities coalescing into distinguishable regions or a populace choosing to proclaim its distinct identity and demarcate its homelands for control, protection and self-governance. In reality, territories have leaders who may seek greater economic advantage and access to valuable resources or religious domination or regional supremacy: boundaries may be disputed; disagreements produce war, invasion, annexation and long-lasting memories of perceived historical injustice. Borders may be redrawn or removed by triumphant victors, nations may disappear, federations of states may disaggregate or reform, and even genocide has tragically been attempted on various occasions to systematically eliminate ethnic differences.

In the midst of such enduring turmoil and the remnants of past discord, the remaining larger and more powerful polities have tried to construct and maintain a system based on formal recognition that strives to provide and protect an agreed international order. Formal recognition may indeed bring membership and a seat at the table of the United Nations. But what of those who have not gained such formal international accreditation or 'club membership', those who argue they are self-governing in defined territories that others do not acknowledge, those who may perceive as enduring what others consider to be, or prefer to be seen as, merely transient?

These are the de facto states: political and territorial entities that are unmistakeable in practice but are not accepted by international society. They aspire to statehood and may have a long history of struggle in support of that goal. They may have evident symbolic bodies and structures, but beyond their likely contentious borders they are officially deemed unofficial, unauthorised,

DOI: 10.4324/9781003178521-1

unsanctioned. Yet they continue to exist. States of uncertainty have become part of the status quo.

The survival and resilience of de facto states in the post-Cold War era has defied initial scholarly predictions that these territorially defined entities seeking external verification and recognition of their political independence and legal protection were destined for a transitory existence. The suggestion that a condition of sustainable non-recognition would become the norm for these state-like entities was at first a unique perspective that eventually drew wider support from de facto state scholars.[1] We are now drawing closer to a consensus that a stasis has formed. But why and how?

In the de facto states literature, rational choice approaches have dominated the analysis of de facto states' international engagement. The nuances of state identity and how it shapes the relationship with international society have yet to be examined in full.[2] Recent moves towards examining the legitimation of de facto states pose a compelling opportunity for such an exploration. However, to date such an opportunity has been restricted by an under-conceptualisation of the social system that de facto states inhabit, limiting the explanatory utility of legitimacy as an analytical tool. Legitimacy is seemingly ambiguous and indisputably complex when conceptualised in a domestic political context; applying it to the anarchic arena of international politics makes it yet more complicated still. But within that inherent complexity, there is powerful explanatory utility that is well placed to support the articulation of a deeper, richer understanding of the relationship between an exclusive society and those deemed unfit to join.

Rather than an anomaly or an aberration, non-recognition in the relationship between de facto states and international society has become almost a standardised form of existence in an indeterminate limbo: the state of non-recognition has proven to be enduring and endurable. Early studies focused heavily on de facto states' foreign relations, an approach complemented by a subsequent turn in later years to examine the intricacies of domestic dynamics, significantly advancing our understanding. Throughout this investigative journey, the utilisation of International Relations Theory has been focused primarily on challenging notions of statehood and sovereignty, with light forays of critique aimed at the notion of international society. There is an under-conceptualisation of the specific relationship between de facto states and international society, undeserving of a phenomenon that continues to challenge central concepts in the discipline of International Relations. This book attempts to address that conceptual need and synthesises constructivist and English School approaches to build a conceptual framework that enables a clearer articulation of the relationship between de facto states and the international society they seek to join.

Our Current Understanding

In the field of International Relations, de facto states were for a long time a relatively understudied phenomenon. Recently, however, it has gained increasing scholarly attention.[3] Following the release of Scott Pegg's watershed 1998 book, *International Society and the De Facto State*,[4] a distinct literature emerged, much of which offers insights using the analytical lenses of identity politics,[5] conflict resolution[6] and comparative politics.[7] The post-Cold War context has also seen the post-Soviet de facto states studied in isolation as a specific regional phenomenon.[8] Comprehensive texts, such as those of Pegg, Kingston and Spears, Tozun Bahcheli et al., Deon Geldenhuys, Dov Lynch and Nina Caspersen, provide valuable case study analyses drawing on original empirical research that has developed a deeper understanding of the commonalities and differences between the varying unrecognised state-like entities that exist in the post-Cold War international arena.[9]

The persistence of de facto states has elicited scholarly curiosity about the strength of their state institutions and governing apparatuses.[10] Where Charles Fairbanks once described de facto states as "the weakest of the weak",[11] and Pål Kolstø claimed that they were condemned, at best, to "transmute into recognized quasi-states" lacking internal authority and functionality",[12] Freedom House ratings have at times considered Northern Cyprus and Taiwan to be "free", while Nagorno Karabakh, Abkhazia, and Somaliland have all been considered as "partly free".[13]

There has been a growth of studies examining the processes of state-building and internal legitimacy construction in territorially defined, politically autonomous, unrecognised entities, inspiring more nuanced and inclusive models of statehood. Caspersen even claims that "unrecognized statehood can be seen as a new form of statehood".[14] For as long as standards of desirable statehood have continued to change, excluded entities have existed: historically, the system has "lived with them".[15] Such an existence leads to a qualitatively different form of state, one that is stuck between the existential need to secure enabling forms of external support to maintain its de facto independence and the need to effectively govern the people who legitimise its status and who will inevitably be unsatisfied so long as their country's sovereignty is denied recognition.[16] The innovative forms of state-building that this condition has given rise to comprise one of the most insightful developments in the de facto states literature, uncovering beacons of success and relative stability in places previously referred to as "pirate states".[17] These unique forms of state-building have challenged the conventional, indivisible view of sovereignty, yet at the same time have struggled with the centrality of it as an integral organisational unit of international society.

The resilience shown by de facto states has inspired an important focus in the literature on their external relations.[18] Following his comprehensive analysis of de facto state-parent state relations,[19] James Ker-Lindsay rigorously details the "spectrum of activity" that para-diplomatic relations of unrecognised entities can take, shedding light on the importance of intent, implication and appearance in his analysis of bilateral and multilateral engagement.[20] The dynamics of "engagement without recognition"[21] have been an insightful research agenda, deepened by analysis of recognised states pursuing their

4 Introduction

national interests without contravening international norms;[22] the spectrum of stigmatisation of de facto states by the international community and how it influences the degree of engagement that can be achieved;[23] how different de facto and parent states view and try to instrumentalise engagement;[24] and how the pursuit of de facto state foreign policy varies in light of patron state relationships and the perceived antipathy of the international community.[25] Meanwhile, Caspersen has built on the existing thread in the literature that focusses on the "recognition game" that de facto states play in their quest for sovereignty.[26] Caspersen has mapped various potential recognition-seeking strategies, providing a timely contribution that distils the dynamics of recognition seeking and international engagement in the aftermath of the partial recognition of Kosovo. Analysis of de facto states' external relations has thus been empirically robust, insightful and especially valuable for policy practitioners. However, there has been a dominance of rational choice approaches that analyse international engagement as a fixed interest. Conceptualising the social system de facto states inhabit, how it interacts with the society they are excluded from, and how this situation in turn shapes identity and interest is still at an embryonic stage.

The Opportunity for Deeper Theorising

Scott Pegg was an insightful and prescient pioneer of the de facto state literature. His book *International Society and the De Facto State* gives a detailed overview of the relationship of the de facto state according to international law, and, as the title suggests, begins to define the de facto state by its status as an autonomous entity excluded from international society.[27] Pegg provides illuminating coverage of the challenges that non-recognition presents, laying down a crucial foundation upon which most of the following analyses have been built, and drawing much-needed focus to the anomalies of the international system that challenge the assumption that "the surface of the earth is portioned into territorially differentiated independent countries".[28] Pegg establishes a strict, highly detailed definition of the de facto state that he claims was not supposed to "serve as a definitive statement on the subject" but instead serve as "a starting point", stating that "future scholars following on from it will seek to add to, modify or challenge its various premises".[29] Pegg's definition has served as a launch pad for continuous debate about how to conceive of, and define, state-like entities that lack international recognition.

The comprehensive scope of Pegg's impressive landmark text, however, limits the depth of his analysis in some areas. Pegg grounds his enquiry in the theoretical framework of the English School; however, there is a theoretical lacuna in his conception of the international system and international society. Pegg provides a clear definition of international society, drawing on Terry Nardin, Hedley Bull and Thomas Franck to define it as a "society of states" that is "a practical association with the mutual recognition of sovereignty as its foundation" and that "is based not on shared goals or purposes, but on a set of minimal rules that allow each state to pursue its own particular aims, subject only to mutually reciprocal constraints on how those aims may legitimately be pursued".[30] This is a compelling and widely accepted definition of international society, which clearly locates the de facto state as the excluded entity. However, Pegg does not accompany it with a clear definition of what constitutes the international state system that he frequently refers to. At times, Pegg even appears to conflate the two, claiming that the "entire states-system is premised upon this mutual recognition of sovereignty"[31] and referring to "how the members of the states-system choose to deal (or not deal) with specific *de facto* states".[32] His seventh chapter is even titled "The *De Facto* State in International Society".[33] The lack of a clear definition leads to a resultant ambiguity in which Pegg conceives of a social structure that de facto states are excluded from, but without simultaneously conceptualising the social structure that they inhabit.

Where Pegg was the early pioneer, Nina Caspersen has become a more recent authority. Caspersen's coruscating book *Unrecognized States: The Struggle for Sovereignty in the Modern International System* delivers one of the major theoretically insightful examinations of how the existence and resilience of de facto states influences conceptions of statehood and sovereignty. Investigating major themes relevant to better understanding what she terms 'unrecognised states', Caspersen's detailed analysis draws on her extensive fieldwork in the Balkans and the Caucasus and combines it with a deep knowledge of other de facto entities. Caspersen's analysis provides a valuable excursus on how state-like entities inform notions of statehood and sovereignty; the major challenges besetting unrecognised states; possible trajectories for unrecognised states; and the process of state-building in a condition of non-recognition. *Unrecognized States* has significantly furthered the research agenda; however, although this penetrating examination of the relationship between internal state-building and the external condition of de facto states has helped to conceptualise statehood with greater accuracy and with attention to its varying forms, the precise details of the social system of which de facto states are a part are still vague, and the structural effects are mostly confined to the logistical challenges that they face. Furthermore, following a trend that pervades the literature, the relationship between de facto states and international society is conceived of through a lens of instrumental rationality; the nuances of normativity are glossed over, and state identity is equated with state interest.

Nina Caspersen and Gareth Stansfield's edited volume, *Unrecognized States in the International System*, seeks to shift the focus away from empirical case-study analysis and towards theorising unrecognised states.[34] One of the most valuable contributions of this book is its compilation of a series of perspectives that reframe the emphasis, treating de facto states as "if not more 'regular' features of the international system, at least ones of a more perennial rather than anomalous nature".[35] As this quote reveals, the de facto state is construed as existing within an international state system alongside recognised states but without clearly demarcating the concepts of system and society, as demonstrated by the opening line of James Harvey and Gareth Stansfield's chapter: "Unrecognised states are anomalous features of the international system and international society".[36] Harvey and Stansfield, and Closson, make important contributions that extend our understanding of the complexities of sovereignty and how de facto states inform this conceptual quagmire. Matan Chorev, Kledja Mulaj and Francis Owtram all provide original analyses of the external relations of de facto states, respectively focusing on their relationship with globalisation, the role of the international community in creating these entities, and their foreign policy goals.[37] These are substantial developments in the breadth and direction of de facto states literature, embracing the need and expected utility of greater theoretical engagement. Even so, the systems-level structural effects that condition the perception and identity of de facto states are still to be elucidated. That theoretical vacuity is where this book intends to enrich our understanding by establishing a clear delineation between the international system and international society that locates the de facto state, establishing a framework within which the relationship with their social constituency and its normative fabric can be examined.

The core purpose of this book is to build on the work of other scholars to propose a framework for considering the normative standing of de facto states, a framework built on a deeper understanding of their relationship with international society and that clearly articulates the social system that they inhabit, not just the society they are excluded from. This is illustrated with the findings of three case studies of de facto states in which this framework is applied and examined. It is a concerted attempt to enrich the de facto state literature with the power of deeper theoretical engagement whilst bridging empirical approaches to ensure its practical utility.

Approach and Methodology

The question driving this research agenda is: how does de facto state identity contribute to the stasis of the relationship with international society? Put simply, why has the relationship between international society and de facto states in the post-Cold War era remained essentially constant and relatively stable? The under-conceptualisation of the relationship between de facto states and international society requires a consequent research question to be answered first: how can the relationship between de facto states and international society be conceptualised to account for the international legitimation of de facto states?

An accurate articulation of this relationship must be able to account for the normative and political components of this relationship. The right to self-determination and the recognition of sovereignty have historically intertwined normative and political dynamics: who *ought* to be a member of international society is an inherently normative question; however, the process of sovereignty recognition has proven to be a heated political contest.

De Facto State Identity and International Legitimation 7

To refer to 'stasis' in the relationship between de facto states and international society is not to imply that the risk of forced reintegration or disintegration is no longer in play. In the case of de facto states, resilience is not strength; they are surviving, not thriving. This reality was demonstrated loud and clear for Nagorno Karabakh in 2020, when, in the Second Karabakh War, Azerbaijan regained control of swathes of land including the critically strategic town of Shushi, which is in a powerful position of elevation above the capital of Stepanakert. Had the ensuing ceasefire not been signed and adhered to, the entire territory may well have fallen to Azerbaijan and Nagorno Karabakh might have no longer existed in the form of a de facto state. Even as part of the status quo, the reality of non-recognition is as harsh and confronting as ever.

A Note on Terminology

This book argues that these territorially autonomous entities are part of the international state system but are excluded from international society. While the terms 'de facto state', 'unrecognised state', 'quasi-state', and 'contested state' have all been used to refer to this corporate apparatus, I choose to employ the term 'de facto state' to focus on what the entity has achieved, rather than on what it is being denied. This decision was made after answering the consequent research question, clearly articulating the social system that the de facto state inhabits and delineating the society from which it is excluded. The term 'international society' will be used to refer specifically to international society as it is defined in Chapters One and Two. The term 'international community' or 'members of the international community' will be used to refer to the recognised states that have legitimate membership in international society. As will become apparent in the following theoretical chapters, the two terms are not interchangeable; international society refers to a specific social structure that is constituted by the existence of certain norms, rules and institutions.

'Nagorno Karabakh' will be used to refer to what is otherwise called 'Nagorno-Karabakh', 'Nagorny Karabakh', or 'Artsakh'. The 'Nagorno Karabakh Republic' (NKR) will be used interchangeably with 'Nagorno Karabakh' to refer to the de facto state in the period following its declaration of independence. The same logic of usage will be applied to 'Somaliland' and the 'Republic of Somaliland'. I aim not to try and preference one side's interpretation over the other's. I am instead using commonly understood or widely accepted terms in English. In the case of Nagorno Karabakh, I use the place names used by the de facto state's representatives when I conducted my fieldwork. This project focusses on each de facto state's recognition narrative; therefore, it is logical to utilise the language used by each entity. It is not expressing support for either side or taking a position on the most accurate terminology when discussing the conflict. The 'Kurdistan Region of Iraq' (KRI) will be used to refer to the de facto state,

8 *Introduction*

distinctive from the 'Kurdistan Regional Government' (KRG), which refers specifically to the government of the de facto state.

In the case of Somali orthography, I decided to follow the lead shown in the works of Ioan Lewis, who, in his various books on the Somali experience, chose to follow standard Somali usage without indicating long vowels or the Arabic letter *ayn*, which is written as 'c' in popular Somali script. The stated rationale, applicable and preferred in this case, is that this "avoids unnecessary linguistic puzzles" and makes text readily accessible to both English and Somali speakers because it does not distort the spoken sound for English-speaking readers and is easily pronounced and understood in context by Somali speakers.[38]

Why These Case Studies?

This book heeds the call for innovative case study selection.[39] The case studies selected to examine the conceptual framework proposed are the KRI, Nagorno Karabakh, and Somaliland. Nagorno Karabakh and Somaliland have been previously described as de facto states; however, since the KRI became a federated region of Iraq in 2005 it has not featured in the literature as frequently as, for example, the post-Soviet states of Abkhazia or South Ossetia.[40] Although it is legally a region of Iraq, the powers that the KRI holds according to the Iraqi Constitution give it the same corporate body, territorial authority and social capacities of a de facto state. By focussing on the social attributes common to three contrasting state apparatuses – one of which is a federated region – the characteristics of statehood that qualify social entities to operate in a state-like manner will be clearly delineated from the juridical status that currently defines them.

The main independent variable that was used in the case study selection was the parent state relationship. A parent state refers to the recognised sovereign state that a de facto state is trying to secede from. The parent state relationship has been considered as the most influential factor in enabling the conduct of de facto states in the international system. In order to understand the structural conditioning of de facto states, it is therefore logical to choose three case studies that have different degrees of enablement through their respective parent state relationships. A patron state is a more powerful, internationally recognised state that provides resources, security and economic lifelines that help to sustain some de facto states. I recognise the important role that, for some de facto states, patron states play in providing protection and access to resources. Turkey's provision for Northern Cyprus and Russia's provision for Abkhazia and Transdniestria are illustrative examples. However, the parent state relationship plays a greater role in influencing the access to international engagement with members of the formally recognised international society; hence, I have chosen it as the most influential criterion for selection.[41]

In the spectrum of de facto states, Nagorno Karabakh is one of the least enabled. For the majority of its existence since the ceasefire in 1994, it has been in a state of 'no peace, no war' with the parent state of Azerbaijan. Somaliland has managed a higher degree of international engagement, which has been driven in large part because its parent state is the failed state of Somalia. The KRI has one of the highest degrees of international engagement, stemming from the unique status of a federated region of Iraq that it has managed to utilise to great effect.[42] Choosing case studies that have varying degrees of international engagement, whether or not they are enabled or disabled by their parent states, allows one's research findings to be more generalisable.

There are further benefits from this unique comparison of case studies. The relationship between legitimacy and legality is not only important to understanding legitimacy in the abstract, it is also a crucial consideration for theorising the conceptual space that de facto states occupy; recognition provides legal protections and rights under international law. The legal frameworks that encompass the varying legal positions of de facto states have therefore also shaped my choice of case studies. The KRI is currently a legally federated region, a point that for some means it should not be considered a de facto state. In Chapter One, I justify in depth why it should be considered such. Somaliland currently has no international recognition, but it was a recognised state in 1960, and this historical precedent is the foundation of its claim to statehood. Nagorno Karabakh has never received international recognition.

Methodology

The question at the heart of this project addresses the recognition narrative and systems-level identity of de facto states as agents, and the social conditioning that exists within their social structure. As such, the project needs a methodology that bridges agency and structure without giving ontological priority to either. Vincent Pouliot's sobjectivism was therefore employed. This methodology best suits the question that this project is trying to answer because it spans agency and structure, captures the subjective understanding held by agents, objectifies these meanings in their structural context and provides the tools to explain the evolution of these meanings.

Sobjectivism is based on three processes. The first process is capturing the subjective meaning of social agents through inductive technique. Theorisation imposes preconceived categories and meanings on the reality as it is understood by the agents being studied; therefore, an inductive methodology is required to accurately capture the subjective meanings. The second process is to objectify these meanings in their intersubjective context through techniques such as archival research and secondary research. This involves adopting an interpretive approach, which is necessary because intersubjective meanings require interpretation to develop understanding. As Pouliot, following Clifford Geertz,[43] points out, "a twitch is not a wink",[44] which is a difference that is entirely social and based on intersubjective understanding. The last process

10 Introduction

is explaining the evolution of these meanings through historicisation, which is crucial because meanings are never fixed or static: they evolve over time. Process and sequence are imperative because social life is inherently temporal. No social realities are natural; they are the result of political and social processes, which is why historicisation must be employed. Narrative construction, a fundamental form of historicisation, will therefore be foundational to my case study analyses. The formation and evolution of each entity's recognition narrative is critical to understanding their systems-level identity, warranting a substantial excursus on the state-formation periods for each empirical chapter. Historical determinants of de facto state formation have previously been documented, but the focus here is on understanding how the formation of each entity has shaped its identity, its legitimation, and what this in turn reveals about its stasis with international society.

To effectively and accurately conduct constitutive analysis of de facto state identity, this project heeds the institutionalist suggestion that actors are influenced by their institutional context in both preference generation and preference change. Sobjectivism is built on a constructivist "style of reasoning",[45] specifically constructivism informed by a post-foundationalist metatheory based on three tenets: knowledge is socially constructed; social reality is constructed; and knowledge and reality are mutually constitutive.[46] The metatheoretical grounding is important because this reveals that sobjectivism shares the same ontological assumptions as constructivist institutionalism, a logical foundation for adopting this institutional framework. Furthermore, historical institutionalism is inadequate for theorising change and sociological institutionalism puts too great an emphasis on structure over agency.

The notion of state agency that underpins the present research is developed at length in Chapter One. To outline the importance of why government individuals have been one of the main interview sources, a summary of the notion of state agency as used is requisite. I accept Alexander Wendt's notion of state agency as being constituted by the commitment of a state's individual members to acting on behalf of the state's collective beliefs, giving states their causal powers.[47] It is important to note that they only have to be committed to acting on behalf of a collective belief. By this logic, a statement made by an official representative of the state can evidence a self-understanding, because as a representative of the state they are employed to represent that state's collective beliefs. As such, interviews with de facto state representatives have formed the basis of much of my initial case-study research. I also examined diplomatic statements in press releases, press conferences, and official speeches, all of which were potential sources of the de facto state's subjective perspective. It is important to make clear at the outset that the central goal of this research is not to uncover radically new information about each of these case studies. Rather, it is to inform the development of a new framework to better understand their relationship with international society.

It must also be acknowledged at the outset that de facto states' ongoing desire to prove their statehood, and often their democratic credentials, means that official documents tend to overstate the governments' ability to make their case. This has not affected the accuracy of the research, because the aim is to discern why these autonomous political entities think that their claims will be deemed legitimate by international society. Therefore, the accuracy of the data (for example, any claims made) is not paramount; it is the concepts and qualities that de facto states are emphasising and how they are emphasising them that are the central concerns.

The interviews cited in this research include interviews with foreign diplomats representing several different states in the KRI. The term 'senior diplomat' is used in citations to describe a diplomatic official of high rank, with ten or more years of experience in representing their country. This clarification is required because some of the diplomats agreed to be interviewed on condition that their name and the name of the country they represent will be excluded from publication.

A Practicable Scope

This book is centred on de facto states' recognition narratives, and seeks to understand the components of state identity that are relevant to those narratives as a means of establishing a comprehensive understanding of the relationship between de facto states and international society. Bringing a theoretically rich approach to the study of de facto states, illustrated with empirical case studies, requires a scope that balances an appreciation of relevant and informative bodies of work without exploring every related field in exhaustive depth.

The recognition narratives of de facto states and their constituent identity components will at times require the consideration of foreign policy; however, this project is not conducting comprehensive foreign policy analysis. Similarly, as many de facto states have grown from or been the product of nationalist self-determination movements, the topic of nationalism will feature throughout my discussions of the identity articulation of the case studies. After all, the relationship between nation and state cannot be avoided when studying de facto states. However, while I may raise questions about this relationship, it is not the central avenue of enquiry. A thorough consideration of nationalism is beyond the scope of this book. I draw on epistemologically compatible frameworks from constructivism and the English School in order to answer the consequent research question. However, this book is a contribution to the field of de facto state studies because uses an original synthesis of theories to develop a deeper understanding of the relationship between de facto states and international society. It is not, however, proposing theoretical challenges to the fields of constructivism and the English School.

Historicisation is a key process in the chosen methodology; however, this project is not a contribution to the field of history and will focus only on the historicisation of the events and developments that are central to the state identity and recognition narrative of each case study. Some of the case studies

12 *Introduction*

share similar state identities and relevant components. The depth and breadth of the examination of each of these components will be specific to the case study and the degree to which each component is relevant to the de facto state's situation. For example, members of the KRG emphasised the development of civil society as a key indicator of democratisation; therefore, the civil society of the KRI has been examined in depth. This contrasts with Somaliland, where elections were emphasised as a key indicator of state development, and therefore the integrity of Somaliland's elections has been examined in greater depth than its civil society, which has not been addressed to the same extent.

Chapter Two develops a framework of normative standing, ultimately incorporating Ian Clark's three conceptual pillars of legality, morality and constitutionality. That framework is applied to three case studies, which requires the legal standing of each case study to be considered. Chapter One locates de facto states in the international system based in part on a somewhat refined definition of the de facto state. This definition requires an entity to meet criteria that map closely to the functions and abilities outlined by the criteria of the 1933 Montevideo Convention on the Rights and Duties of States.[48] As such, when considering the legal pillar of each case study, I will not focus on the applicability of the Montevideo criteria, for meeting these criteria is antecedent to being a de facto state as defined in Chapter One.

Outline of the Book

The first two chapters form the theoretical core of the book, and address the research question: how can the relationship between de facto states and international society be conceptualised to account for the international legitimation of de facto states?

Chapter One examines existing approaches to defining de facto states, including conceptions of statehood and sovereignty, and proposes a refined definition. It critiques current approaches and models in the literature for locating de facto states in the international system and their relationship with international society, including recent constructivist theories about identity that can be applied to de facto states. In synthesising relevant components from previous theoretical contributions, the chapter identifies the need for a systems-level framework to better account for de facto states, and positions the concept of legitimacy as a promising platform for such an analytical framework.

Chapter Two examines existing approaches to legitimacy as a subject of scholarly enquiry, its extension into international jurisdictions, its meaning and implications for de facto states, and the limitations and strengths of previous approaches to the issue in the existing literature. The chapter proposes a definition of international legitimacy that forms the foundation of an enhanced theoretical framework for interpreting the relationship between de facto states and international society. As this theoretical framework is a contribution to the de facto state literature by virtue of its producing an original synthesis of International Relations Theory that provides explanatory utility, Chapters One and Two each require a more in-depth examination of theoretical approaches – namely constructivism, the English School and legitimacy – than is conventional or commonly found in the de facto state literature. This is not an indulgence; rather, it is a necessity to demonstrate that the framework is robust. Such examinations are much-needed supports in any attempt to build a bridge between theory, on the one hand, and empirical approaches, on the other. Chapter Two culminates in creating and positioning that bridge, a conceptual framework of normative standing that can be used to examine de facto states by locating them in the international system and explicating their exclusion from international society, the latter being what defines the contours of normative standing.

Chapters Three, Four and Five utilise the framework constructed in Chapters One and Two to address the primary research question: how does de facto state identity contribute to the stasis of the relationship with international society? To achieve this, the book presents and examines three selected case studies with varying degrees of international engagement and contrasting parent state relationships. In each case study, the formation and development of state identity is examined on the basis of fieldwork research conducted in each of these locations. Insights gained from applying the analytical lens of state identity are then used to assess the normative standing of each entity, revealing drivers, dimensions and dynamics of the stasis with international society.

The Conclusion evaluates the findings from the application of the conceptual framework across all three case studies. It synthesises and critiques the insights that have been provided into a better understanding of the stasis of the relationship between de facto states and the international community; it considers implications for the distinction made between the international system and international society; and it explores further possible areas of research that could add value to the generalisability and the functionality of the framework for the study of de facto states.

Notes

1 Scott Pegg first raised this prospect, stating that "there are a number of reasons to suspect that non-transformation or stasis may be the most likely outcome for these entities"; see Scott Pegg, *International Society and the De Facto State* (Aldershot, UK: Ashgate, 1998) 209. In 2004, Pegg made this argument more explicitly; see Scott Pegg, "From De Facto States to States-Within-States: Progress, Problems, and Prospects", in Paul Kingston and Ian S. Spears, eds., *States-Within-States: Incipient Political Entities in the Post-Cold War Era* (Basingstoke, UK: Palgrave Macmillan, 2004). Pegg's perspective was at first unique; however, wider support for this notion gathered slowly and is now one of the foundations upon which the 'engagement without recognition' research agenda – discussed below – has flourished.
2 Mikulas Fabry has made insightful inroads exploring the concept of national identity in de facto states and how non-recognition can strengthen it, a position I agree with, albeit through a different lens on identity articulated in Chapter One. See Mikulas Fabry, "Unrecognized States and National Identity", in Martin Riegl

14 Introduction

and Bohumil Doboš, eds., *Unrecognized States and Secession in the 21st Century* (New York: Springer, 2017).
3 James Ker-Lindsay, "Engagement without Recognition: The Limits of Diplomatic Interaction with Contested States", *International Affairs* 91:2 (2015) 267.
4 Pegg, *International Society and the De Facto State*.
5 Rachel Clogg, "The Politics of Identity in Post-Soviet Abkhazia: Managing Diversity and Unresolved Conflict", *Nationalities Papers* 36:2 (2008) 305–329.
6 International Crisis Group, "Abkhazia: The Long Road to Reconciliation" (Europe Report No. 224, 10 April 2013); Esmira Jafarova, *Conflict Resolution in South Caucasus* (Lanham, MD: Lexington Books, 2015); Stefan Wolff, "A Resolvable Frozen Conflict? Designing a Settlement for Transnistria", *Nationalities Papers*, 39:6 (2011) 863–870; Laurence Broers, ed., *The Limits of Leadership: Elites and Societies in the Nagorny Karabakh Peace Process* (London: Conciliation Resources, 2006).
7 John O'Loughlin et al., "Inside the Post-Soviet De Facto States: A Comparison of Attitudes in Abkhazia, Nagorny Karabakh, South Ossetia, and Transnistria", *Eurasian Geography and Economics* 55:5 (2014) 423–456; Alex Jeffrey, Fiona McConnell and Alice Wilson, "Understanding Legitimacy: Perspectives from Anomalous Geopolitical Spaces", *Geoforum* 66:1 (2015) 177–183.
8 Helge Blakkisrud and Pål Kolstø, "Dynamics of De Facto Statehood: The South Caucasian De Facto States between Secession and Sovereignty", *Southeast European and Black Sea Studies* 12:2 (2012) 281–289; Laurence Broers, "Recognising Politics in Unrecognised States: 20 Years of Enquiry into the De Facto States of the South Caucasus", *Caucasus Survey* 1:1 (2013) 59–74; Silvia von Steinsdorff and Anna Fruhstorfer, "Post-Soviet De Facto States in Search of Internal and External Legitimacy", *Communist and Post-Communist Studies* 45:1 (2012) 117–121; Galina Yemelianova, "Western Academic Discourse on the Post-Soviet De Facto State Phenomenon", *Caucasus Survey* 3:3 (2015) 219–238.
9 Pegg, *International Society and the De Facto State*; Tozun Bahcheli et al., *The Quest for Sovereignty* (London: Routledge, 2004); Deon Geldenhuys, *Contested States in World Politics* (Basingstoke, UK: Palgrave Macmillan, 2009); Dov Lynch, *Engaging Eurasia's Separatist States: Unresolved Conflicts and De Facto States* (Washington, DC: United States Institute of Peace Press, 2004); Nina Caspersen, *Unrecognized States: The Struggle for Sovereignty in the Modern International System* (Cambridge: Polity, 2012).
10 Eiki Berg, "Parent States versus Secessionist Entities: Measuring Political Legitimacy in Cyprus, Moldova and Bosnia & Hercegovina", *Europe-Asia Studies* 64:7 (2012) 1271–1296; Pål Kolstø and Helge Blakkisrud, "Living with Non-Recognition: State and Nation-Building in South Caucasian Quasi-States", *Europe-Asia Studies* 60:3 (2008) 483–509; Kristin Bakke et al., "Convincing State-Builders? Disaggregating Internal Legitimacy in Abkhazia", *International Studies Quarterly* 58:3 (2014) 591–607; Razmik Panossian, "The Irony of Nagorno-Karabakh: Formal Institutions versus Informal Politics", in James Hughes and Gwendolyn Sasse, eds., *Ethnicity and Territory in the Former Soviet Union* (London: Frank Cass, 2002); Daria Isachenko, *The Making of Informal States: Statebuilding in Northern Cyprus and Transdniestria* (Basingstoke, UK: Palgrave Macmillan, 2012); Nina Caspersen, "Separatism and Democracy in the Caucasus", *Survival: Global Politics and Strategy* 50:4 (2008) 113–136; Rebecca Richards and Robert Smith, "Playing in the Sandbox: Statebuilding in the Space of Non-Recognition", *Third World Quarterly* 36:9 (2015) 1717–1735.
11 Charles Fairbanks, "Weak States and Private Armies", in Mark Beissinger and Crawford Young, eds., *Beyond State Crisis? Postcolonial Africa and Post-Soviet Eurasia in Comparative Perspective* (Washington, DC: Johns Hopkins University Press, 2002).

12 Pål Kolstø, "The Sustainability and Future of Unrecognized Quasi-States", *The Journal of Peace Research* 43:6 (2006) 725.
13 Freedom House, "Freedom in the World 2015", https://freedomhouse.org/report/freedom-world/freedom-world-2015#.WG3IWFV96Uk.
14 Caspersen, *Unrecognized States*, 11.
15 Stephen D. Krasner, "Abiding Sovereignty", *International Political Science Review* 22:3 (2001) 243.
16 Caspersen, *Unrecognized States*, 118.
17 Vladimir Kolossov and John O'Loughlin, "Pseudo-States as Harbingers of a New Geopolitics: The Example of the Trans-Dniester Moldovan Republic (TMR)", in David Newman, ed., *Boundaries, Territory and Postmodernity* (London: Frank Cass, 1999) 152.
18 Nina Caspersen, "Playing the Recognition Game: External Actors and De Facto States", *The International Spectator* 44:4 (2009) 47–60; Eiki Berg and Raul Toomla, "Forms of Normalisation in the Quest for De Facto Statehood", *International Spectator* 44:4 (2009) 27–45; Laurence Broers, "Mirrors to the World: The Claims to Legitimacy and International Recognition of De Facto States in the South Caucasus", *Brown Journal of World Affairs* 20:11 (2014) 145–159; Nina Caspersen, "Degrees of Legitimacy: Ensuring Internal and External Support in the Absence of Recognition", *Geoforum* 66:1 (2015) 184–192; Bridget Coggins, "Friends in High Places: International Politics and the Emergence of States from Secession", *International Organization* 65:3 (2011) 433–467; Alexander Cooley and Lincoln Mitchell, "Engagement without Recognition: A New Strategy toward Abkhazia and Eurasia's Unrecognized States", *Washington Quarterly* 33:4 (2010) 59–73.
19 James Ker-Lindsay, *The Foreign Policy of Counter Secession: Preventing the Recognition of Contested States* (Oxford: Oxford University Press, 2012).
20 Ker-Lindsay, "Engagement without Recognition", 284.
21 Ibid.
22 Eiki Berg and Scott Pegg, "Scrutinizing a Policy of 'Engagement without Recognition': US Requests for Diplomatic Actions With *De Facto* States", *Foreign Policy Analysis* 14:3 (2018) 388–407.
23 James Ker-Lindsay, "The Stigmatisation of De Facto States: Disapproval and 'Engagement without Recognition'", *Ethnopolitics* 17:4 (2018) 362–372.
24 Nina Caspersen, "Recognition, Status Quo or Reintegration: Engagement with De Facto States", *Ethnopolitics* 17:4 (2018) 373–389.
25 Eiki Berg and Kristel Vits, "Quest for Survival and Recognition: Insights into the Foreign Policy Endeavours of the Post-Soviet De Facto States", *Ethnopolitics* 17:4 (2018) 390–407.
26 Nina Caspersen, "The Pursuit of International Recognition after Kosovo", *Global Governance* 21:1 (2015) 393–412.
27 Pegg, *International Society and the De Facto State*, 15–16.
28 Robert Jackson, *Sovereignty* (Cambridge: Polity, 2007) 150.
29 Pegg, *International Society and the De Facto State*, 246–247.
30 Ibid., 14–15.
31 Ibid., 16.
32 Ibid., 173.
33 Ibid.
34 Nina Caspersen and Gareth Stansfield, "Introduction: Unrecognized States in the International System", in Nina Caspersen and Gareth Stansfield, eds., *Unrecognized States in the International System* (London: Routledge, 2011) 7.
35 Ibid.
36 James Harvey and Gareth Stansfield, "Theorizing Unrecognized States: Sovereignty, Secessionism, and Political Economy", in Nina Caspersen and Gareth Stansfield, eds., *Unrecognized States in the International System* (London: Routledge, 2011) 11.

16 *Introduction*

37 Matan Chorev, "Complex Terrains: Unrecognized States and Globalization"; Klejda Mulaj, "International Actions and the Making and Unmaking of Unrecognized States"; Francis Owtram, "The Foreign Policies of Unrecognized States", in Nina Caspersen and Gareth Stansfield, eds., *Unrecognized States in the International System* (London: Routledge, 2011).
38 Ioan Lewis, *Making and Breaking States in Africa: The Somalia Experience* (Trenton, NJ: Africa World Press, 2010) xi.
39 Scott Pegg, "Twenty Years of De Facto State Studies: Progress, Problems, and Prospects", in *Oxford Research Encyclopedia of Politics* (Oxford: Oxford University Press, 2017).
40 The KRI is especially absent from comparative studies. For an insightful examination that argues that the KRI is a de facto state, see Yaniv Voller, *The Kurdish Liberation Movement in Iraq: From Insurgency to Statehood* (London: Routledge, 2014). For an authoritative exploration of post-Soviet de facto states, see Tomáš Hoch and Vincenc Kopeček, eds., *De Facto States in Eurasia* (London: Routledge, 2020).
41 The dynamics of patron state relations have been studied in depth. See Pål Kolstø, "Authoritarian Diffusion, or the Geopolitics of Self-Interest? Evidence from Russia's Patron-Client Relations with Eurasia's De Facto States," *Europe-Asia Studies* 72:3 (2020) 1–23; Berg and Vits, "Quest for Survival and Recognition: Insights into the Foreign Policy Endeavours of the Post-Soviet de facto States"; and Caspersen, "Recognition, Status Quo or Reintegration: Engagement with De Facto States".
42 The specific details of this arrangement are explored in detail in Chapter One.
43 Clifford Geertz, *The Interpretation of Culture: Selected Essays* (New York: Basic Books, 1973) 6.
44 Vincent Pouliot, "'Sobjectivism': Toward a Constructivist Methodology", *International Studies Quarterly* 51:2 (2007) 365.
45 Ibid., 361.
46 Ibid.
47 Alexander Wendt, *Social Theory of International Politics* (Cambridge: Cambridge University Press, 1999) 219.
48 Hurst Hannum, *Autonomy, Sovereignty and Self-Determination: The Accommodation of Conflicting Rights* (Philadelphia: University of Pennsylvania Press, 1990) 15–16.

Bibliography

Bahcheli, Tozun, et al. *The Quest for Sovereignty* (London: Routledge, 2004).
Bakke, Kristin, et al. "Convincing State-Builders? Disaggregating Internal Legitimacy in Abkhazia", *International Studies Quarterly* 58:3 (2014) 591–607.
Berg, Eiki. "Parent States versus Secessionist Entities: Measuring Political Legitimacy in Cyprus, Moldova and Bosnia & Hercegovina", *Europe-Asia Studies* 64:7 (2012) 1271–1296.
Berg, Eiki, and Pegg, Scott. "Scrutinizing a Policy of 'Engagement Without Recognition': US Requests for Diplomatic Actions with De Facto States", *Foreign Policy Analysis* 14:3 (2018) 388–407.
Berg, Eiki, and Toomla, Raul. "Forms of Normalisation in the Quest for De Facto Statehood", *The International Spectator: Italian Journal of International Affairs* 44:4 (2009) 27–45.
Berg, Eiki, and Vits, Kristel. "Quest for Survival and Recognition: Insights into the Foreign Policy Endeavours of the Post-Soviet De Facto States", *Ethnopolitics* 17:4 (2018) 390–407.

Blakkisrud, Helge, and Kolstø, Pål. "Dynamics of De Facto Statehood: The South Caucasian De Facto States between Secession and Sovereignty", *Southeast European and Black Sea Studies* 12:2 (2012) 281–298.

Broers, Laurence, ed. *The Limits of Leadership: Elites and Societies in the Nagorny Karabakh Peace Process* (London: Conciliation Resources, 2006).

Broers, Laurence. "Recognising Politics in Unrecognised States: 20 Years of Enquiry into the De Facto States of the South Caucasus", *Caucasus Survey* 1:1 (2013) 59–74.

Broers, Laurence. "Mirrors to the World: The Claims to Legitimacy and International Recognition of De Facto States in the South Caucasus", *Brown Journal of World Affairs* 20:11 (2014) 145–159.

Caspersen, Nina. "Separatism and Democracy in the Caucasus", *Survival: Global Politics and Strategy* 50:4 (2008) 113–136.

Caspersen, Nina. "Playing the Recognition Game: External Actors and De Facto States", *The International Spectator* 44:4 (2009) 47–60.

Caspersen, Nina. *Unrecognized States: The Struggle for Sovereignty in the Modern International System* (Cambridge: Polity, 2012).

Caspersen, Nina. "Degrees of Legitimacy: Ensuring Internal and External Support in the Absence of Recognition", *Geoforum* 66:1 (2015) 184–192.

Caspersen, Nina. "The Pursuit of International Recognition after Kosovo", *Global Governance* 21:1 (2015) 393–412.

Caspersen, Nina. "Recognition, Status Quo or Reintegration: Engagement with de facto States", *Ethnopolitics* 17:4 (2018) 373–389.

Caspersen, Nina, and Stansfield, Gareth. "Introduction: Unrecognized States in the International System", in Nina Caspersen and Gareth Stansfield, eds., *Unrecognized States in the International System* (London: Routledge, 2011) 1–8.

Chorev, Matan. "Complex Terrains: Unrecognized States and Globalization", in Nina Caspersen and Gareth Stansfield, eds., *Unrecognized States in the International System* (London: Routledge, 2011).

Clogg, Rachel. "The Politics of Identity in Post-Soviet Abkhazia: Managing Diversity and Unresolved Conflict", *Nationalities Papers* 36:2 (2008) 305–329.

Coggins, Bridget. "Friends in High Places: International Politics and the Emergence of States from Secession", *International Organization* 65:3 (2011) 433–467.

Cooley, Alexander, and Mitchell, Lincoln. "Engagement without Recognition: A New Strategy toward Abkhazia and Eurasia's Unrecognized States", *Washington Quarterly* 33:4 (2010) 59–73.

Fabry, Mikulas. *Recognizing States: International Society and the Establishment of New States since 1776* (Oxford: Oxford University Press, 2010).

Fabry, Mikulas. "Unrecognized States and National Identity", in Martin Riegl and Bohumil Doboš, eds., *Unrecognized States and Secession in the 21st Century* (New York: Springer, 2017).

Fairbanks, Charles. "Weak States and Private Armies", in Mark Beissinger and Crawford Young, eds., *Beyond State Crisis? Postcolonial Africa and Post-Soviet Eurasia in Comparative Perspective* (Washington, DC: Johns Hopkins University Press, 2002).

Freedom House, "*Freedom in the World 2015*", https://freedomhouse.org/report/freedom-world/freedom-world-2015#.WG3IWFV96Uk.

Geertz, Clifford. *The Interpretation of Culture: Selected Essays* (New York: Basic Books, 1973).

18 Introduction

Geldenhuys, Deon. *Contested States in World Politics* (Basingstoke,UK: Palgrave Macmillan, 2009).

Hannum, Hurst. *Autonomy, Sovereignty and Self-Determination: The Accommodation of Conflicting Rights* (Philadelphia: University of Pennsylvania Press, 1990).

Harvey, James, and Stansfield, Gareth. "Theorizing Unrecognized States: Sovereignty, Secessionism, and Political Economy", in Nina Caspersen and Gareth Stansfield, eds., *Unrecognized States in the International System* (London: Routledge, 2011).

Hoch, Tomáš, and Kopeček, Vincenc, eds., *De Facto States in Eurasia* (London: Routledge, 2020).

International Crisis Group, "Abkhazia: The Long Road to Reconciliation", Report No. 224, https://www.crisisgroup.org/europe-central-asia/caucasus/abkhazia-georgia/abkhazia-long-road-reconciliation (10 April 2013).

Isachenko, Daria. *The Making of Informal States: Statebuilding in Northern Cyprus and Transdniestria* (Basingstoke, UK: Palgrave Macmillan, 2012).

Jackson, Robert. *Sovereignty* (Cambridge: Polity, 2007).

Jafarova, Esmira. *Conflict Resolution in South Caucasus* (Lanham, MD: Lexington Books, 2015).

Jeffrey, Alex, McConnell, Fiona, and Wilson, Alice. "Understanding Legitimacy: Perspectives from Anomalous Geopolitical Spaces", *Geoforum* 66:1 (2015) 177–183.

Ker-Lindsay, James. *The Foreign Policy of Counter Secession: Preventing the Recognition of Contested States* (Oxford: Oxford University Press, 2012).

Ker-Lindsay, James. "Engagement without Recognition: The Limits of Diplomatic Interaction with Contested States", *International Affairs* 91:2 (2015) 1–16.

Ker-Lindsay, James. "The Stigmatisation of De Facto States: Disapproval and 'Engagement without Recognition'", *Ethnopolitics* 17:4 (2018) 362–372.

Kolossov, Vladimir, and O'Loughlin, John. "Pseudo-States as Harbingers of a New Geopolitics: The Example of the Trans-Dniester Moldovan Republic (TMR)", in David Newman, ed., *Boundaries, Territory and Postmodernity* (London: Frank Cass, 1999).

Kolstø, Pål. "The Sustainability and Future of Unrecognized Quasi-States", *The Journal of Peace Research* 43:6 (2006) 723–740.

Kolstø, Pål. "Authoritarian Diffusion, or the Geopolitics of Self-Interest? Evidence from Russia's Patron-Client Relations with Eurasia's De Facto States", *Europe-Asia Studies* 72:3 (2020) 1–23.

Kolstø, Pål, and Blakkisrud, Helge. "Living with Non-Recognition: State and Nation-Building in South Caucasian Quasi-States", *Europe-Asia Studies* 60:3 (2008) 483–509.

Krasner, Stephen D. "Abiding Sovereignty", *International Political Science Review* 22:3 (2001) 229–251.

Lewis, Ioan. *Making and Breaking States in Africa: The Somalia Experience* (Trenton, NJ: Africa World Press, 2010).

Lynch, Dov. *Engaging Eurasia's Separatist States: Unresolved Conflicts and De Facto States* (Washington, DC: United States Institute of Peace Press, 2004).

Mulaj, Klejda. "International Actions and the Making and Unmaking of Unrecognized States", in Nina Caspersen and Gareth Stansfield, eds., *Unrecognized States in the International System* (London: Routledge, 2011) 41–57.

O'Loughlin, John, et al. "Inside the Post-Soviet De Facto States: A Comparison of Attitudes in Abkhazia, Nagorny Karabakh, South Ossetia, and Transnistria", *Eurasian Geography and Economics* 55:5 (2014) 423–456.

Owtram, Francis. "The Foreign Policies of Unrecognized States", in Nina Caspersen and Gareth Stansfield, eds., *Unrecognized States in the International System* (London: Routledge, 2011).

Panossian, Razmik. "The Irony of Nagorno-Karabakh: Formal Institutions versus Informal Politics", in James Hughes and Gwendolyn Sasse, eds., *Ethnicity and Territory in the Former Soviet Union* (London: Frank Cass, 2002).

Pegg, Scott. *International Society and the De Facto State* (Aldershot, UK:Ashgate, 1998).

Pegg, Scott. "From De Facto States to States-Within-States: Progress, Problems, and Prospects", in Paul Kingston and Ian S. Spears, eds., *States-Within-States: Incipient Political Entities in the Post-Cold War Era* (Basingstoke, UK: Palgrave Macmillan, 2004).

Pegg, Scott. "Twenty Years of De Facto State Studies: Progress, Problems, and Prospects", in *Oxford Research Encyclopedia of Politics* (Oxford: Oxford University Press, 2017), https://oxfordre.com/politics/view/10.1093/acrefore/9780190228637.001.0001/acrefore-9780190228637-e-516.

Pouliot, Vincent. "'Sobjectivism': Toward a Constructivist Methodology", *International Studies Quarterly* 51:2 (2007) 359–384.

Richards, Rebecca, and Smith, Robert. "Playing in the Sandbox: Statebuilding in the Space of Non-Recognition", *Third World Quarterly* 36:9 (2015) 1717–1735.

Steinsdorff, Silvia von, and Fruhstorfer, Anna. "Post-Soviet De Facto States in Search of Internal and External Legitimacy", *Communist and Post-Communist Studies* 45:1–2 (2012) 117–121.

Voller, Yaniv. *The Kurdish Liberation Movement in Iraq: From Insurgency to Statehood* (London: Routledge, 2014).

Wendt, Alexander. *Social Theory of International Politics* (Cambridge: Cambridge University Press, 1999).

Wolff, Stefan. "A Resolvable Frozen Conflict? Designing a Settlement for Transnistria", *Nationalities Papers* 39:6 (2011) 863–870.

Yemelianova, Galina. "Western Academic Discourse on the Post-Soviet De Facto State Phenomenon", *Caucasus Survey* 3:3 (2015) 219–238.

1 De Facto States and the International System

De Facto States and Sovereignty

A key component of de facto state research that grounds its importance within the discipline of International Relations concerns how the existence of de facto states informs conceptions of statehood and sovereignty. Since the end of the Cold War and the dissolution of the Soviet Union and Yugoslavia, contrasting interpretations of sovereignty have proliferated.[1] An exhaustive analysis of the evolution of interpretations of sovereignty is beyond the scope of this chapter; it is a clear conceptualisation of sovereignty in relation to de facto states that is crucial.

The classical view of sovereignty perceives it as an absolute and exclusive authority covering a clearly demarcated territory.[2] This view is mirrored by the constitutive approach to international law, claiming that if a polity's juridical independence is not recognised, then it cannot be a state.[3] Supporters of this view, such as Kalevi Holsti, claim that sovereignty is an externally recognised legal status that is an "absolute category and not a variable".[4] Others, such as Robert Jackson, analyse the internal and external components of sovereignty, but claim that it is not divisible because external recognition is intrinsic and enabling, arguing that "supremacy and independence cannot exist separately".[5] Jackson's view enables the analysis of juridical states lacking internal sovereignty, which he refers to as "quasi-states".[6]

The existence of autonomous unrecognised territories challenges the classical perception of sovereignty. The Kurdistan Region of Iraq (KRI) is a de facto state that has not even declared independence,[7] yet due to the empowered position of wielding a relatively stable state-like entity in a rather anarchic neighbourhood, it is not only reshaping the regional balance of power between Iraq, Iran, Turkey and the Government of Syria, but the extensive foreign support in Syria means that the KRI is now also wedged between the great power struggles of the United States and Russia. This exemplifies the need to challenge the classical view of juridical states as the only territorially defined, authoritative agents in international politics. Post-Cold War scholarship has paralleled the opposing legal opinions represented by the constitutive and declaratory approaches to statehood. Attempts to develop a more sophisticated comprehension of de facto states has led to the challenging of the belief that sovereignty is indivisible and absolute.

Scott Pegg uses Jackson's notions of positive and negative sovereignty to ground his analysis of de facto states.[8] Positive sovereignty is a political and logistical rather than legal quality, describing a government that "possesses the wherewithal to provide political goods" to its populace.[9] Negative sovereignty refers to external recognition by other states, in theory providing assurance of non-intervention.[10] Pegg's definition of de facto states classifies them as having achieved the former but not the latter.[11] This distinction has been employed elsewhere, where it is referred to as the difference between empirical sovereignty and juridical sovereignty.[12]

Nina Caspersen and Deon Geldenhuys divide sovereignty into internal and external categories. Caspersen's external sovereignty is the same as Jackson's negative sovereignty: the recognition of juridical independence. Caspersen's definition of internal sovereignty is similar to Jackson's positive sovereignty, though it moves beyond "formal authority" to include "the supply of public services and the enjoyment of popular legitimacy".[13] Similar to those who consider domestic sovereignty and legitimacy to be inseparable, Caspersen argues that recognition by the populace – and not just control – is a key component of internal sovereignty (which is occasionally deemed to be popular sovereignty).[14] Where Jackson has shown the existence of states possessing external sovereignty without its internal counterpart, thus allowing the view of sovereignty as indivisible because only recognition matters, Caspersen has shown that internal sovereignty can exist without external recognition.[15]

Divisibility of sovereignty is closely associated with the work of Stephen Krasner, especially his seminal text *Sovereignty: Organized Hypocrisy*.[16] In their analysis of unrecognised states, James Harvey and Gareth Stansfield utilise Krasner's division of sovereignty into the components of international-legal, Westphalian, domestic and interdependence.[17] International-legal sovereignty is the legal recognition by other states and international organisations.[18] Westphalian sovereignty refers to the authority of an entity to prohibit the interference of actors over the domestic authority structures within its territory.[19] Domestic sovereignty refers to structures of authority within a state and their ability to regulate behaviour.[20] Interdependence sovereignty is the ability of states to control their borders and movement across them.[21] Krasner contends that the different components are not mutually constituted; one can exist on its own or in combination with others.[22]

Krasner also challenges the notion that sovereignty is absolute, underpinning his contention that states have never been as sovereign as has often been assumed.[23] Krasner argues that Westphalian sovereignty has been compromised through contracts, conventions, coercion and imposition.[24] The latter two are also violations of international-legal sovereignty, whereas the former two confirm it because entering into a convention is voluntary and a state has the right to exit a contract.[25] Any variation in these circumstances would equate to imposition or coercion.

Krasner's Westphalian, international-legal and domestic sovereignties are concerned primarily with authority. Interdependence sovereignty refers only to control. Although Krasner's segmenting of sovereignty deviates from the classical conception from which the term originates, I argue that to create a category of sovereignty purely about control is a bridge too far. Positive, negative, internal, external, domestic, Westphalian and international-legal are categories of sovereignty that are employed in an attempt to comprehend the evolution of the concept. These terms all have one characteristic in common: the primacy of authority. The focus of Krasner's *Sovereignty: Organized Hypocrisy* is Westphalian and international-legal sovereignty. Krasner dedicates barely two pages to analysing interdependence sovereignty, telling how scholars have claimed that the decreasing ability of states to control the movement of people, goods, diseases and ideas across borders has been *described* as a loss of sovereignty.[26] In alignment with Holsti's interpretation of authority as the defining characteristic of sovereignty,[27] this book argues that interdependence sovereignty is not sovereignty at all. Krasner has developed a phrase to describe an idea that stemmed from misguided interpretations.[28]

The resilience of de facto states has inspired a sustained problematisation of the condition of sovereignty, a nebulous concept that de facto state experts continue to grapple with. A position on this defining agential criterion cannot be reached independently from considering the structure within which it operates.

In order to clarify the relationship of de facto states with international society, the social system that they occupy must be considered. The de facto state literature refers to "international society",[29] the "international system"[30] and the "international community"[31] almost interchangeably. Pegg grounds his analysis in a Grotian-inspired, English School interpretation of international society, which, although more specific than much of the literature, does not state precisely what it is that de facto states inhabit.[32] Eiki Berg and Ene Kuusk offer an "empirical approach" to international society that provides a more detailed systems-level schematic;[33] however, I argue that their approach is premised on a misunderstanding about what constitutes a society by overlooking the intrinsic, normative component of rightful membership.[34] Chapter Two explores the concept of an international society specifically, settling on Ian Clark's legitimist interpretation, which provides the most insightful explanation of the social constituency that de facto states are excluded from. Detailing the social system that they actually inhabit, though, is the task to which this chapter now turns.

Defining the De Facto State

Defining the social system of which de facto states are a functioning part requires first asking: what exactly constitutes a de facto state? The growing body of literature that examines territorially defined, self-governing entities that lack juridical recognition in the international system has developed with minimal definitional consensus to encompass the growing number of anomalous entities. Providing an important and recognised "starting point", Pegg centres his definition of the de facto state on secessionist origins.[35] Pegg's definition is one of the most widely cited:

> Organized political leadership which has risen to power through some degree of indigenous capability; receives popular support; and has achieved sufficient capacity to provide government services to a given population in a specific territorial area, over which effective control is maintained for a significant period of time. The de facto state views itself as capable of entering into relations with other states and it seeks full constitutional independence and widespread international recognition as a sovereign state. It is, however, unable to achieve any degree of substantive recognition and therefore remains illegitimate in the eyes of international society.[36]

Dov Lynch's terminology and framework mirror those of Pegg, while Tozun Bahcheli et al. avoid the issue and interchange "de facto state" with "unrecognized state".[37] Paul Kingston and Ian Spears centre their study on "states-within-states", which they have deliberately "left imprecise" in order to broaden the parameters of the evolving dialogue.[38] Geldenhuys introduces the phrase "contested states", strictly limiting his study to entities seeking recognition.[39] Pål Kolstø's "unrecognized quasi-state" must also be seeking international recognition as well as maintaining control over most of the territory to which it may lay claim, and it must have been active in this "state of non-recognition" for at least two years.[40]

Actively seeking recognition is the major definitional point of departure. Caspersen, Harvey and Stansfield use the term "unrecognised states" to refer to entities that have established de facto independence for at least two years, including territorial control over at least two-thirds of the territory it claims and including its key city and main region; have received no or only partial recognition from international society; and demonstrated a desire for independence, "either through a formal declaration of independence, through the holding of a referendum, or through other actions or declarations that show a clear desire for a separate existence".[41] Caspersen has added to her definition the criterion of attempting to develop state institutions.[42] Requiring only the desire for independence rather than official declaration provides a broader conceptual base for analysing state-like actors. Although this book focusses on multiple case studies, it also promotes an English-School-inspired distinction of the international system as different to the international society, which in combination with Wendt's identity framework will be used to better understand individual de facto states as well as their collective position within the international system. Therefore, Caspersen's inclusive definition and terminology will be used as a starting point, with one key adjustment: a crucial platform for theorising an increasingly important subject in a context that has been largely devoid of systemically conscious theorising.

The issue of recognition is inescapably important when it comes to understanding de facto states; however, centering the definition on recognition limits the concept's explanatory power. So long as the subjects of the study have declared independence or harbour such aspirations, it is logical for a definition to include these components, but differentiating these entities based on how many states have recognised them is only useful if that recognition causes or constitutes some degree of significant qualitative change. The most enabling benchmark of recognition is the recognition required to gain entry into the United Nations. This empowers states by equipping them with the status required to obtain international legal protection, and it ensures access to major international organisations. This empowering status is considered to be the touchstone that erases any question about a polity's rights as a state.[43] Hence in practice, the United Nations has become equivalent to a "collective arbiter of statehood".[44]

On that basis, I propose making one key adjustment to Caspersen's definition. Rather than specifying that an entity must have no or only partial recognition by international society, I suggest that an entity must not have recognition which is sufficient to gain entry into the United Nations.[45] This simpler definition draws a clear distinction that removes borderline cases. Under this definition, Taiwan and Kosovo are considered to be de facto states because they do not have recognition sufficient to gain entry into the United Nations. Parsimony is not reason enough to adjust the definition. The primary reason for changing this criterion is the conceptual clarity that it enables. To unlock the analytical power of a more nuanced and applicable conceptualisation of the normative relationship between de facto states and international society, a clear distinction between those included and excluded from international society is needed. As Chapter Two demonstrates, a legitimate member of international society is one who has been *empowered* with rights through the social sanctioning of rights-holding constituents. An unambiguous distinction between rights-holding constituents and everyone else is therefore essential. This does not mean reverting to a simplistic, reductionist confirmation of the recognised state as the only kind of state. On the contrary, it is an enabling move towards constructing a framework that allows for a deeper understanding of the relationship between recognised states, the society they form, and excluded de facto states.

To clarify, an entity is considered to be a de facto state if:

1. It has established de facto independence for at least two years, including territorial control of at least two-thirds of its territory and its key city and main region.
2. It has not been recognised as a full member of the United Nations.
3. It has demonstrated a desire for independence.
4. It is in the process of developing independent state institutions.

De Facto States in the International System

The concept of an international system is deployed more frequently than it is clearly defined. Hedley Bull's archetypal international system "is formed when two or more states have sufficient contact between them, and have sufficient impact on one another's decisions to cause them to behave – at least in some measure – as parts of a whole".[46] Bull's demarcation of system and society is essentially a disaggregation of Martin Wight's notion of a system, which is defined as "constituting a valid society of mutual rights and obligations".[47] Bull's conception of an international system, however, is limited by a characteristic that it shares with Kenneth Waltz's materialist definition of the state system as a distribution of capabilities:[48] an under-conceptualisation of the social structures that exist within the system. A key difference between Bull's theory and Waltz's model is that Bull at least accounts for the importance of the inherently social rules, values and institutions in his framework of an international society.[49] Meanwhile, Christian Reus-Smit has taken issue with the system–society distinction and has subsequently offered a solution to this problem.

Reus-Smit's issue with the system–society distinction is "not conceptual, it is historical".[50] He argues that a close examination of the last 600 years shows that rarely does a "textbook example" of Bull's international system exist, "let alone one that transformed with the advent of mutual recognition into an international society", which is what "conventional accounts suggest".[51] Reus-Smit proffers a model of the international system that "has always had fundamental social dynamics" and that did not emerge prior to international society because "system and society emerged simultaneously".[52] For Reus-Smit, the international system develops social structures, specifically "relatively stable constitutional norms and attendant reproductive practices that define the terms of legitimate statehood and the parameters of rightful state action".[53] International society describes the orders that evolve around these constitutional structures. Reus-Smit's conception of the international system as encompassing the orders that coalesce as international societies provides a logical and useful starting point for a framework.[54]

Reus-Smit's model of the international system was conceived for the purpose of his investigation into the development of rights and the role this played in the evolution of the international system. This book's focus on the identity of de facto states requires a model of the international system that follows Reus-Smit's logic but with greater detail that accounts for unrecognised statehood without resorting to an ambiguous position on the issue of sovereignty. The framework of Wendt's state system provides another related and appropriate contribution to a new framework.

Wendt's state system is based on his refined model of the essential state, which consists of five criteria:

1 An institutional-legal order.
2 An organisation claiming a monopoly on the legitimate use of organised violence.
3 An organisation with sovereignty.
4 A society.
5 Territory.[55]

As the above discussion established, sovereignty is a heavily contested concept, and Wendt employs a specific definition of sovereignty to underpin his model, a definition that this book accepts and adopts.[56] Wendt divides sovereignty into internal and external components.[57] Internal sovereignty refers to the state having the ultimate authority within society; recognition is the key.[58] Internal sovereignty is about being recognised by society as having authority.[59] Autonomy is not sovereignty: wielding forceful power over society is only internal sovereignty if that power is recognised by the people. This political bargain can take different forms with examples ranging from democratic to rentier or totalitarian.

External sovereignty refers to the absence of any external authority that can supersede that of the state.[60] Wendt claims that the recognition of external sovereignty by other states is not a prerequisite.[61] Recognition bestows certain freedoms and establishes legal rights for a state, which is supremely enabling and therefore desirable; however, external sovereignty is simply having independence from an outside authority.[62] This aligns with Jackson's distinction that posits that recognition establishes juridical statehood but that without recognition there is still empirical statehood.[63] Wendt's refined model of the essential state therefore provides a fitting framework from which to theorise the socially constituted identity of a de facto state.

A clearly reasoned justification for using this framework is required, given that Wendt himself states that the purpose of the essential state is only to "provide the necessary platform or 'body' to begin doing systemic theory".[64] Wendt also admits that the state "has borderline cases".[65] The de facto state is surely the epitome of a borderline case. Theorising about agents that self-organise in anomalous circumstances is complex.[66] Much of the de facto state literature has employed empirical approaches that are too exclusionary to provide a comprehensive framework for theorising the relationship between de facto states and international society. Excluding international-legal sovereignty from the defining criteria of the state is an approach echoed in Dominik Zaum's analysis of sovereignty.[67] The essential state is also similar to the definition found in the 1933 Montevideo Convention on the Rights and Duties of States, which classifies a state as an autonomous entity with a permanent population that exists in a defined territory, consisting of a government that is legitimated by the recognition of its citizens, with the capacity to enter into relations with other states.[68] The only significant difference is Montevideo's inclusion of the capacity for foreign relations, which in the case of de facto states cannot be conducted through the conventional diplomatic avenues.[69]

Wendt's framework is designed to explain the cultures of anarchy at a systemic level and is insufficient for revealing state identity in its entirety because it does not account for domestic forces. Wendt acknowledges the importance of inner state workings; they are simply beyond the scope of his research.[70] There are significant components of the research in this book that consider sub-state-level identity forces and domestic actors in the case studies; however, using

Wendt's framework is still justifiable because the book is not using this framework to explain these intra-state workings. Rather, it adopts this substantive framework, with a specific focus on the essential state as an entity to which identities and interests can be attributed, to form the first conceptual layer: the international system.[71] In Chapter Two, Clark's legitimist interpretation of international society will be employed, forming the second conceptual layer. With these two concepts firmly in place, I will locate de facto states as units in the international system that are excluded from the international society, and that are heavily influenced by the culture and norms of the international society that they are seeking to join. This is the conceptual foundation upon which I will build the framework of normative standing.

Adopting this framework also requires a thorough assessment of the KRI's complex positioning. Although the KRI has a formalised legal relationship with the Government of Iraq (GoI), the division of authority makes it more complicated to fit the KRI into models of sovereignty and statehood in comparison to other de facto states. Iraq's Constitution recognises the authority of the KRI over all administrative requirements of the region including internal security. The laws of the Kurdistan region, implemented by the Kurdistan Parliament, bind the KRI.[72] The KRI therefore clearly satisfies the criterion of an institutional-legal order. The claim to having a monopoly on the legitimate use of organised violence is evidenced by the functioning of the Kurdistan police force, the internal security force known as the Asayish, and their military, the Peshmerga. The vibrant Kurdish identity is displayed throughout society, and the KRI's territorial authority over Dohuk, Erbil and Sulaymaniyah is recognised in the Constitution.[73] The KRI clearly meets the criteria of society and territory. I argue that the criterion of sovereignty is met, but that the way in which it is met is rather complicated and requires deeper clarification.

The internal sovereignty of the KRI is indisputable. The institutional-legal order, effective provision of security and recognition displayed by successful democratic elections are a testament to this. The KRI is not entirely free of external authority; however, I argue that the establishment and development of authority structures within Kurdistan represents relevant components of such freedom. Article 115 of Iraq's Constitution clearly states that regions have the power to amend the application of federal law on matters outside the exclusive authority of the federal government,[74] and Article 110 delineates those exclusive authorities. The fourth, sixth and ninth points of Article 110 are too minor to affect the authority structures of the KRI. The third and seventh points show that the GoI can influence the financial and business sectors in Iraq, but power and influence do not equate to *authority*.[75] The three points that specify GoI supremacy are the following:

Article 110:
   The federal government shall have the exclusive authorities in the following matters:

28 *De Facto States and the International System*

>First: Formulating foreign policy and diplomatic representation; negotiating, signing and ratifying international treaties and agreements; negotiating, signing, and ratifying debt policies and formulating foreign sovereign economic and trade policy … Fifth: Regulating issues of citizenship, naturalization, residency, and the right to apply for political asylum … Eighth: Planning policies relating to water sources from outside Iraq and guaranteeing the rate of water flow to Iraq and its just distribution inside Iraq in accordance with international laws and conventions.

These points outline the GoI's supremacy over the KRI in managing foreign relations. The KRI's capability to conduct diplomacy and manage citizenship is limited, and these limitations show the GoI's authority over the KRI's relations with other states and international organisations. The GoI has no authority over the structures that govern the *domestic* affairs of Kurdistan. The authority that the GoI holds over the KRI is directly related to the GoI's international-legal sovereignty. These are empowering functions that recognition bestows, the same recognition that other more commonly accepted de facto states are also denied. The KRI's limited ability to conduct diplomatic foreign relations does not diminish its authority over the political and legal structures within its territory. The KRI therefore has the external sovereignty required to be considered a de facto state.

De Facto State Identity in the International System

The 'social turn' in International Relations has spawned a vast and diverse array of constructivist theories about identity. International Relations scholarship over the last 30 years is replete with complementing and contrasting sociologically grounded theories. The importance of identity has become a staple, from foreign policy analysis through to systems-level theorising. A baseline point of agreement for many constructivists is the claim that the basis of state interests is state identity.[76] An extensive review of the entire constructivist library is beyond the scope of this project; rather, what is required is an understanding that will enable a rigorous assessment of de facto states' relationship with international society by providing the tools to study their state identity. I utilise Wendt's multi-layered identity framework for the same reason that his essential state model has been embraced: the explanatory utility for illuminating the social positioning of de facto states at the system level. This chapter will now proceed to detail this framework and defend the Wendtian approach against criticism that, I argue, can actually be embraced for the task at hand to elaborate Wendt's state identity model.

Wendt considers identity to be a "property of intentional actors that generates motivational and behavioural dispositions".[77] Identity is grounded in the self-understanding held by an actor, which has an intersubjective character because the meaning of that self-understanding is often reliant on whether other actors reflect that meaning by representing it accordingly: identities are created by ideas held by the Self and the Other.[78] Both internal and external structures constitute identities. Wendt divides identity into four categories, which are built upon his essential state framework: corporate, type, role and collective. In the state system, the corporate identity is considered to be pre-social, while the last three are socially constructed.[79]

Corporate identity is the foundation for the other identities and consists of the properties that make an actor a distinct body constituted by "self-organizing, homeostatic structures".[80] This includes the material foundation of an actor and, for intentional actors such as humans or states, having a state of consciousness and memory.[81] Summed up aptly by Wendt, corporate identity is the "body and experience of consciousness".[82] Because the corporate identity is self-organising, it is exogenous to the social structure within which it exists; hence, Wendt classifies it as pre-social. The classification of the corporate identity as pre-social is a problem that I will examine below.

Type identity is a category of shared traits that are social in content and meaning.[83] The determining characteristics of type identities are intrinsic to the actor, meaning that although the trait must have social meaning to be identified as a type it must also exist whether or not another actor is there to recognise it.[84] An actor can have multiple type identities, but just because a characteristic is shared does not mean that it will create a type identity.[85] For instance, the United Kingdom and New Zealand are both made up of islands; however, this aspect of their corporate identity has no social meaning, whereas both states are democratic, which is of categorical social consequence in international society and therefore constitutes a type identity.

In comparison to corporate and type identities, role identities are purely social, existing only in relation to the Other.[86] To have a role identity, an agent must fill a position in a social structure, behaving towards an Other according to the norms that constitute the former's identity and the latter's counter-identity. Role identities are based on shared expectations, which for many roles can be institutionalised in a social structure before certain agents have interacted. The use of Mead's concept of the "Me", being "the self as it sees itself through the Other's eyes", is a key to understanding the function of role identity.[87] The internalisation of these expectations by an agent leads to that structure being reflected in the structure of the "Me", a process called "alter-casting". The existence of a role identity in the agent's consciousness allows an agent to assume a role identity.

Wendt includes collective identity as the third social sub-class of identity. Collective identity is a unique configuration of type and role identities that has the "causal power to induce actors to define the welfare of the Other as part of that of the Self".[88] Collective identity is fundamental for Wendt in extrapolating his grand theory of international politics. However, it is peripheral to the purpose of this project, and, as Cederman and Daase have highlighted in their critique of Wendt, role and corporate identities can exist in both individual and collective terms.[89] As such, collective identity needs no further elaboration.

The power of any identity cannot be fully understood without the interests it is attached to. Interest is founded in identity.[90] Sometimes an identity may be selected to serve an interest, but in this case the interest concerned presupposes a stronger identity in the actor's hierarchy of Self.[91] Identities alone are not sufficient to explain behaviour, meaning that interests are not reducible to identity: "Without interests identities have no motivational force, without identities interests have no direction".[92] The explanatory power of each is interdependent on the other, and one alone cannot be fully understood in isolation.[93]

There are two types of interest, subjective and objective. Objective interests are the elements that are functionally essential for the reproduction of an identity.[94] This is applicable to Wendt's four identity types.[95] For instance, if New Zealand were to relinquish its monopoly on organised violence, then it would cease reproducing the corporate identity of a state. If the Australian army were to overthrow the government by force, then Australia would lose its democratic type identity. These needs are objective because they are essential to an identity regardless of whether or not the New Zealand government recognises this.[96] Actors have to continuously reproduce an internalised identity. To do so, they must realise the needs that must be satisfied to reproduce an identity before acting on that realisation.[97]

Subjective interests are the beliefs that actors hold about how to satisfy their identity needs. These are subjective because they rely on an actor's perception, which may be inaccurate. Just because an actor tries to understand their identity needs does not mean that they will be accurately discerned. An important distinction must be made here: a subjective interest is a preference for achieving a goal, not a preference as to how best to achieve that goal.[98] Subjective interests are motives, not strategies; therefore, actions are not sufficient indicators of preferences.

The Ontological Status of the State

The essential state model and the accompanying identity framework have been subject to much criticism, of which the most relevant regards the ontological status of the state. Wendt claims that "states are ontologically prior to the state system. The state is presocial to other states in the same way that the human body is presocial".[99] This ontological claim provides the epistemological freedom required to execute his grand systems theory; however, as Friedrich Kratochwil asserts, it excludes his theory from engaging with the changes in political boundaries and the politics of inclusion and exclusion.[100] For a systems theory to be unable to address questions regarding how and why actors and systems get reconstituted is a significant shortcoming.[101] The underlying issue is the "rump" materialist ontology that underpins Wendt's essential state, conceiving of the materialism–idealism question as a Cartesian separation of mind and body.

The fact that Wendt considers consciousness and memory to exist in the homeostatic structures of intentional actors is a strong indication that his model is amenable to a monist reinterpretation. *Social Theory of International Politics* is a theory of the state system, not the state, and as such Wendt treats states as units in the system. Wendt draws a line around the state for the purpose of systemic theorising; however, he admits that this "is not to say that we cannot study how these internal structures reproduce themselves, just as we can study how the body sustains itself".[102] Although Wendt's justification for focussing on systemic theorising is sound for the purpose of his theory, the separation of "difference from without" and "sameness within" is where, for the present project to capture state identity, the barrier must be broken down. A definitive separation of the internal and external, the claim that state agency is exogenous, disregards the potential effects of the external on the internal and vice-versa. Domestic decision-makers thinking about international action will not only consider the causes stemming from, and the consequences flowing into, the international sphere. It is unclear whether or not Wendt recognises this problem, for in order to theorise the system he does not need to. To study de facto state identity, however, this project must go a layer deeper.

Positing the state as *cogito* is indefensible outside of a systems theory. Erik Ringmar points out that the question of recognition "presupposes recognisability",[103] a point that can be colourfully illustrated using de facto states. One cannot point to a time when any de facto state was a *tabula rasa*; de facto states are – as all states are – the products of multi-dimensional political and ideological struggles.[104] De facto states, however, are defined in the eyes of international society as unacceptable pariahs because of the nature of those formative transformations. This book examines the relationship between the systems-level interactions of de facto states and the consequences they have on the internal processes, and similarly in reverse. Given that de facto states are secessionist movements, most of which have developed with or from a strong foundation of sub-state or trans-state nationalism, and considering that their proclaimed systems-level identity has been rejected by the society within which they seek to establish themselves, overcoming this divide is imperative.

This book examines the relationship between specific units in the international system, and the relationship that exists between these units and international society. In order to effectively appraise this, it must address both unit- and systems-level influences. Wendt's identity framework will therefore be utilised at the systems level, for as this chapter previously pointed out, the type, role and collective identities are all still directly applicable. In order to study the key components of sub-state identity, the corporate identity will still be accepted as a corporate identity; however, in a shift towards accepting a monist ontology the structures, processes and forces that constitute the internal workings of the corporate identity, and specifically how they shape the state identity, will also be considered.

Achieving this requires a clear statement on the ontological status of the state and its relationship to the system. The state is not pre-social. Rejecting the claim that it is 'ideas all the way down' does not require committing to a separation of the *cogito* and the *persona*. I accept that the internal structures and processes that take place to self-organise a state are composed of individuals who together hold a collective knowledge of the international sphere. Hence, at the point in time when the state will have self-organised – that is, when the criteria of the essential state will have been met – the corporate structures will have already been holding views and developing collective knowledge about the international system and the other units within it. In the contemporary context, perceptions of the international system can in fact be formative influences in the process of state creation.

Furthermore, the state is not considered to be ontologically prior to the system. As Wendt admitted in an earlier extended quotation, conceding to the cogent arguments posed by critics,[105] state identity largely concerns the differentiation of the Self from the Other. As such, claiming ontological priority is indefensible. However, I argue that the state, and consequently the state system, is ontologically prior to an international society. The distinction between system and society will be fleshed out and finalised in Chapter Two. Briefly, in order to progress, it is sufficient to state that I agree with Wendt's state system, which is composed of states that are intentional actors, and that the system itself is anarchic. At this stage, I will not commit to Wendt's proclamation that the system's structure is defined in cultural terms. Wendt's conception of the system is built for trans-historic theorising in a way that transcends the distinction between international system and international society that, I will argue, can take place in a specific form at a fixed place in time.

Wendt's cultural system is defined by the type of ideas that are shared in the system, replacing Bull's distinction of society as the degree of shared knowledge that exists across the system. Since 1945, those shared ideas have included a very narrow definition of who should be empowered with the rights of sovereign statehood. As such, the system of self-organising units has continued to reconstitute itself alongside an international society enforcing strict rules about who is a legitimate member. Following Reus-Smit's logic, the system and society exist simultaneously, a condition that is crucial for understanding the socialisation of de facto states. Hence, I draw a clear distinction between the system and society. A key characteristic of this distinction that must be identified at this point is that the difference between a system and a society is purely social. Although there is much debate about the different qualities that can be considered definitive of an international society, the one criterion that is widely agreed to be intrinsic is that an international society is formed out of member states which recognise each other's sovereignty, which empowers them with the right to act in that society.[106] Identifying the key principle of difference as a purely social act based on intersubjective meaning draws focus to the need for the history of the practice of recognition to be outlined. This is a vital step for understanding the conditionality of membership and the context in which de facto states' normative claims have been made and subsequently rejected. The history of recognition is also, in part, the history of international society.

International Society and the Politics of Recognition

De Facto States in International Law

International law is widely accepted as an institution of international society. De facto states exist in a zone between international politics and international law.[107] It is therefore imperative to understand how statehood, the central frame of reference, is conceived in each body of thought. The two poles in the "great debate"[108] of understanding statehood are the declaratory and constitutive approaches.[109] The declaratory approach claims that, for a state to be a state, it must fulfil certain criteria.[110] The criteria most widely used as a frame of reference are derived from 1933 Montevideo Convention on the Rights and Duties of States, which classifies a state as an autonomous entity, with a permanent population that exists in a defined territory, consisting of a government that is legitimated by the recognition of its citizens, and possessing the capacity to enter into relations with other states.[111] According to the declaratory approach, recognition is a purely political act; a state is constituted purely by the above-mentioned essential empirical attributes.

The constitutive approach to statehood claims that a state is constituted by other states recognising its sovereignty.[112] Recognition is more than supremely enabling political support, it is an "absolute category" of legal status, from which the concept of statehood cannot be untethered.[113] Where the declaratory approach conceives of statehood as objective status recognition, the constitutive position views statehood as intersubjective status creation. Proponents of the constitutive approach argue that, although a political entity can function like a state without being recognised, others must verify an entity's self-understanding in order for it to be validated and maintained.[114]

The difference between the constitutive and declaratory theories has been widely accepted as a distinction between empirical facts and social reality, a distinction that has led to the development of both theories stagnating and securing an impasse.[115] The very nature of this debate illuminates the political and existential quagmire that de facto states inhabit. Declaratory theorists argue that if statehood is not understood as the satisfaction of empirical criteria, then the empowering act of recognition will become the pawn of great power politics to be wielded as the rulers of the day see fit. Constitutive theorists counter this argument by claiming that rendering statehood as a purely empirical establishment fails to grasp the inherent normative basis of statehood; recognition is reserved for those entities who *ought* to be empowered with the rights and protections afforded by the status.

For the field of International Relations, the declaratory and constitutive theories are both insufficient theories of statehood, given that quasi states and de facto states both exist as exceptions to these theories. Indeed, I argue that there can be no single theory of statehood that is so strict in its parameters. I also reject the categorisation of the constitutive as the normative theory and the declaratory as the empirical theory, for these are untenable in

International Relations. There can be no one theory of statehood, for there is no one statehood. The international state system has evolved over time, just as the parameters of international society have shifted along normative and political lines. The practical way forward is to suggest a theory of statehoods that appreciates and accounts for the difference between the co-existing international state system and international society.

The Practice of State Recognition

The waves of decolonisation and new state creation that were the fertile ground giving seed to contemporary de facto states took place in the post-1945 chapter of the twentieth century. The narrative of recognition and self-determination that was central to how this unfolded is often restricted to this time period as well. However, understanding the background to this journey helps to elucidate the complexities of the post-1945 recognition discourse.

The Latin American independence movements of the early nineteenth century played a crucial part in building the foundation of contemporary practices of state recognition. The question of 'who is allowed to join the family of nations?' was thrust upon international society by the Spanish American revolutions, consequently giving rise to two practices that have remained central to state recognition ever since: de facto statehood and *uti possidetis juris*. De facto statehood saw that, although an established state was rightful in demanding that other states respect its territorial integrity, this right was forfeit if the established state was internally replaced by a de facto state.[116] Mikulas Fabry offers a tight summary of what this practice soon came to mean:

> The *de facto* state has a right to independence vis-à-vis international society. As such, it has the right to obtain foreign recognition and third parties have a corresponding obligation to extend it. A third party can postpone recognition, but neither arbitrarily nor indefinitely: there must be compelling reasons for the delay.[117]

The significance of de facto statehood as the defining criterion of nascent states marked the definitive shift away from dynastic legitimacy.

The guiding principle of *uti possidetis juris* was adopted in conjunction with the pillar of de facto statehood. The principle is derived from the Roman property law *uti possidetis, ita possideatis*, literally meaning "as you possess, so you may possess".[118] In the context of nineteenth-century Latin America, the United States and Britain applied this principle to incipient states, determining their borders to be the jurisdictional borders they had previously held as non-sovereign entities.[119] This move was designed to protect the territorial integrity of all the polities that had established de facto statehood; hence, the two concepts are considered to have gone hand in hand in this period (the contemporary practice of *uti possidetis juris* has changed considerably, and will be explored in detail below). *Uti possidetis juris* did not play a part in deciding which entities were to be recognised; rather, it demarcated the juridical boundaries of emerging polities and protected their infantile sovereignty, helping to secure order in the wake of political tumult.

The next key turning point in the practice of state recognition came in the aftermath of the First World War, following the Wilsonian re-conceptualisation of self-determination. Although when the narrative of contemporary self-determination is recounted it often begins with him, in fact Woodrow Wilson was responsible for the internationalisation of the concept, not the formulation of the concept itself.[120] While the idea has deep roots in the liberal political tradition, it was Lenin who first "conceptually and politically" introduced the concept of self-determination into the wartime antagonism.[121] Rita Knudsen even goes so far as to suggest that Lenin's focus on self-determination was a key motivating factor for Wilson's attempt to shape the international self-determination discourse. Wilson sought to establish a perception of the concept as being strictly rooted in the liberal purview, in stark contrast to Lenin, whose radical notion of self-determination was loaded with socialist meaning.

In moving to own the internationalisation of the concept, Wilson attempted to reshape its meaning altogether. Where inceptive states in the nineteenth century practised self-determination as a negative right, Wilson sought to progress towards a twentieth-century conception of self-determination as a positive international right.[122] No longer were the established members of international society to simply respect foreign self-determination projects by not intruding in the trajectory of realisation. Now, Wilson postulated that states had a duty to aid fledgling polities in bringing their desired status to fruition. Wilson's ideology, however, was quickly perceived to risk opening a Pandora's Box of nationalist claims.

A considerable disconnect eventuated between Wilson's indeterminate, idealistic self-determination rhetoric and the actual practice of state recognition. The key change that saw the interwar period as a turning point in the history of recognition was not the realisation of self-determination as a positive right, but rather the elimination of the right of conquest. This was the first time that the process of state creation was considered integral to a state's case for recognition. What soon became known as the Stimson Doctrine was recognised in an addendum to the League of Nations Covenant's Article 10: states should adopt a policy of *non-recognition* towards entities that are created through invasion or forced adjustment of borders.[123] This meant that, despite Wilson's rhetoric, the practice of recognition in the interwar period built on the practices of the past, consisting of two main distinguishing features of state recognition in the wake of the First World War. The first was their prior de facto emergence; and the second their formation of an integral juridical section of the state from which they originated. The contours of international society had experienced a definitive shift beyond the age of conquest.

During the interwar period, the right to self-determination was still withheld from the non-settler colonies of Africa and Asia on the basis that they were deemed to fall short of what was known as the 'standard of civilisation'. The 'standard of civilisation' is a concept that has manifested itself in a diverse array of societies dating back to ancient Greece and is evident in the history of China and Islamic empires.[124] Most commonly, and in the context of international relations, it refers to the admission and recognition of new states into international society.[125] Put simply, the gatekeepers of international society had to be satisfied that a prospective entity satisfied certain governing and cultural practices. It is most colourfully illustrated by the Western-colonial international society of the nineteenth century, where colonised people were considered to be 'under tutelage' on matters such as law, human rights and good governance, while non-colonised entities such as China and the Ottoman Empire were not recognised and admitted until international society had deemed them to have satisfied the standard.[126]

It was only in the early 1960s that, accompanying the acknowledgement and acceptance of colonialism as illegitimate, the 'standard of civilisation' was abandoned, to be superseded by the belief in the self-determination and independence for people who had been the victims of colonisation. This gave way to an enormous wave of new sovereign states being created through the process of decolonisation. Not only was the 'standard of civilisation' abandoned, but none of these entities were even required to demonstrate the basic de facto statehood that had been so crucial to the practice of recognition since the beginning of the nineteenth century. In fact, United Nations Resolution 1514 stated that "inadequacy of political, economic, social, or educational preparedness should never serve as a pretext for delaying independence".[127] The ability to govern had been shed as a deciding factor, replaced instead by a narrow focus on the origins of the state.[128] As Jackson aptly put it: "To be a sovereign state today one needs only to have been a formal colony yesterday".[129] This opened the door to the most rapid expansion of states being confirmed as members of international society. In 1945, there were 51 member states of the United Nations; by 1970, this number had surged to 127.

This new approach led to a markedly different interpretation of *uti possidetis juris* being employed in the post-1945 era. Jackson offers an encompassing formulation that outlines the constitution of recognition practice since 1945:

1. Existing interstate borders are legitimate, legal, and inviolable.
2. Change of borders by force is illegitimate and illegal.
3. If borders are to be changed, all states affected by the change must give their consent.
4. In the absence of general consent to change borders, if secession is to occur international boundaries of seceding states should follow the internal administrative boundaries of the state from which they seceded.

5   Ethnonations have no inherent right of self-determination, and the only recognized nation-state is the population group residing within borders defined by juridical boundaries, that is, the political or civic nationality.[130]

The exception to this practice during the Cold War was the case of Bangladesh. The recognition of Bangladesh was the first instance of what has since come to be known as 'remedial secession'. Pakistan, by committing gross human rights violations against its own people, was deemed to have forfeited its sovereignty; its right to govern was removed by the international community. The ethnic distinction and geographic separation from the rest of Pakistan aided the case for self-determination; however, James Crawford points out that there is evidence to suggest that the United Nations perceived the recognition of Bangladesh as an inevitability rather than as a case of self-determination, effectively preventing any precedent from being set.[131]

Recognition after the Cold War

The end of the Cold War was a significant turning point for state recognition. For the duration of the Cold War, international society was "closed at both ends" to all entities that were not former colonies.[132] New, non-colonial states did not form, and incumbent states did not 'fail', regardless of their capacity to govern.[133] The dissolving of the Soviet Union and the dissolution of Yugoslavia, however, saw the right to self-determination being granted to polities that had a non-colonial background. Far from creating an open-door policy, the right was now more specifically extended to former republics, legitimising state dissolution as a path to statehood. Theoretically, the republics' statehood was conditional on meeting certain normative criteria, a policy that came to be known as "standards before status".[134] The baseline standards put forward by the Badinter Arbitration Commission that had to be met by the Yugoslav republics concerned human rights, general democratic criteria and the protection of minority rights.[135] Even though these normative standards have since featured in the policy that enabled Kosovo's formation, not to mention their steadfast roots in international society's democratisation discourse, they have never been applied consistently.[136]

The partial recognition of Kosovo has been the most significant provocateur in post–Cold War debates about state recognition. Serbia was not in the process of dissolution, and although Kosovo had been an autonomous region in the former Yugoslavia – autonomy that had strong legal grounding – it was not the same full republican title that had enabled the other former Yugoslav states to attain recognised statehood. The "standards before status" policy was put forward by the UN mission in Kosovo in an attempt to coax the authorities into improving their governance and protection of human rights to align with the United Nations' ideal of best practice by using conditional recognition as the promised fruit.[137] While these standards were supposed to be progressing, mediation efforts with Serbia continued but to no avail; the parent state refused to agree to any solution that gave Kosovo the right to full independence. A motion was put to the UN General Assembly recommending that Kosovo be given independence but on the provision that the United Nations oversaw its development towards meeting the previously outlined standards of practice.[138] By June 2008, 42 states including the United States and most European states recognised Kosovo's independence.[139] It is important to note, however, as Caspersen points out, that in the recognition of Kosovo the Western powers focussed primarily on the exceptionality of the case.[140] This echoed the Bangladeshi case, for even though the Kosovar people were victims of gross human rights violations, the primary foundation for recognition was its unique situation, warranting and facilitated by external intervention.[141] Kosovo is yet to obtain recognition sufficient to gain entry into the United Nations, and is categorised by many as a 'borderline case' in the de facto state literature.[142] Although there was disagreement among the major powers about Kosovo's right to self-determination, the one component of this question upon which a consensus was clear was that Kosovo did not set a precedent.

There has always been a balance between the normative ideals and political reality that shapes the practice of state recognition, but Kosovo's partial recognition put politics at the front and centre of the debate. Kosovo's failure to achieve the standards that were supposed to come before its status did not inhibit the Western powers from recognising its independence. Furthermore, in the wake of the 2008 war with Georgia, and emboldened by the monohemispheric recognition of Kosovo, Russia recognised the independence of South Ossetia and Abkhazia. This was a significant change in position, as Russia had previously positioned itself to respect the sovereignty of parent states and had practised adherence to the norms of international law. Russia did not reference any normative criteria, nor did it extend this right of self-determination to Somaliland, Nagorno Karabakh or the Turkish Republic of Northern Cyprus. If there was any doubt about the political nature of this move, Russia quashed it when it directly compared its recognition of the Georgian secessionist movements to the West's recognition of Kosovo, stating that if Kosovo was a credible exception, then so too were Abkhazia and South Ossetia.[143] Consequently, the practice of state recognition outside of the *uti possidetis juris* framework stipulated by Jackson, outlined above, is now seen by many to be predominantly the manoeuvring of pieces on the political chessboard of great powers.[144]

The history of recognition shows that the conditions allowing a polity the right to self-determine have evolved along with the norms and practices of international society.[145] As a right, self-determination is inherently normative; however, it cannot be untethered from the political contestations of great powers.[146] When there is agreement and unanimous recognition, such as with South Sudan in 2011, these cases are in alignment with conventions and expectations that have been spawned and shaped by great power politics. As noted above, there is even a strong argument claiming that Wilson's desire to project self-determination into the international arena was initially, in part, a pre-emptive move to stunt the prospect of a Leninist notion of self-determination taking root.[147] Prioritising stability and order over justice, international society has long been cautious of granting a generous open-door approach to self-determination. The post-Cold War era demonstrates an especially steadfast stasis, and this has led Uriel Abulof to quip that "modern states may have pulled the normative rug from beneath their own feet, suspending their system in moral mid-air".[148] So long as international society sustains this stasis, de facto states will continue to navigate the amorphous intersection between international politics and international law, which is suspended in the unwavering volatility that requires new and innovative analytical lenses to develop a more comprehensive understanding of their existence and relationships.

Conclusion

The resilience of de facto states has led to a steady growth of literature in a still relatively understudied but developing field. Scholars such as Scott Pegg, Nina Caspersen, James Ker-Lindsay, James Harvey and Gareth Stansfield have laid a solid foundation of penetrating theory that has challenged basic assumptions of International Relations, and drawn much-needed academic attention to a political phenomenon that reveals important insights about the international political arena, from the level of sub-state social mobilisation through to challenging systems-level models. However, de facto states have yet to be accurately factored into a systems-level framework, limiting observers' understandings of their relationship with international society. This chapter made a concerted move towards establishing a systems-level framework that accounts for de facto states, employing the Wendtian essential state model and adopting Reus-Smit's international system logic. Adjusting and utilising the Wendtian identity framework, I adopted a position to more accurately conceptualise the state identity of de facto states by enabling the framework to consider systems-level and sub-state-level influences. Finally, reviewing the politics of recognition highlighted the competing forces of political interests and normative ideals that determine the rules of membership in international society. This revealed the need for a more complete conception of the relationship between international society and the international system, one that can embody these qualities. Legitimacy is a social phenomenon that encompasses both the political and the normative and is therefore a suitable lens through which to construct the final conception of this relationship, which is the task of the next chapter.

Notes

1 For a comprehensive overview, see Hent Kalmo and Quentin Skinner, eds., *Sovereignty in Fragments* (Cambridge: Cambridge University Press, 2010).

2 Nina Caspersen, *Unrecognized States: The Struggle for Sovereignty in the Modern International System* (Cambridge: Polity, 2012) 4–5.
3 Ibid., 13.
4 Kalevi J. Holsti, *Taming the Sovereigns: Institutional Change in International Politics* (Cambridge: Cambridge University Press, 2004) 114.
5 Robert Jackson, *Sovereignty* (Cambridge: Polity, 2007) 12.
6 Robert Jackson, *Quasi-States: Sovereignty, International Relations and the Third World* (Cambridge: Cambridge University Press, 1990).
7 The KRI did hold an independence referendum in September 2017; however, it was non-binding and at the time of writing a declaration of independence has so far not been made.
8 Scott Pegg, *International Society and the De Facto State* (Aldershot, UK: Ashgate, 1998) 51–52.
9 Jackson, *Quasi-States: Sovereignty, International Relations and the Third World*, 29.
10 Ibid., 27.
11 Pegg, *International Society and the De Facto State*, 26–30.
12 Stacy Closson, "What Do Unrecognized States Tell Us about Sovereignty?" in Nina Caspersen and Gareth Stansfield, eds., *Unrecognized States in the International System* (London: Routledge, 2011) 66. Eva Erman disagrees with the use of this terminology. See Eva Erman, "The Recognitive Practices of Declaring and Constituting Statehood", *International Theory* 5:1 (2013) 129–150.
13 Caspersen, Unrecognized States, 15.
14 A position also held by Zaum. See Dominik Zaum, *The Sovereignty Paradox* (Oxford: Oxford University Press, 2007).
15 Caspersen, *Unrecognized States*, 21.
16 Stephen D. Krasner, *Sovereignty: Organized Hypocrisy* (Princeton, NJ: Princeton University Press, 1999).
17 James Harvey and Gareth Stansfield, "Theorizing Unrecognized States: Sovereignty, Secessionism, and Political Economy", in Nina Caspersen and Gareth Stansfield, eds., *Unrecognized States in the International System* (London: Routledge, 2011).
18 Krasner, *Sovereignty: Organized Hypocrisy*, 14.
19 Ibid., 20.
20 Ibid., 11.
21 Ibid., 12.
22 Ibid., 9–10.
23 Ibid., 24.
24 Ibid., 25–27.
25 Ibid., 25–27.
26 Ibid., 12–14.
27 Holsti, *Taming the Sovereigns: Institutional Change in International Politics*, 114.
28 For instance, on the effects of globalisation on the state and sovereignty, see Jessica Matthews, "Power Shift", *Foreign Affairs* 76:1 (1997) 50–66; and Jean L. Cohen, *Globalization and Sovereignty* (Cambridge: Cambridge University Press, 2012).
29 Pegg, International Society and the De Facto State; Eiki Berg and Ene Kuusk, "What Makes Sovereignty a Relative Concept? Empirical Approaches to International Society", *Political Geography* 29:1 (2010) 40–49; Eike Berg and Raul Toomla, "Forms of Normalisation in the Quest for De Facto Statehood", *The International Spectator: Italian Journal of International Affairs* 44:4 (2009) 27–45.
30 Caspersen, *Unrecognized States;* Caspersen and Stansfield, *Unrecognized States in the International System.*

De Facto State Identity and International Legitimation   41

31 Daria Isachenko, *The Making of Informal States: Statebuilding in Northern Cyprus and Transdniestria* (Basingstoke, UK: Palgrave Macmillan, 2012); Pål Kolstø, "The Sustainability and Future of Unrecognized Quasi-States", *The Journal of Peace Research* 43:6 (2006) 734; Charles King, "The Benefits of Ethnic War: Understanding Eurasia's Unrecognized States", *World Politics* 53:1 (2001) 526.
32 Pegg, *International Society and the De Facto State*, 14–15.
33 Berg and Kuusk, "What Makes Sovereignty a Relative Concept?".
34 Chapter Two addresses this in detail. For a detailed assessment of the varying approaches to interpreting an international society, see Tim Dunne, "Sociological Investigations: Instrumental, Legitimist and Coercive Interpretations of International Society", *Millennium: Journal of International Studies* 30:1 (2001) 67–91; Barry Buzan, *From International to World Society? English School Theory and the Social Structure of Globalization* (Cambridge: Cambridge University Press, 2004); and Cornelia Navari, ed., *Theorising International Society: English School Methods* (New York: Palgrave Macmillan, 2009).
35 Pegg, *International Society and the De Facto State*, 26–28.
36 Ibid., 13.
37 Dov Lynch, *Engaging Eurasia's Separatist States: Unresolved Conflicts and De Facto States* (Washington, DC: United States Institute of Peace Press, 2004) 13–16; Bahcheli et al., *De facto States: The Quest for Sovereignty* (London: Routledge, 2004) 2–9.
38 Ian S. Spears, "States-within-States: An Introduction to Their Empirical Attributes", in Paul Kingston and Ian S. Spears, eds. *States-within-States: Incipient Political Entities in the Post-Cold War Era* (New York: Palgrave Macmillan, 2004) 16.
39 Deon Geldenhuys, *Contested States in World Politics* (Basingstoke, UK: Palgrave Macmillan, 2009) 4.
40 Kolstø, "The Sustainability and Future of Unrecognized Quasi-States", 725–726.
41 Caspersen, *Unrecognized States*, 11; Harvey and Stansfield, "Theorizing Unrecognized States: Sovereignty, Secessionism, and Political Economy", 3–4.
42 Caspersen, *Unrecognized States*, 11.
43 Joshua Keating, "How to Start Your Own Country in Four Easy Steps", *Foreign Policy* (February 2008), https://foreignpolicy.com/2008/02/26/how-to-start-your-own-country-in-four-easy-steps/.
44 James Ker-Lindsay, *The Foreign Policy of Counter Secession: Preventing the Recognition of Contested States* (Oxford: Oxford University Press, 2012) 131.
45 This may not work for a more historical analysis, and I accept this limitation.
46 Hedley Bull, *The Anarchical Society* (London: Macmillan, 1977) 9–10.
47 Martin Wight, *Systems of States*, ed. Hedley Bull (Leicester: Leicester University Press, 1977) 39.
48 Kenneth Waltz, *A Theory of International Politics* (Reading, MA: Addison-Wesley Publishing, 1979).
49 Bull, *The Anarchical Society*, 13.
50 Christian Reus-Smit, *Individual Rights and the Making of the International System* (Cambridge: Cambridge University Press, 2013) 17.
51 Ibid.
52 Ibid., 18–19.
53 Ibid., 19.
54 As noted above, the finer details of this distinction will be fleshed out in Chapter Two.
55 Alexander Wendt, *Social Theory of International Politics* (Cambridge: Cambridge University Press, 1999) 202.

42   De Facto States and the International System

56 As the other four criteria are self-explanatory, only sovereignty is explored in detail here. The question of sovereignty and de facto states is addressed above.
57 See Robert Jackson and Carl Rosberg, "Why Africa's Weak States Persist: The Juridical and the Empirical in Statehood", *World Politics* 35:1 (1982) 1–24.
58 Wendt, *Social Theory of International Politics*, 207.
59 Ibid.
60 Ibid., 208.
61 Ibid.
62 Ibid., 209.
63 Ibid., 209; Jackson and Rosberg, "Why Africa's Weak States Persist: The Juridical and the Empirical in Statehood".
64 Wendt, *Social Theory of International Politics*, 201.
65 Ibid., 202.
66 Pegg, *International Society and the De Facto State*, 229.
67 Zaum, *The Sovereignty Paradox*, 32–34.
68 Hurst Hannum, *Autonomy, Sovereignty and Self-Determination: The Accommodation of Conflicting Rights* (Philadelphia: University of Pennsylvania Press, 1990) 15–16.
69 See James Ker-Lindsay, "Engagement without Recognition: The Limits of Diplomatic Interaction with Contested States", *International Affairs* 91:2 (2015) 1–16.
70 Alexander Wendt, "Social Theory as Cartesian Science: An Auto-Critique from a Quantum Perspective", in Stefano Guzzini and Anna Leander, eds., *Constructivism and International Relations: Alexander Wendt and His Critics* (London: Routledge, 2006) 208.
71 Wendt acknowledges the divisibility of his substantive framework from his theory of international politics. See Wendt, "Social Theory as Cartesian Science", 181.
72 Kurdistan Regional Government, "The Kurdistan Parliament", http://www.KRI.org/p/p.aspx?l=12&s=030000&r=319&p=229.
73 Iraqi Constitution, http://www.wipo.int/wipolex/en/text.jsp?file_id=230000 (2005).
74 Ibid.
75 On this point, see Holsti, *Taming the Sovereigns: Institutional Change in International Politics*, 114.
76 Mlada Bukovansky, "American Identity and Neutral Rights from Independence to the War of 1812", *International Organization* 51:2 (1997) 210; Rodney Hall, *National Collective Identity: Social Constructs and International Systems* (New York: Columbia University Press, 1999).
77 Wendt, *Social Theory of International Politics*, 224.
78 Ibid.
79 Alexander Wendt, "Collective Identity Formation and the International State", *The American Political Science Review* 88:2 (1994) 385–386.
80 Wendt, *Social Theory of International Politics*, 224.
81 Ibid.
82 Wendt, "Collective Identity Formation and the International State", 385.
83 Wendt, *Social Theory of International Politics*, 226.
84 Ibid.
85 Ibid.
86 Ibid., 227.
87 Ibid.
88 Ibid., 229.
89 Lars-Erik Cederman and Christopher Daase, "Endogenizing Corporate Identities: The Next Step in Constructivist IR Theory", *European Journal of International Relations* 9:1 (2003) 7.

90 Alexander Wendt, "Anarchy Is What States Make of It", *International Organization* 46:2 (1992) 389.
91 Wendt, *Social Theory of International Politics*, 231.
92 Ibid., 234.
93 Audie Klotz and Cecilia Lynch, *Strategies for Research in Constructivist International Relations* (London: Routledge, 2007) 86.
94 Wendt, *Social Theory of International Politics*, 232.
95 Ibid.
96 Ibid.
97 Ibid.
98 Ibid.
99 Ibid., 198.
100 Friedrich Kratochwil, "Constructing a New Orthodoxy? Wendt's Social Theory of International Politics and the Constructivist Challenge", in Stefano Guzzini and Anna Leander, eds., *Constructivism and International Relations: Alexander Wendt and His Critics* (London: Routledge, 2006) 43.
101 Hall, *National Collective Identity*.
102 Ibid.
103 Erik Ringmar, "How the World Stage Makes Its Subjects: An Embodied Critique of Constructivist IR Theory", *Journal of International Relations and Development* 19:1 (2016) 104.
104 For a detailed analysis of the domestic and international forces contributing to the creation of secessionist entities and de facto states, see Ryan D. Griffiths, *The Age of Secession* (Cambridge: Cambridge University Press, 2016).
105 Cederman and Daase, "Endogenizing Corporate Identities"; Kratochwil, "Constructing a New Orthodoxy?".
106 Bull, *The Anarchical Society*; Buzan, *From International to World Society?*; Christian Reus-Smit, *The Moral Purpose of the State* (Princeton, NJ: Princeton University Press, 1999).
107 I disagree with Martti Koskenniemi's notion of international politics and international law as inseparable. See Martti Koskenniemi, *Politics of International Law* (Oxford: Hart, 2011).
108 James Crawford, *The Creation of States in International Law* (Oxford: Clarendon Press, 1979) 16.
109 Erman, "The Recognitive Practices of Declaring and Constituting Statehood".
110 Cedric Ryngaert and Sven Sobrie, "Recognition of States: International Law or Realpolitik? The Practice of Recognition in the Wake of Kosovo, South Ossetia and Abkhazia", *Leiden Journal of International Law* 24:1 (2011) 470.
111 Hannum, *Autonomy, Sovereignty and Self-Determination*, 15–16.
112 William Worster, "Law, Politics and the Conception of the State in State Recognition Theory", *Boston University International Law Journal* 115 (2009) 119.
113 Holsti, *Taming the Sovereigns: Institutional Change in International Politics*, 114.
114 Erik Ringmar, "Introduction: The International Politics of Recognition", in Thomas Lindemann, ed., *The International Politics of Recognition* (Boulder, CO: Paradigm, 2011) 11–12.
115 Erman, "The Recognitive Practices of Declaring and Constituting Statehood", 135.
116 Mikulas Fabry, *Recognizing States: International Society and the Establishment of New States since 1776* (Oxford: Oxford University Press, 2010) 69.
117 Ibid.
118 Robert Jackson, *The Global Covenant* (Oxford: Oxford University Press, 2000) 327.

119 Fabry, *Recognizing States*, 76.
120 For an in-depth discussion of this point, see Rita Augestad Knudsen, "Moments of Self-Determination: The Concept of 'Self-Determination' and the Idea of Freedom in 20th and 21st Century International Discourse" (PhD Dissertation: The London School of Economics and Political Science, 2013).
121 Knudsen, "Moments of Self-Determination", 89.
122 Fabry, *Recognizing States*, 118.
123 Ibid., 135.
124 Barry Buzan, "The 'Standard of Civilisation' as an English School Concept", *Millennium – Journal of International Studies* 42:3 (2014) 578.
125 See Gerrit Gong, *The Standard of "Civilization" in International Society* (Oxford: Clarendon Press, 1984).
126 Buzan, "The 'Standard of Civilisation' as an English School Concept", 583.
127 United Nations Resolution 1514, http://www.un.org/en/decolonization/declaration.shtml.
128 Barry Bartmann, "Political Realities and Legal Anomalies: Revisiting the Politics of International Recognition", in Tozun Bahcheli et al., *De Facto States: The Quest for Sovereignty* (London: Routledge, 2004) 12–13.
129 Jackson, *Quasi-States: Sovereignty, International Relations and the Third World*, 17.
130 Jackson, *The Global Covenant*, 328.
131 Crawford, *The Creation of States*, 415–416.
132 Caspersen, "The Pursuit of International Recognition after Kosovo", *Global Governance* 21:1 (2015) 394.
133 Jackson, *Quasi-States: Sovereignty, International Relations and the Third World*, 17.
134 See Anne-Marie Gardner, "Beyond Standards before Status: Democratic Governance and Non-State Actors," *Review of International Studies* 34:3 (2008) 531–552.
135 Caspersen, "Separatism and Democracy in the Caucasus", *Survival: Global Politics and Strategy* 50:4 (2008) 113–136.
136 Caspersen, "The Pursuit of International Recognition after Kosovo", 395.
137 James Ker-Lindsay, "The 'Final' Yugoslav Issue: The Evolution of International Thinking on Kosovo, 1998–2005", in Dejan Djokic and James Ker-Lindsay, eds., *New Perspectives on Yugoslavia* (London: Routledge, 2011) 184–185.
138 United Nations, Report of the Special Envoy of the Secretary-General on Kosovo's Future Status, http://www.un.org/en/ga/search/view_doc.asp?symbol=S/2007/168 (2007).
139 James Hughes, "Russia and the Secession of Kosovo: Power, Norms and the Failure of Multilateralism", *Europe Asia Studies* 65:5 (2013) 1011.
140 Caspersen, *Unrecognized States*, 20. For an insightful overview of the shift in focus from autonomy to independence by external powers, see Ker-Lindsay, "The 'Final' Yugoslav Issue". For a compelling case against the exceptionality of Kosovo's case, see James Ker-Lindsay, "Preventing the Emergence of Self-Determination as a Norm of Secession: An Assessment of the Kosovo 'Unique Case' Argument," *Europe-Asia Studies* 65:5 (2013) 837–856.
141 Ibid.
142 Caspersen, *Unrecognized States*, 12; Harvey and Stansfield, "Theorizing Unrecognized States", 11.
143 Closson, "What Do Unrecognized States Tell Us about Sovereignty?", 60.
144 See Caspersen, "The Pursuit of International Recognition after Kosovo", 396–397.
145 For a thorough overview, see Tanisha M. Fazal and Ryan D. Griffiths, "Membership Has Its Privileges: The Changing Benefits of Statehood", *International Studies Review* 16:1 (2014) 79–106.

146 Bridget Coggins, "Friends in High Places: International Politics and the Emergence of States from Secession", *International Organization* 65:1 (2011) 461–462.
147 Knudsen, "Moments of Self-Determination", 89.
148 Uriel Abulof, "We the Peoples? The Strange Demise of Self-Determination", *European Journal of International Relations* 22:3 (2016) 559.

Bibliography

Abulof, Uriel. "We the Peoples? The Strange Demise of Self-Determination", *European Journal of International Relations* 22:3 (2016) 536–565.
Bahcheli, Tozun, *et al.*, eds., *The Quest for Sovereignty* (London: Routledge, 2004).
Bartmann, Barry. "Political Realities and Legal Anomalies: Revisiting the Politics of International Recognition", in Tozun Bahcheli, *et al.*, eds., *The Quest for Sovereignty* (London: Routledge, 2004).
Berg, Eiki, and Kuusk, Ene. "What Makes Sovereignty a Relative Concept? Empirical Approaches to International Society", *Political Geography* 29:1 (2010) 40–49.
Berg, Eiki, and Toomla, Raul. "Forms of Normalisation in the Quest for De Facto Statehood", *The International Spectator: Italian Journal of International Affairs* 44:4 (2009) 27–45.
Bukovansky, Mlada. "American Identity and Neutral Rights from Independence to the War of 1812", *International Organization* 51:2 (1997) 209–233.
Bull, Hedley. *The Anarchical Society* (London: Macmillan, 1977).
Buzan, Barry. *From International to World Society? English School Theory and the Social Structure of Globalization* (Cambridge: Cambridge University Press, 2004).
Buzan, Barry, "The 'Standard of Civilisation' as an English School Concept", *Millennium – Journal of International Studies* 42:3 (2014) 576–594.
Caspersen, Nina. "Separatism and Democracy in the Caucasus", *Survival: Global Politics and Strategy* 50:4 (2008) 113–136.
Caspersen, Nina. *Unrecognized States: The Struggle for Sovereignty in the Modern International System* (Cambridge: Polity, 2012).
Caspersen, Nina. "The Pursuit of International Recognition after Kosovo", *Global Governance* 21:1 (2015) 393–412.
Caspersen, Nina, and Stansfield, Gareth. "Introduction: Unrecognized States in the International System", in Nina Caspersen and Gareth Stansfield, eds., *Unrecognized States in the International System* (London: Routledge, 2011) 1–8.
Cederman, Lars-Erik, and Daase, Christopher. "Endogenizing Corporate Identities: The Next Step in Constructivist IR Theory", *European Journal of International Relations* 9:1 (2003) 5–35.
Closson, Stacy. "What Do Unrecognized States Tell Us about Sovereignty?", in Nina Caspersen and Gareth Stansfield, eds., *Unrecognized States in the International System* (London: Routledge, 2011) 50–78.
Coggins, Bridget. "Friends in High Places: International Politics and the Emergence of States from Secession", *International Organization* 65:1 (2011) 433–467.
Cohen, Jean L. *Globalization and Sovereignty* (Cambridge: Cambridge University Press, 2012).
Crawford, James. *The Creation of States in International Law* (Oxford: Clarendon Press, 1979).

Dunne, Tim. "Sociological Investigations: Instrumental, Legitimist and Coercive Interpretations of International Society", *Millennium – Journal of International Studies* 30:1 (2001) 67–91.

Erman, Eva. "The Recognitive Practices of Declaring and Constituting Statehood", *International Theory* 5:1 (2013) 36–56.

Fabry, Mikulas. *Recognizing States: International Society and the Establishment of New States since 1776* (Oxford: Oxford University Press, 2010).

Fazal, Tanisha M., and Griffiths, Ryan D. "Membership Has Its Privileges: The Changing Benefits of Statehood", *International Studies Review* 16:1 (2014) 79–106.

Gardner, Anne-Marie. "Beyond Standards before Status: Democratic Governance and Non-State Actors," *Review of International Studies* 34:3 (2008) 531–552.

Geldenhuys, Deon. *Contested States in World Politics* (Basingstoke, UK: Palgrave Macmillan, 2009).

Gong, Gerrit. *The Standard of "Civilization" in International Society* (Oxford: Clarendon Press, 1984).

Griffiths, Ryan D. *The Age of Secession* (Cambridge: Cambridge University Press, 2016).

Hall, Rodney. *National Collective Identity: Social Constructs and International Systems* (New York: Columbia University Press, 1999).

Hannum, Hurst. *Autonomy, Sovereignty and Self-Determination: The Accommodation of Conflicting Rights* (Philadelphia: University of Pennsylvania Press, 1990).

Harvey, James, and Stansfield, Gareth. "Theorizing Unrecognized States: Sovereignty, Secessionism, and Political Economy", in Nina Caspersen and Gareth Stansfield, eds., *Unrecognized States in the International System* (London: Routledge, 2011) 11–26.

Holsti, Kalevi J. *Taming the Sovereigns: Institutional Change in International Politics* (Cambridge: Cambridge University Press, 2004).

Hughes, James. "Russia and the Secession of Kosovo: Power, Norms and the Failure of Multilateralism", *Europe Asia Studies* 65:5 (2013) 992–1016.

Iraqi Constitution, http://www.wipo.int/wipolex/en/text.jsp?file_id=230000 (2005).

Isachenko, Daria. *The Making of Informal States: Statebuilding in Northern Cyprus and Transdniestria* (Basingstoke, UK: Palgrave Macmillan, 2012).

Jackson, Robert. *Quasi-States: Sovereignty, International Relations and the Third World* (Cambridge: Cambridge University Press, 1990).

Jackson, Robert. *The Global Covenant* (Oxford: Oxford University Press, 2000).

Jackson, Robert. *Sovereignty* (Cambridge: Polity, 2007).

Jackson, Robert, and Rosberg, Carl. "Why Africa's Weak States Persist: The Juridical and the Empirical in Statehood", *World Politics* 35:1 (1982) 1–24.

Kalmo, Hent, and Skinner, Quentin, eds. *Sovereignty in Fragments* (Cambridge: Cambridge University Press, 2010).

Keating, Joshua. "How to Start Your Own Country in Four Easy Steps", *Foreign Policy* (February 2008), https://foreignpolicy.com/2008/02/26/how-to-start-your-own-country-in-four-easy-steps/.

Ker-Lindsay, James. "The 'Final' Yugoslav Issue: The Evolution of International Thinking on Kosovo, 1998–2005", in Dejan Djokic and James Ker-Lindsay, eds., *New Perspectives on Yugoslavia* (London: Routledge, 2011) 176–192.

Ker-Lindsay, James. *The Foreign Policy of Counter Secession: Preventing the Recognition of Contested States* (Oxford: Oxford University Press, 2012).

Ker-Lindsay, James. "Preventing the Emergence of Self-Determination as a Norm of Secession: An Assessment of the Kosovo 'Unique Case' Argument", *Europe-Asia Studies* 65:5 (2013) 837–856.

Ker-Lindsay, James. "Engagement without Recognition: The Limits of Diplomatic Interaction with Contested States", *International Affairs* 91:2 (2015) 1–16.
King, Charles. "The Benefits of Ethnic War: Understanding Eurasia's Unrecognized States", *World Politics* 53:1 (2001) 143–172.
Klotz, Audie, and Lynch, Cecilia. *Strategies for Research in Constructivist International Relations* (London: Routledge, 2007).
Knudsen, Rita Augestad. "Moments of Self-Determination: The Concept of 'Self-Determination' and the Idea of Freedom in 20th and 21st Century International Discourse" (PhD Dissertation: London School of Economics and Political Science, 2013).
Kolstø, Pål. "The Sustainability and Future of Unrecognized Quasi-States", *The Journal of Peace Research* 43:6 (2006) 723–740.
Koskenniemi, Martti. *Politics of International Law* (Oxford: Hart, 2011).
Krasner, Stephen D. *Sovereignty: Organized Hypocrisy* (Princeton, NJ: Princeton University Press, 1999).
Kratochwil, Friedrich. "Constructing a New Orthodoxy? Wendt's *Social Theory of International* Politics and the Constructivist Challenge", in Stefano Guzzini and Anna Leander, eds. *Constructivism and International Relations: Alexander Wendt and His Critics* (London: Routledge, 2006) 21–47.
Kurdistan Regional Government. "The Kurdistan Parliament", http://www.KRI.org/p/p.aspx?l=12&s=030000&r=319&p=229.
Lynch, Dov. *Engaging Eurasia's Separatist States: Unresolved Conflicts and De Facto States* (Washington, DC: United States Institute of Peace Press, 2004).
Matthews, Jessica. "Power Shift", *Foreign Affairs* 76:1 (1997) 50–66.
Navari, Cornelia, ed. *Theorising International Society: English School Methods* (New York: Palgrave Macmillan, 2009).
Pegg, Scott. *International Society and the De Facto State* (Aldershot, UK: Ashgate, 1998).
Reus-Smit, Christian. *The Moral Purpose of the State* (Princeton, NJ: Princeton University Press, 1999).
Reus-Smit, Christian. *Individual Rights and the Making of the International System* (Cambridge: Cambridge University Press, 2013).
Ringmar, Erik. "Introduction: The International Politics of Recognition", in Thomas Lindemann, ed., *The International Politics of Recognition* (Boulder, CO: Paradigm, 2011) 3–24.
Ringmar, Erik. "How the World Stage Makes Its Subjects: An Embodied Critique of Constructivist IR Theory", *Journal of International Relations and Development* 19:1 (2016) 101–125.
Ryngaert, Cedric, and Sobrie, Sven. "Recognition of States: International Law or *Realpolitik*? The Practice of Recognition in the Wake of Kosovo, South Ossetia and Abkhazia", *Leiden Journal of International Law* 24:1 (2011) 467–490.
Spears, Ian S. "States-within-States: An Introduction to Their Empirical Attributes", in Paul Kingston and Ian S. Spears, eds., *States-within-States: Incipient Political Entities in the Post–Cold War Era* (New York: Palgrave Macmillan, 2004) 15–34.
United Nations, *Report of the Special Envoy of the Secretary-General on Kosovo's Future Status*, http://www.un.org/en/ga/search/view_doc.asp?symbol=S/2007/168 (2007).
United Nations Resolution 1514. http://www.un.org/en/decolonization/declaration.shtml.
Waltz, Kenneth. *A Theory of International Politics* (Reading, MA: Addison-Wesley Publishing, 1979).

Wendt, Alexander. "Anarchy Is What States Make of It", *International Organization* 46:2 (1992) 391–425.
Wendt, Alexander. "Collective Identity Formation and the International State", *The American Political Science Review* 88:2 (1994) 384–396.
Wendt, Alexander. *Social Theory of International Politics* (Cambridge: Cambridge University Press, 1999).
Wendt, Alexander. "*Social Theory* as Cartesian Science: An Auto-Critique from a Quantum Perspective", in Stefano Guzzini and Anna Leander, eds., *Constructivism and International Relations: Alexander Wendt and His Critics* (London: Routledge, 2006) 178–216.
Wight, Martin. *Systems of States*, ed. Hedley Bull (Leicester: Leicester University Press, 1977).
Worster, William. "Law, Politics and the Conception of the State in State Recognition Theory", *Boston University International Law Journal* 115 (2009) 115–171.
Zaum, Dominik. *The Sovereignty Paradox* (Oxford: Oxford University Press, 2007).

2 International Legitimacy and the Normative Standing of De Facto States

Legitimacy is frequently employed as a functional construct to authorise, sanction or discredit political status and conduct, yet it remains a remarkably tenuous concept, often subject to the perspective or convenience of the user. Can de facto states exhibit legitimate behaviour? Can they *be* legitimate or *have* legitimacy in the international sphere? If not, how do we conceive of their actions which mirror those of states that are deemed by other recognised states to be legitimate? If so, can their actions or status be conceived of as more or less legitimate than those of recognised states? Are there degrees of legitimacy?

In order to examine the prospective legitimacy of de facto states, and in order to determine how to assess it in less nebulous and more systematic ways, I propose a framework that synthesises concepts and notions from existing analyses of legitimacy and explicitly reject other proposed frameworks, concepts and notions. The robustness of this framework is essential to the concept of normative standing that will be constructed and presented below; therefore, an explanation of the framework's key tenets is required to bolster its defensibility and its generalisability.

What Is Legitimacy?

This chapter aims to answer questions surrounding the prospect of international legitimacy. In order to achieve this goal, I will trace the study of legitimacy, the varying contexts in which it is evident and how it has been conceived in those contexts, so that we may better understand its contemporary applications vis-à-vis the international sphere. Legitimacy is a relational concept, and the dynamics of the international field within which legitimacy lies are distinct from the relations of government and the governed. However, theories of legitimacy were spawned from studies of state–society relations, and therefore this study's consideration of conceptual precedents begins in the domestic sphere. In order to account for the many influences that have shaped understandings of legitimacy, this discussion will extend beyond the restrictive confines of Political Science and International Relations to include various sociological and philosophical contributions to the subject.

DOI: 10.4324/9781003178521-3

Bridging the Empirical–Normative Divide

The majority of literature examining legitimacy is focussed on the domestic political sphere.[1] Weber's conception of legitimacy has proven to be an enduring frame of reference, a concept that "theorists have found themselves unable to live comfortably either with, or wholly without".[2] Max Weber describes social action as being "guided by the belief in the existence of a legitimate order".[3] He describes a political regime as legitimate when its subjects believe it to be so: "The basis of every system of authority, and correspondingly of every kind of willingness to obey, is a belief, a belief by virtue of which persons exercising authority are lent prestige".[4] Weber famously claimed that this belief in the legitimacy of a regime arises from three main sources: the long-standing status of the regime (tradition), the charisma of the ruler, and the regime's rational-legal basis.[5] Weber's greatest contribution to the study of legitimacy, however, is his move to locate legitimacy in the belief of the people. While much of his theory has been debated and rejected, the centrality of belief as both a vehicle for and a source location of legitimacy has endured, and has become central to an array of definitions.[6]

A frequently overlooked component of Weber's conceptualisation is the relationship between legitimacy at the group level and legitimacy at the individual level. When a group considers norms, values and practices as legitimate, Weber refers to this as "validity";[7] it forms the foundation of a valid social order. This order becomes an object in itself that regulates the behaviour of the people. For Weber, legitimation is therefore inherently collective. As Morris Zelditch states, for Weber "legitimacy is a collective product of many psychologies, not one".[8] Even for an individual who does not believe in the order's legitimacy, the individual knows that it regulates the behaviour of the group, and is aware of how their own behaviour relates to the norms, values, beliefs and practices of that social order. The order is considered binding by nature. What begins as intersubjective understanding is then objectified through externalisation, becoming lasting and pervading the form and function of that society. Compliance often becomes habitual, but it can also be motivated by expedience.[9]

Weberian notions of legitimacy, and the empirical approaches they have inspired,[10] have been criticised for their inadequate consideration of the moral fibre that legitimacy denotes. Normative approaches argue that, by studying the beliefs of the people, observers erroneously draw the focus away from the rightfulness of the regime's actions, consequently hollowing the concept of moral substance.[11] This risks equating legitimacy to something as fickle and equivocal as sentiment.[12] The early champions of this approach argue that legitimacy ought to be measured against a set of normative standards and not be reduced to simple acquiescence or consensus. They argue that legitimacy is not the same as consensus; rather, it is a unique kind of consensus to which *the right* to rule is intrinsic.[13] Empirical approaches, they argue, obfuscate the right to rule by confusing it with a regime's ability to "persuade members of its own appropriateness",[14] which risks justifying the authority of a regime that manipulates its people to perceive its potentially immoral power as adequate.[15]

As the legitimacy literature unfolded, the concepts of authority and legitimacy were so closely linked that, until relatively recently, a disregard for the need to discern and clarify them as being pragmatically distinctive was pervasive. This is understandable given the logic underpinning the widely accepted Weberian approach to this matter, which interprets authority to be the status of the relationship between an institution and an actor when the actor deems that institution to be legitimate.[16] Political authority, according to this view, is therefore the marriage of power with this "legitimate social purpose";[17] to classify an institution as having legitimate authority would therefore be tautological.[18]

The most prevalent view on the relationship between legitimacy, authority and obligation is that legitimate authority creates political obligations for the subjects of that authority.[19] This perspective was originally derived from John Locke's conception of political obligation.[20] Weberian empiricists, who perceive the effect of the legitimacy of a regime to be the obligation that it elicits at the individual level, have perpetuated it further. Even for those who make the distinction between authority and legitimacy, it is commonly accepted that, so long as both have been established, binding obligations have been created.

An opposing view is that obligations are derived from one's membership in a collective – either a "biological or social group" – rather than from their relationship with a regime.[21] This does not discount the existence of a general obligation to obey a political authority, but this obligation arises from the normative binding of the community, not as a direct duty to the authority. Some justice scholars extrapolate this further.[22] John Rawls argues that a "natural" binding duty exists within a just community, rather than an explicit duty to obey the law purely because it has been implemented by the state.[23] For Rawls, this duty to "support and comply" with institutions only exists if the institution is "just (or fair)" and the individual has "voluntarily accepted the benefits of the arrangement or taken advantage of the opportunities it offers".[24] In this instance, subjects can be obligated to a legitimate authority, but such an obligation is not automatic. In response to these rejections of any general principle of obligation, George Klosko argues that the idea of a general principle is in itself the problem; there are multiple principles of obligation that exist in varying moral and political relationships between governments and those governed.[25] For a concept now widely accepted by social scientists as being multifaceted, it is fitting that, if the function of obligation is to be included, it is only one piece of the puzzle and not the essential defining criterion.[26]

The empirical and normative approaches to legitimacy have been deemed by many to be insufficient and problematically narrow in their conception.[27] David Beetham recognises that, in their criticism, the normativists overstate their case by making a flawed distinction between "people's beliefs" and their "*grounds* or *reasons*" for holding these beliefs, for these could well be morally founded.[28] Beetham's critique of Weberian empiricism argues that it misrepresents the relationship between legitimacy and people's beliefs: "A given power relationship is not legitimate because people believe in its legitimacy, but because it can be *justified in terms of* their beliefs".[29] The values and standards of the people are the measure of the regime. This interpretation avoids the ambiguities of the abstract normative approaches while embodying the very moral substance that they have sought to install. For Beetham, if a political system conforms to the normative expectations of the people, then and only then can it be considered to be legitimate.

In this framework, the rules of power form the first level, referring to the legal validity of the means through which power is obtained and the practices through which it is exercised. The second level is the justification for the rules of power based on the beliefs of the society. This encompasses the competence of the powerholder, the source of their authority, and the ability of the system of power relations to serve the common interest. The third level is the consent of the subordinate, which must be evidenced by an explicit action. The event of explicit action is a crucial component that this study argues must be incorporated into any theory of international legitimacy. The nature of legitimacy in a social structure devoid of the governed–government relationship demands such overt statements because the dynamics and political context of the international society are far more fluid than those of the domestic sphere. At the international level, it is not consent that is being expressed, it is the agreement or approval of other actors' behaviours that need to be explicit.

Incorporating Sources of Legitimacy

The analytical distinction between procedural and substantive legitimacy permeates studies of legitimacy. The former refers to an outcome that is deemed legitimate due to adherence to procedural factors, frequently referred to as "input legitimacy".[30] In the domestic sphere, this generally refers to the mechanisms that convert the beliefs of the people into political action. Elections are a prime example of a mechanism that, in a democratic context, provides the people with an instrument to exercise their preferences through explicit action.[31] Hence, one criterion of a *legitimate* democracy is the practice of free and fair elections. The significance of procedural factors is central to legal-rational conceptions of legitimacy, where rules or authority are accepted because of the "formal legality" that is affixed to them.[32]

Substantive legitimacy – also commonly described as "output legitimacy"[33] – refers to the acceptance of a rule, institution or outcome because it embodies certain principles or ideals,[34] or because it achieves a desirable result.[35] For instance, Fritz Scharpf considers the extent to which a government performs effectively to be a fair measure of its output legitimacy.[36] If an institution is satisfying the basic functions that it exists to serve, then it is substantively legitimate. This correlates to the requisite competence and common interest in the second level of Beetham's framework, which clearly infers that the effectiveness of government contributes significantly to its legitimacy.

It is important to note that both procedural and substantive conceptions of legitimacy can be normative in nature, and indeed most are. This is the case when rules or institutions derive their input legitimacy through the perception of certain procedures satisfying the requirements to be a "rightful source of authority",[37] just as it is the case when output legitimacy is obtained because of the "fundamental extra-legal values" that the rule or institution appeals to.[38] Similarly, procedural and substantive notions are not mutually exclusive. Although there have been many efforts to identify which brings the greatest legitimacy in varying situations,[39] prominent theories of legitimacy such as those of Beetham and Franck incorporate both. The applicability is contingent on the social constituency and the central issue of legitimation.

The concept of consensus is integral to legitimacy. The notion of consensus as a legitimating force dates back to the work of Aristotle, and permeates the social contract theories of Locke and Rousseau.[40] At the consensus-relevant end of the spectrum, Rawls argues that an order is legitimate when it is guided by a collection of basic standards that "citizens as free and equal may reasonably be expected to endorse", equating to an "overlapping consensus".[41] It is important to note, given the nature of Rawls' work, that this "overlapping consensus" is not an abstract ideal; rather, it is an observable social phenomenon that can exist in liberal democratic communities. At the consensus-centric end of the spectrum, there are normative theorists such as Talcott Parsons and Seymour Lipset who have developed approaches based on the core component of the perception that the group interest, or consensus that reflects this group interest, defines what is rightful and therefore legitimate.[42]

As I noted above, in acknowledging the key function of consensus, one must not make the mistake of reducing legitimacy solely to consensus. Legitimacy is not the same as consensus; it is a unique kind of consensus in which the right to rule is elemental.[43] There are varying accounts of the role that consensus plays in legitimation; however, there is broad agreement that, no matter how its role is defined, it is indeed intrinsic.[44] Even theorists who do not explicitly state the centrality of consensus, such as Ian Hurd, focus on the perceptions of the subjects and, in effect, study the patterns of normative beliefs and the degree to which they correspond with one another.[45] This pattern signifies, at the very least, a degree of consensus and demarcates its purview. At the international level, the element of consensus becomes even more important because the overtly hierarchical relationship between the government and the governed does not exist. International legitimacy, in this sense, exists between subjects.

The interplay between actors' interests and that which they consider to be legitimate raises the following question: can an observer discern whether an actor is following rules, or acting in accordance with socially sanctioned norms, because of a self-interested motivation, rather than because they are complying with their society's expectations? A clear distinction between contextually defined interest and self-interest is required to answer this question.

Legitimacy is an innately contested concept. As a quality, legitimacy can be used to describe a practice, behaviour, rule or institution. As a status, legitimacy refers to an agent's right to behave in certain ways and in specific forums. Although the normative–empirical divide is still present, the most accepted way forward is a hybrid approach that embraces the power of belief and recognises the normative grounding underpinning this belief. The study of deeply contested concepts spurs such divides. Embracing the utility of the descriptive approach enables scholars to study and understand a phenomenon that is now largely accepted to be normative in nature. These are the contours that I will now navigate in search of a practicable understanding of international legitimacy.

International Legitimacy

It is relatively recently that the concept of legitimacy has come to be closely examined in the international realm. The absence of scholarship on the subject was not due to academic neglect but to "a positive rejection of a concept widely considered inappropriate to an international setting".[46] Put simply, a concept that was commonly understood to mean 'the right to rule' was deemed redundant for analysing the dynamics of a system defined by the absence of government.[47] While the dominant International Relations theories of the twentieth century focussed on great power politics and perceived the international sphere as being dominated by the amoral contest of competing national agendas, there was little interest in interrogating the beliefs of states as to how they should act, or in assessing their actions against external normative yardsticks.

Much of the earlier work that broke ground on international legitimacy came from legal theorists, who followed the vein of Inis Claude. Claude's seminal piece sought to snatch legitimacy out of the hands of the philosophers, and utilise it as a tool to better understand the processes of "collective legitimisation" that bore international approval, focussing on the underlying institutions and procedures of the United Nations.[48] Claude's work highlighted the positive and negative effects of the authority carried by the United Nations' stamp of approval, and drew attention to the gap between international law and international legitimacy, concluding that the former does not necessarily equate to the latter. It was another 20 years before this gap received adequate scholarly attention, when Thomas Franck turned a distinct spotlight on it.[49] This laid the foundation for subsequent legal theorists, who have since constructed more comprehensive models of international legitimacy.[50]

Allen Buchanan brought analytical, moral and political philosophy to bear on his examination of the relationship between the morality of international law and international legitimacy. Buchanan's holistic theory grounds his interpretation of international legitimacy in justice, expounding the argument that a legitimate institution is one that operates with just procedures for protecting the rights of individuals.[51] This issue of justice and how it relates to legitimacy colourfully illustrates the division between purely empirical and normative approaches. The question of when an institution can be considered just is fundamentally grounded in an observer's judgement about 'justness'. This is a very separate question to that of when an institution is perceived as legitimate by those subject to it. Equating legitimacy with 'justness' deprives the former of its explanatory utility.[52] Shifting the focus from the belief of the people to the assessment of the observer is useful for the philosopher seeking universal explanations or for the social scientist comparing the democratic credentials of domestic political systems against a global trend or norm. If the aim is to understand the motivations, behaviours, and relationships of actors within a social system, then a purely normative conception of legitimacy based on justice is inadequate. This does not mean, however, that to study legitimacy empirically one must exclude any notion of morality. On the contrary, legitimacy is an inherently normative concept.

A more nuanced and diagnostic approach comes from Franck, another of the legal theorists, who divorces legitimacy from justice. In Franck's disaggregation, he lays the moral foundation first, defining legitimacy as "a property of a rule or rule-making institution which itself exerts a pull towards compliance on those addressed normatively".[53] This definition adopts the Weberian notion of an actor's subjective belief, but then extends it to include the moral grounding as constitutive of the normative compliance pull. It is important to note here that Franck is not strictly referring to states as "those addressed", but includes any major international actors, including international organisations and leadership elites.[54] Franck proceeds to add a significant qualifier, stipulating the importance of "the perception of those addressed by a rule or rule-making institution that the rule or institution has come into being and operates in accordance with generally accepted principles of right process".[55] The compliance pull is driven in part by the procedural correctness that confers the rightful authority. This echoes the justification found in Beetham's second level, but here it is conceived in more procedural terms.

Franck seeks to understand legitimacy at a deeper level than that of simple institutional and procedural approaches. His layered framework claims to uncover the sources of what he accepts to be a value judgement. Franck's articulation of legitimacy is founded on rules that are built on four layers. The first layer is determinacy, which states that rules must be as explicit and univocal as possible. The second is symbolic validation, addressing the degree to which a judgement has been made through "proper channels". Coherence forms the third layer, describing the extent to which a rule coheres with accepted and honoured conventions. The final layer is adherence, and is concerned with the motivations of states: have they abided by the rule because of an elemental, latent identification as a member of a community?

The practice of legitimacy is at the heart of Franck's framework: validations of the past set expectations for validation in the present and future. The idea of how international actors should behave is built on the improvement of previously approved behaviour. International society, as a project, is therefore continuously refining legitimate practice, rather than classifying that which is legitimate by measuring actions and decisions against an exogenous set of values. John Williams' critique of this argument is insightful, claiming that Franck sees "legitimacy as being clouded by the introduction of value systems, despite these providing the foundations for the mechanisms, which he sees as constituting legitimacy".[56] Williams' charge against Franck is that his move to detach value judgements from "value systems" is arbitrary and problematic. Williams views the system of values to be a requisite metaphysical framework upon which a value judgement draws. Franck's choice to separate legitimacy from justice explicitly rejects such a position. Focussing on the practice of legitimacy reveals a political locus that is divorced from the ideals of a universal morality. I agree with Franck and argue that political competition is intrinsic to the contours of international legitimacy. The politics of recognition, as explored in the previous chapter, demonstrate the omnipresent political undercurrents that saturate international legitimation debates and contestations.

Disregarding an overarching value system does not mean jettisoning the role of values; legitimacy is, after all, an identifiable entity's value judgement. This is particularly clear in Franck's later work, where he contends that an important output of legitimate institutions and practice is a belief in the fairness of their outputs.[57] Abram Chayes and Antonia Chayes also focus on the relationship between fairness and legitimacy; however, they suggest an inverse relationship to that of Franck, claiming that it is the actors' beliefs in the fairness of a rule or institution that elicit compliance.[58] Fairness, in their interpretation, is a fundamental value that exists in the procedures, applications and output of legitimate institutions. Legitimacy is only achieved in the wake of fairness.

I choose to separate legitimacy from fairness, just as I choose to divorce legitimacy from justice. Fairness is a value that may play a vital part in certain processes of legitimation, and indeed in certain situations it may be a legitimate or desired outcome. However, I argue that it is not intrinsic to the legitimation process because legitimacy is discernible from any value based on its constitution by social recognition. Christian Reus-Smit illustrates this argument poignantly in relation to justice: "An actor might plausibly describe his or her actions as *just*, regardless of the level of social endorsement".[59] Hurd supports this position, stating that one should not conflate the question of "when is an institution legitimate?" with "when can we say that an institution is just?".[60] This logic can be applied to any and every value that may be relevant or present in the process of legitimation. As Beetham cogently points out, "legitimacy for social scientists is always legitimacy-in-context, rather than absolutely, ideally, or abstractly".[61] The values pertaining to any given legitimation process or contest will be contingent on the context and especially on the norms and legitimate practices of the relevant social constituency. In this instance, Franck's original logic is adhered to; normative judgements do not require omnipresent value systems. It is in the interplay of values and norms that legitimacy is contested, a contestation that is subject to political manoeuvring, if not manipulation.

The legitimacy of international regimes has been a fruitful subject of enquiry that has inspired significant contributions to understanding international legitimacy.[62] An insightful proponent is Hurd, who defines legitimacy in a Weberian vein as an "actor's normative belief that a rule or institution ought to be obeyed".[63] With belief still as the kernel of legitimacy, Hurd discards Weber's creation of obligation because it is the actor's "feeling" of a "compliance pull" that guides behaviour, not a mandated political duty.[64] The belief in the rightfulness of a norm and the consequent action of following that norm have no inherent relationship with abiding by the law or generally complying with a regime's regulations. Legitimacy can in fact drive an individual to break a law because that law asks them to act in a manner contrary to their own normative persuasion.[65] This is the predominant motivation behind acts of civil disobedience such as the famous actions of Rosa Parks. It is only when the laws of the state are deemed to be in accordance with the normative convictions of the people that legitimacy contributes to state-backing law and order.[66] This notion of the compliance pull is very much aligned with Beetham's second layer, where a regime must justify the rules of power in alignment with the beliefs of the people. Furthermore, I argue that the notion of a compliance pull rather than a mandated obligation is the most applicable notion in an anarchical valid social order.[67]

For Hurd, legitimacy is explicitly subjective and normative, manifesting as a feeling that shapes the perception of an actor or group of actors. The fact that one actor deems a rule legitimate has no implication for how that rule is perceived by other actors, as it is held internally. Legitimacy can of course still be intersubjective. The motivation for complying with a rule is a sense of "rightness and obligation"; the essential action of legitimation, for Hurd, is the internalisation of an extrinsic principle that causes the actor's interests to be reconfigured in light of the rule.[68] In order to forward this approach, centred on subjectivity, Hurd accepts the possibility of conflicting perceptions of legitimacy being held by different actors. Hurd's internalisation thesis is well designed for analysing rules and institutions, but its explanatory utility is limited to this task. The focus on internalisation as the key mechanism of legitimacy, and the consequent behaviour as the key marker of legitimacy, cannot extend to explaining the behaviour between actors and is consequently insufficient for understanding legitimacy within an international society or community. The central reason for this point needs to be made clear, given that I agree with other key components of Hurd's approach.

First, although I accept the Wendtian agent-structure framework and notion of state agency that underpins Hurd's theory, Hurd has misinterpreted one key feature of Wendt's theory of state identity. He claims that adopting this approach "suggests that states, by virtue of being corporate entities, have strong beliefs about their interests, and they pursue strategies to maximize them".[69] Thus far, we are in agreement. However, he continues: "But they are also corporate entities only by virtue of the social recognition of that identity by the community, and so their understandings of their interests are shaped by the expectations of the community".[70] Hurd is correct in claiming that the social recognition by the community shapes their understanding of their interests; however, Wendt states that the *corporate* identity of the state is constituted by "self-organizing, homeostatic structures".[71] Because the corporate identity is self-organising, it is exogenous to the social structure within which it exists; hence, Wendt classifies it as pre-social. As I pointed out in the previous chapter, the corporate identity exists prior to recognition, and to confuse this point is to make a mistaken ontological statement about the state system and about state creation. Hurd's misinterpretation makes it impossible for his theory to understand the social currency of agents with varying levels of recognition, but it is also problematic for analysing the dynamics of a community or society; it is only capable of explaining the internalisation of a rule, norm or authority, because this internalisation influences the agent's behaviour. Although internalisation is the key mechanism for Hurd, his object of study is the consequent behaviour.[72] In many situations, a state is capable of making an internal normative appraisal without necessarily acting on it. Conversely, using Wendtian logic, states are incapable of forming their interests without considering the motivations and actions of other states, which is incompatible with Hurd's "operative process" of a consequent reconfiguration of "his or her interests".[73]

To effectively analyse the legitimacy of actors in relation to one another, there must be a separation between the adjustment of one's own interests in relation to those of others and the explicit normative appraisal of another's identity that leads to such an adjustment. Reus-Smit captures this when he claims that "an actor can be said to command legitimacy, therefore, when its decisions and actions (and I would contend identities and interests) are *socially sanctioned*".[74] For such an identity or interest to be socially sanctioned, it is not the appraisal of single actors that equates to this; it is "when society ordains this quality" that an actor can be said to command legitimacy.[75] Consensus is fundamental. The expression of this consensus through explicit action is crucial. Positing that legitimacy gives an agent the right to act means that some form of consensus must be present because "the very idea of a right presupposes the existence of a community".[76] An actor's belief in the rightfulness of their action is not the same as a community appraising it as legitimate. This point is evidenced by the approach of contemporary international society to norms of territorial integrity and nuclear non-proliferation. The community's recognition of an agent's right to act is most accurately described as a "process of consensual empowerment".[77] The relationship between power and legitimacy, therefore, needs closer examination.

Reus-Smit led an interrogation into the relationship between international legitimacy and power in a pioneering agenda that sought to define the contours of that which can be considered a 'crisis of legitimacy', a phrase frequently used yet infrequently clarified. Prior to this effort, scholars of international relations typically made a clear distinction between power and legitimacy, viewing the former through a Waltzian lens of material capability and the latter as a mere mantle of social acquiescence sought to justify the wielding of this might.[78] Reus-Smit problematises this distinction by first dismantling the reductionist assumption that power is equal to the sum of resources commanded. Drawing on Weber, he defines a powerful actor as one who has "the capacity to realise their objectives" and a powerful institution as having "transformative capacity" with the "ability to engender behavioural change in those within its jurisdiction".[79] Material factors are relevant to power, but they are rarely defining of it; rather, they demarcate the limits of possibility.[80] The meaning of the material is contingent upon the intersubjective norms and beliefs of the society. Legitimacy is an appraisal made by members of the society about the actions and identity of other members in reference to the intersubjective norms that exist within the society. Legitimation contests are, therefore, integral to the social fibres and dynamics that condition "the nature and exercise of power".[81] Establishing oneself as rightful, and acting in accordance with established norms, means that an actor can draw on the support of other legitimate members; they can expect compliance from those members pertaining to legitimated practices or rules; and they can operate with minimal resistance from the community.[82] As indicated above, legitimacy is empowering.

Clarifying the intrinsic relationship between empowerment and legitimacy, and outlining the process of legitimation lay the foundation for Reus-Smit's definition of a crisis of legitimacy, "that critical turning point when decline in an actor's or institution's legitimacy forces adaptation (through re-legitimation or material inducement) or disempowerment".[83] The temporality of crises can be short and intense, or it can be long and sustained.[84] Actors can be conscious of their crisis of legitimacy, but they do not have to be. An actor can very easily misperceive the basis of their legitimacy, just as an illegitimate actor can misinterpret the legitimation processes of the community within which they seek to be legitimised. The political sphere within which an entity seeks to act will determine the social constituency that the entity needs in order to engage in a process of legitimation. Hence, for an actor aspiring to legitimacy, their position could be outside of this political arena and they may be operating with a resultant ignorance of crucial norms and practices, or of ideational barriers blockading their quest for legitimacy.

Rightful Membership and Rightful Conduct

One of the enduring conceptions of legitimacy in international relations scholarship has been the recognition of sovereignty by other states. Martin

Wight was one of the earliest scholars to focus on international legitimacy, putting it at the centre of his analysis of the evolution of the international state system and as considering it a grounding force for understanding the constitution of international society:

> Let us define international legitimacy as the collective judgement of international society about rightful membership of the family of nations; how sovereignty may be transferred; how state succession should be regulated, when large states break up into smaller, or several states combine into one. It concerns the presuppositions of the region of discourse that international lawyers seek to reduce to juridical system when they write about the recognition of states.[85]

Wight sought to trace how this practice of reciprocal recognition has developed throughout history. He propelled the idea of recognition as being more than just an expression of the acceptable standards of statehood; it is the empowerment of a polity with international legitimacy.[86] This view strongly supports the constitutive interpretation of sovereignty, explicitly stating that sovereignty is not a status or condition that a state can simply achieve through its own volition. Rather, it is a reciprocated appraisal.[87] This mutuality is not only defining of the condition, it is a telling insight into the "very nature" of international society.[88] Since Wight first made this claim, equating recognition with rightful membership into the 'family of nations' has been widely agreed upon as one clear measure of international legitimacy by scholars of international society and by those who support the constitutive theory of statehood.[89] Of course, this is only a measure of status, and implies little about practice.

The distinction between legitimate status and the practice of legitimacy is at the heart of Clark's theory of legitimacy in international society. Clark promotes the Wightian premise that "the core principles of international legitimacy express rudimentary social agreement about who is entitled to participate in international relations", but importantly he adds that it is "also about appropriate forms in their conduct".[90] Clark's theory seeks not only to clarify international legitimacy, but also to articulate a clearer conception of international society, which he describes as "a set of historically changing principles of legitimacy" that are "not necessarily expressed as institutions" and that are "often too informal to be classed as rules".[91] For Clark, the existence of legitimacy denotes the existence of international society. International society is the subject of international legitimacy; legitimation is the ongoing process that, in part, constitutes that society. Put succinctly, "legitimacy lies at the very heart of what is meant by an international society".[92] Clark states that an argument about international legitimacy cannot be made outside of the framework of international society "or near equivalent".[93] As an inherently social concept, this is seemingly hard to argue with, and it aligns with the requisite relationship between legitimacy and community which was discussed above.

Clark's conception posits legitimacy as a "first-order" quality or principles of international society; it is necessary for an international society to exist. The "second-order" qualities describe the activities that the society will permit.[94] There is a clear distinction between legitimacy as constituting international society and the norms that pertain to the second-order behaviour. Clark details the interplay of three second-order qualities that are central to this understanding: the international norms of legality, morality and constitutionality. Legality, in the most basic sense, refers to the widely held view that international legitimacy indicates adherence to the law. For an action or decision to be legitimate, it must be in accordance with international law. This is a logical starting point, given the word 'legitimate' has etymological roots in *legislate*.[95] Legality is an important force in the dynamics of international legitimacy, but the two are by no means synonymous. An illustrative example of this can be found in the Independent International Commission on Kosovo (IICK), which stated that the military intervention by the North Atlantic Treaty Organisation (NATO) in 1998–1999 was "illegal but legitimate" – illegal because it was not approved by the United Nations Security Council but legitimate because "all diplomatic avenues had been exhausted and because the intervention had the effect of liberating the majority population of Kosovo".[96] International law, in this case, is clearly an insufficient source for mapping the terrain of international legitimacy. Rightful action in this case was guided by principles of morality as well.

The pillar of morality can be understood in a similar vein to the justice-grounded theories of legitimacy. In Buchanan's analysis of the Kosovo intervention, he highlights the shortcomings of international law, as it does not allow "what morality requires".[97] In Buchanan's portrayal of the gap between the law and morality, he moves to equate legitimate action with this moral imperative. The example of Kosovo does lend itself to conceiving legitimacy in terms of extrajudicial morality; however, it is only one example, and the limitations of this approach have already been highlighted. The 2003 United-States-led invasion of Iraq provides a more contentious example, where the moral arguments in support of the intervention have split observers.[98] Clark claims that, even though the moral arguments were perceived as "ambiguous and indeterminate", the crisis of legitimacy arose from the invasion's incongruity with the norm of constitutionality.[99]

Constitutionality is a more amorphous phenomenon than the other two cognate concepts or norms, but one that has considerable explanatory utility for those who perceive legitimacy to be more than the relationship between legality and morality. Constitutionality refers to the reciprocated political beliefs and assumptions of international society that influence behaviour, that are not enshrined in law, and that are not equivalent to moral principles. Clark succinctly argues that the concept refers to "the political realm of conventions, informal understandings, and mutual expectations".[100] Constitutionality, this study argues, largely encompasses Franck's layer of coherence, and it incorporates his component of adherence. For a state to take action that is contrary to the conventional, consensually expected behaviour of international society is to shun part of its identification with that society. In this sense, whether states are abiding by these expectations or acting in discordance with them, constitutionality is inherently political. As such, it is the most complicated component because it can be subject to swift changes in the global system, and because it is always contingent on the power relations within society. Constitutional behaviour can maintain a state's position of power, but the constitution itself is conditioned by the distribution of power and the actions of those who wield it.[101]

The 2003 United-States-led invasion of Iraq is a clarifying example of a crisis in constitutionality. The legal case for military intervention in Iraq was no stronger than the one presented for Kosovo, and it is arguable that the moral case was equally problematic. The facts of the case for invading Iraq placed before the members of international society were more troubling than those for Kosovo, not only because of the ambiguities, but also because the proposal fell against a backdrop of increasing unilateralism in US foreign policy: "The crisis over Iraq would not have been so serious had it not been regarded as the *culmination* of a tendency, rather than as an isolated departure".[102] Considerations of supporting the intervention happened in a political context that was already riddled with concerns about the increasingly unilateral US foreign policy and exacerbated by its 'war on terror'. This reveals the inherently political nature of legitimacy, which is expressed as "the exercise of choice in a realm of indeterminate values".[103]

Constitutionality has powerful explanatory utility because it captures this contextual contingency of legitimacy, embracing its political locus without rejecting the normative dynamics embodied by the pillars of morality and legality. International legitimacy indicates the presence of these norms and a substantive degree of harmony between them. Yet, it can also be that which exists in between the tension of these norms when they are at odds with one another. It is important to be clear about this key feature: the tension, which can result in questions arising about the legitimacy of the relevant subject, is between each of these norms, not between any one norm and legitimacy itself. To frame such a crisis as being between that which is legitimate and that which is legal or moral is a contradiction in terms. This is a clear point of difference between Franck's framework and that of Clark, for Franck describes the IICK report as "bridging the gap" between legitimacy and legality.[104] Exploring another key component of Clark's theory will help to elucidate this complex relationship between legitimacy and these cognate norms.

In addition to the balance held between these normative standards, international legitimacy is still deeply connected to the notion of consensus. Legitimacy has already been shown to exist in relation to the norms of legality, morality and constitutionality, but it is not the mere sum of these parts, nor is it so closely related to them that each norm is indistinguishable from legitimacy itself. Rather, legitimacy includes the crucial quality of political negotiation and compromise, establishing an accommodation between the contesting normative poles that is expressed on a spectrum of consensus. This consensual component denotes the standing of legitimacy as distinct and distanced from these norms upon which it draws.[105]

In this sense, consensus is not inherently valuable as a stand-alone phenomenon. Consensus is valuable and integral to international legitimacy because it marks a political accommodation that corresponds to the norms that guide rightful international practice. The centrality of consensus and its normative grounding challenges the traditional normative theories, for it posits that legitimacy "does not possess its own independent standard against which actions can be measured".[106] By acknowledging the political dynamic of legitimation contests and embracing the normative foundations upon which they rest, Clark's central thrust of equating international society with the existence of international legitimacy becomes abundantly clear.

Theories of international legitimacy have developed to embrace its moral fibre, but in a more practical manner than those authored by moral philosophers, contextualising legitimacy's meaning in the dynamics of a specific social structure at a given time. Clark has achieved this convincingly with his theory of legitimacy in international society, though Beetham, Franck, Hurd and Reus-Smit have all provided useful theoretical tools with which to interrogate the legitimacy of an international entity. Before this study can draw on these insights to clearly outline the framework that it will use to question the notion of a de facto state's international legitimacy, it will first need to explore the use of legitimacy as an elucidatory concept within the de facto state literature.

De Facto States and International Legitimacy

The recent move by scholars of de facto states to elaborate their analyses by introducing the concept of legitimacy as an illuminating lens has developed without yet fully engaging the rich tapestry of legitimacy theory. The work done so far has carved out a path upon which this study seeks to fruitfully expand by engaging the literature on legitimacy to explore and detail the place of de facto states in international political systems. Insights from the forays of scholars into the international legitimacy of de facto states provide a logical starting point.

International legitimacy, commonly referred to as 'external legitimacy' in the de facto state literature, has predominantly been examined in relation to internal legitimacy, the object of study being how the lack of external legitimacy impacts the development of internal legitimacy and vice versa.[107] A 2012 special issue of *Communist and Post-Communist Studies* led the charge in this investigation by looking into the post-Soviet de facto states, bringing their internal political developments to the fore. Following Scott Pegg's initial distinction of internal and external legitimacy, this issue equates external legitimacy with international recognition, and focusses on the success of domestic legitimation in the absence of recognition.[108] Pegg and Kolstø's astute analysis of Somaliland's robust internal legitimacy follows in this vein, embracing what is a common position in the literature.[109]

Some attempts have been made to separate external legitimacy from international recognition by focussing on the extent of economic, cultural and diplomatic engagements that de facto states have managed to secure.[110] It is important to note that the literature focussing on the international engagement of de facto states addresses behaviours and activities that are specific to the practice of para-diplomacy. Para-diplomacy is defined by Noé Cornago as:

> non-central governments' involvement in international relations through the establishment of permanent or ad-hoc contacts with foreign public or private entities, with the aim to promote socioeconomic or cultural issues, as well as any other foreign dimension of their constitutional competences.[111]

This book accepts this definition, and consequently perceives all relations between a de facto state government and any foreign private or public entity to be a form of para-diplomacy. As such, all discussion of international engagement, and its relationship to legitimacy, by extension, encompasses the practice of para-diplomacy as a perceived form of legitimation.

James Ker-Lindsay has thoroughly interrogated the dynamics of international engagement, and although his work is not centred specifically on legitimacy he claims that the creative measures that recognised states are willing to use to engage de facto states do confer "a degree of legitimacy" without going as far as "to extend formal recognition".[112] Nina Caspersen has since used this notion of degrees of legitimacy as a springboard to launch a detailed analysis of the tensions that exist between internal and external legitimation strategies. Caspersen's analysis draws much-needed attention to the difficulties that the pursuit of different forms of international engagement can pose for de facto state leaders and their means of securing popular domestic support. Although Caspersen's examination of this relationship is insightful and a significant contribution that elucidates the struggles of de facto states, Caspersen's conceptualisation of legitimacy is restrictive, limiting its theoretical utility and explanatory power.

Caspersen defines external legitimacy as "support from external sources, be it from state or non-state actors", adding the criteria that there is no single measure of support and that the support must be "active, voluntary support".[113] Caspersen addresses the distinction between normative and empirical legitimacy, acknowledging that "normative criteria ... affect both external and internal legitimacy" and stating that "the extent of this impact and the type of normative standards that matter are expected to depend on the audience in question".[114] This is a suitably pragmatic definition for answering what Caspersen considers to be "an empirical question".[115] The present study recognises that the question asked is indeed empirical, and acknowledges the utility of examining the tension between internal legitimation and external engagement. However, it also argues that to equate external legitimacy with international engagement is to oversimplify legitimacy: they are not one and the same.

Caspersen's Weberian conception of support is problematic at the international level for two reasons. First, support can be motivated strongly by the supporter's own political interest. This is not inherently problematic, however, as demonstrated by the case of Russia's recognition of and support for Abkhazia and South Ossetia; this support can actually be disempowering, which directly contradicts the very heart of what legitimacy is and the reason that de facto states are seeking it. Second, this definition does not specify the role of the community within which this legitimation is happening, a crucial limitation given their symbiotic relationship outlined above. Even Hurd, who operationalises a similarly Weberian notion of legitimacy that focusses on the subjective perspective of supporters, considers a community to be a number of actors that "share a common definition of what is legitimate".[116] Even when asking an empirical question, for support to be considered a measure of legitimacy the role and function of that support within the community must be explicit. To discard the notion of a valid social order, or a community, or a society, is to nullify the concept of legitimacy.

Legitimacy is, as demonstrated above, an inexorably contested concept, and it an inherently complex one. But that is no reason to try and simplify it. On the contrary, simplifying legitimacy only limits the extent to which the subjects engaged in the practice of legitimacy, or in legitimation strategies, can be understood. This is especially pertinent for the more ambiguous political entities such as de facto states. Existing in imposed exclusion from international society does not preclude them from engaging in processes of legitimation. On the contrary, their ongoing legitimation struggles are defining of their very existence and are constitutive of their identity. De facto state experts have made a valuable move in opening the door for research into the international legitimation of these entities. However, in order for the question of their external legitimacy to be raised, the following question must first be asked: what is the social constituency within which they are embedded?

The nature of the relative social constituency is of central importance to understanding any notion of legitimacy; there is scholarly consensus that legitimacy is hollowed of substance in the absence of community.[117] The importance of the social constituency to legitimacy is straightforward, given the fact that legitimacy cannot be understood separately from the notion of rights, which by definition constitute a relational phenomenon.[118] This is clearly outlined in Mark Suchman's definition, which is drawn on by both Hurd and Reus-Smit in the development of their own conceptions of legitimacy: "a generalized perception or assumption that the actions of an entity are desirable, proper, or appropriate within some socially constructed system of norms, values, beliefs, and definitions".[119] The complexity lies in articulating those qualities of the social system at any given point in time, and in how they relate to actors' perceptions of legitimacy or to the practices of legitimacy that are being adhered to. As Chapter One demonstrated, de facto states function within the international state system, but this is a self-organising system that does not inherently produce the cohesion of community or order for the existence of legitimacy to be assumed. Clark's conception of legitimacy within international society, discussed above, clearly demonstrates this.

Clark argues that international society exists when the state system has formed a club of rightful members that recognise each other's sovereignty and that are partaking in the legitimation of practices of rightful conduct. Rightful conduct therefore presupposes rightful membership. Working deductively, this means that the absence of rightful membership denotes the absence of international society and the existence of only the states system. This contrasts with Eiki Berg and Ene Kuusk's "empirical approach" to international society that,[120] while providing valuable insights about the concept of sovereignty and entities that aspire to it, overlooks the inherently normative component that is intrinsic to a society: the granting of rightful membership.

Given the evident realities of the current international relations landscape, consequent questions inevitably follow: what is the status of a state-like entity that is a functioning component of the state system, and is in the legitimating process of trying to become a member of the recognised states society but has not yet attained that status? If a state located in this void adheres to practices of rightful conduct, does this make them any more or less legitimate? What is the social structure of which they are a part, and can this be considered a community? These questions are at the core of enquiry for this study, and they require the articulation of a clear framework for analysing and interpreting international legitimacy that accounts for de facto states' experience of it.

A Conceptual Framework for Normative Standing

I embrace Clark's legitimist definition of international society; however, I do not accept his legitimacy framework as complete or exhaustive. Clark admits that his theory is insufficient for analysing that which happens outside of international society. In order to examine the prospective legitimacy of de facto states, this study draws upon the discussion so far to construct the following framework as a starting point from which to conduct this investigation:

1 Legitimacy is a consensual appraisal within a community that empowers actors and sanctions actions.
2 Legitimacy is intersubjective and normative, and its contestation can be political.
3 Legitimacy is irreducible to any norm or combination of norms.
4 The community of legitimate practice is binding, to the extent that it is an object of cognitive orientation.
5 The right to act is constituted by recognition from other rights-holding constituents.

The framework follows Clark's logic of legitimation, and the framework includes a permutation of Weber's validity, but only to an extent of being binding, not eliciting strict obligation, because it accepts that the conditions of rightful conduct are continuously being contested; variations in the form or substance of legitimacy are always contingent. On these same grounds, it rejects Franck's layers of symbolic validation and coherence. It also rejects Franck's concept of determinacy, which is not applicable because it is grounded in a steadfast concept of rules which together can only apply as a second-order product. Franck's layer of adherence, however, has been incorporated with Weber's validity to state that the community is an object of cognitive orientation.

This framework specifically employs Clark's triad of second-order norms of morality, legality and constitutionality as the procedural design upon which to assess a de facto state's normative standing. How closely the conduct of de facto states within the international system aligns to these second-order norms of international society is what from now on will be referred to as their normative standing. This raises the question: how can de facto states be assessed against the norms of a society from which they are excluded?[121] This is where the fourth criterion of my framework on international legitimacy is crucial: *the community of legitimate practice is binding, to the extent that it is an object of cognitive orientation*. So long as this community is binding, in that any entity with the corporate identity of a state perceives it as a valid order, it can become a cognitive object of orientation regardless of whether or not that entity has been accepted as a legitimate member. Being bound to that order means that the institutions and norms of the order also become cognitive objects of orientation. In other words, the norms and institutions of international society observably govern the behaviour of de facto states in the international system.

A core contribution of the present study, put simply, is that the critical and practicable nexus of morality, constitutionality and legality comprises a conceptual framework that provides unique explanatory utility for analysing de facto states. The relationship between legality and morality is at the very centre of the de facto state problem. Legally, there are the opposing views of declaratory and constitutive statehood. Morally, there is the tension in the high ground that many de facto states take in often comparing their democratic credentials to those of their parent state, but there is also contrasting morality relating to violent secession, territorial integrity, greater security, and stability. Furthermore, the pillar of constitutionality provides a lens through which to interpret the changing attitudes to secession. The most formal depiction of this is *uti possidetis juris*, but this category encompasses the attitude towards territorial integrity, and it is more appropriate than the legal category because the concepts of self-determination and secession fall under a legal grey area that is often determined by political practice instead of clear legal doctrine.

The distinction between the international system and international society is the starting point from which any assessment of normative standing utilising this proposed framework must begin. The international system is still social, as I articulated in Chapter One. The definition of international system is in fact significantly more social than Bull's original English School definition. Although it is similar to the English School definition, in that the system has ontological priority, the significant difference is that there is no sequential specificity. This difference allows for the co-existence of system and society that provides the conceptual clarity required to detail the relationship between de facto states and international society. De facto states are corporate entities in the international system, as are recognised states. Recognised states, however, are accepted and acknowledged members of international society. They have rightful membership. To refer directly to the definition of international legitimacy, they are socially sanctioned members. The international system has ontological priority over international society; the society cannot exist without the system, whereas, in theory, the system could exist without the society. When there is an international society, the system and the society coalesce. This distinction provides the conceptual clarity required to develop an in-depth understanding of the relationship between de facto states and international society.

An important clarification for the purpose of this investigation is that a recognition narrative and normative standing are not one and the same thing. De facto states appeal to principles of international law, moral norms and political interests with aspirations to influence the members of international society, but they can get this wrong. They can also manipulate their case and misread the political expectations of the time. An illustrative example of this is the case of Eritrea, which strategically delayed proclaiming independence to ensure the appropriate support was in place for a successful declaration. This can be compared to any of the post-Soviet de facto states, or indeed to Somaliland, that have declared independence informed by an understanding of rightful membership that differed from the practice of rightful membership as defined by the balance between morality, constitutionality and legality at that point in time. Further to this point, normative standing is not the same as the likelihood of successfully gaining recognition. This can change all too easily with a miscalculation by a de facto state or indeed by a change in the political dynamics within international society.

Normative standing is not a yardstick by which de facto states can be ranked, and the proposed theoretical approach is not intended to measure but rather to analyse, interpret and understand, and this point will be evident when it is applied in the case studies that follow. To attempt to construct a metric by which to rank de facto states' normative standing would be a reductionist treatment of the complex dynamics of the second-order qualities or norms. Entities can be compared, and it may be fair to say that one case study makes a stronger case than another if there is significant differentiation. However, a definitive ranking would be conceptually negligent.

Institutions are the cognitive objects of orientation for de facto states; institutions observably govern their behaviour. This does not challenge the notion that de facto states adopt practices due to a perceived benefit of increasing their palatability as prospective members of international society. Institutions are the mode through which the norms of international society are communicated within the international system. The available spectrum of actions that de facto states may adopt in response to those norms is vast. The motivations behind these responses can be instrumental, as can be observed in the examples used by scholars who forward the notion of earned sovereignty. Motivations are also driven by interests that are constituted by type and role identities belonging to de facto states. The practical application of these concepts will next be presented and analysed through the framework of normative standing in three distinctive regional case studies.

Notes

1 The literature on political legitimacy is vast. For a solid introduction, see Richard E. Flathman, "Legitimacy", in Robert E. Goodin and Philip Pettit, eds., *A Companion to Contemporary Political Philosophy* (Oxford: Blackwell, 1993).
2 Ian Clark, *Legitimacy in International Society* (Oxford: Oxford University Press, 2005) 18.
3 Max Weber, *Economy and Society: An Outline of Interpretive Sociology*, Guenther Roth and Claus Wittich, eds. (Berkeley: University of California Press, 1978) 31.
4 Max Weber, *The Theory of Social and Economic Organization*, Talcott Parsons, ed. (New York: Free Press, 1968) 382.
5 For a detailed assessment of this, see Martin E. Spencer, "Weber on Legitimate Norms and Authority", *British Journal of Sociology* 21:2 (1970).
6 Richard Merelman, "Learning and Legitimacy", *American Political Science Review* 60 (1966) 548; Jean-Marc Coicaud, "Legitimacy, Across Borders and Over Time", in Hilary Charlesworth and Jean-Marc Coicaud, eds., *Fault Lines of International Legitimacy* (Cambridge: Cambridge University Press, 2010) 17.
7 Weber, *Economy and Society*, 31–33.
8 Morris Zelditch, Jr., "Theories of Legitimacy", in John T. Jost and Brenda Major, eds., *The Psychology of Legitimacy: Emerging Perspectives on Ideology, Justice, and Intergroup Relations* (Cambridge: Cambridge University Press, 2001) 44.
9 Ibid.
10 Empirical legitimacy is sometimes referred to as 'descriptive'.
11 Hanna Pitkin, *Wittgenstein and Justice* (Berkeley: University of California Press, 1972) 280–285.
12 John Schaar, "Legitimacy in the Modern State", in William Connolly, ed., *Legitimacy and the State* (Oxford: Basil Blackwell, 1984) 110. Robert Grafstein, "The Failure of Weber's Concept of Legitimacy", *Journal of Politics* 43 (1981) 456.
13 Carl Joachim Friedrich, *Man and His Government: An Empirical Theory of Politics* (New York: McGraw-Hill, 1963) 23.
14 Schaar, "Legitimacy in the Modern State", 109.
15 Helmut Breitmeier, *The Legitimacy of International Regimes* (Farnham, UK: Ashgate, 2008) 19.
16 Weber, *Economy and Society*, 212–217.
17 John Ruggie, *Constructing the World Polity: Essays on International Institutionalization* (London: Routledge, 1998) 64. A more thorough interrogation of the

70 *International Legitimacy and the Normative Standing of De Facto States*

relationship between legitimacy and power will be conducted later in this chapter, for it is most relevant to this study in the international context.
18 Nicholas Onuf and Frank F. Klink, "Anarchy, Authority, and Rule", *International Studies Quarterly* 33:2 (1989) 152.
19 'Political obligations' are generally accepted to include moral obligations. For a detailed discussion on this topic, see Joseph Raz, *The Morality of Freedom* (Oxford: Oxford University Press, 1986); A. John Simmons, *Moral Principles and Political Obligations* (Princeton, NJ: Princeton University Press, 1979); and William Edmundson, *Three Anarchical Fallacies* (Cambridge: Cambridge University Press, 1998).
20 George Klosko, "Legitimacy, Authority and Political Obligation", in Achim Hurrelmann, et al., eds., *Legitimacy in an Age of Global Politics* (Basingstoke, UK: Palgrave Macmillan, 2007) 58.
21 Ronald Dworkin, *Law's Empire* (Cambridge, MA: Harvard University Press, 1986) 191–196.
22 John Rawls, *A Theory of Justice* (Cambridge, MA: Harvard University Press, 1971); Herbert L.A. Hart, "Are There Any Natural Rights?", *The Philosophical Review* 64:2 (1955).
23 Rawls, *A Theory of Justice*, 111–115. Buchanan, for instance, considers authority to exist when the subjects of its jurisdiction have "an obligation to that entity to obey it". See Allen Buchanan, *Justice, Legitimacy, and Self-Determination: Moral Foundations for International Law* (Oxford: Oxford University Press, 2004); and Jean-Marc Coicaud, *Legitimacy and Politics: A Contribution to the Study of Political Right and Political Responsibility* (Cambridge: Cambridge University Press, 2002).
24 Ibid.
25 Klosko, "Legitimacy, Authority and Political Obligation", 72.
26 I will take a clear position on this issue later in this chapter.
27 See, for example, Jurgen Habermas, *Communication and the Evolution of Society* (London: Heinemann, 1979).
28 David Beetham, *The Legitimation of Power* (Atlantic Highlands, NJ: Humanities Press, 1991) 10–12. The moral foundation of people's beliefs is central to Hurd's definition; see Ian Hurd, *After Anarchy* (Princeton, NJ: Princeton University Press, 2007). For a detailed discussion on the relationship between the moral validity of a state and its political authority, see A. John Simmons, *Justification and Legitimacy: Essays on Rights and Obligations* (Cambridge: Cambridge University Press, 2001).
29 Beetham, *The Legitimation of Power*, 11.
30 Fritz W. Scharpf, *Governing in Europe: Effective and Democratic?* (Oxford: Oxford University Press, 1999); Friedrich Kratochwil, "On Legitimacy", *International Relations* 20:3 (2006) 302; Breitmeier, *The Legitimacy of International Regimes*.
31 See G. Bingham Powell, *Elections as Instruments of Democracy: Majoritarian and Proportional Visions* (New Havenm CT: Yale University Press, 2000).
32 Spencer, "Weber on Legitimate Norms and Authority", 133.
33 Scharpf, *Governing in Europe*; Kratochwil, "On Legitimacy"; Breitmeier, *Legitimacy in International Regimes*.
34 David Beetham and Christopher Lord, *Legitimacy and the EU* (London: Routledge, 1998) 3.
35 Kratochwil, "On Legitimacy", 302.
36 Scharpf, *Governing in Europe*, 6.
37 Beetham and Lord, *Legitimacy and the EU*, 3.
38 Spencer, "Weber on Legitimate Norms and Authority", 133.

39 See Erik Voeten, "The Political Origins of the UN Security Council's Ability to Legitimize the Use of Force", *International Organization* 59:3 (2005); and Eva Erman, "Global Political Legitimacy beyond Justice and Democracy?", *International Theory* 8:1 (2016) 29–62.
40 Zelditch, "Theories of Legitimacy", 35; John Locke, *Two Treatises on Government*, Peter Laslett, ed. (New York: New American Library, 1965); Robert N. Bellah, "Rousseau on Society and the Individual", in Susan Dunn, ed., *Jean-Jacques Rousseau, The Social Contract; and The First and Second Discourses* (New Haven, CT: Yale University Press, 2002) 266–275.
41 John Rawls, *Political Liberalism* (New York: Columbia University Press, 1993) 133–137.
42 Talcott Parsons, *Structure and Process in Modern Societies* (New York: Free Press, 1960); Seymour Martin Lipset, "Some Social Requisites of Democracy: Economic Development and Political Legitimacy", *The American Political Science Review* 53:1 (1959).
43 Friedrich, *Man and His Government*, 23.
44 Jens Steffek, "Legitimacy in International Relations: From State Compliance to Citizen Compliance", in Achim Hurrelmann et al., eds., *Legitimacy in an Age of Global Politics* (Basingstoke, UK: Palgrave Macmillan, 2007) 180.
45 Hurd, *After Anarchy*.
46 Clark, *Legitimacy in International Society*, 11.
47 John Williams, *Legitimacy in International Relations and the Rise and Fall of Yugoslavia* (London: Macmillan,1998) 1.
48 Inis L. Claude, "Collective Legitimization as a Political Function of the United Nations", *International Organization* 20:3 (1966) 367.
49 Thomas Franck, "Why a Quest for Legitimacy?", *U.C. Davis Law Review* 21:3 (1988).
50 For a more recent overview, see Jean-Marc Coicaud, "Deconstructing International Legitimacy", in Hilary Charlesworth and Jean-Marc Coicaud, eds., *Fault Lines of International Legitimacy* (Cambridge: Cambridge University Press, 2010).
51 Allen Buchanan, "Political Legitimacy and Democracy", *Ethics* 112:1 (2002) 718–719; Buchanan, *Justice, Legitimacy, and Self-Determination*. For a similar and thorough approach to the legitimacy of international institutions, see Allen Buchanan and Robert Keohane, "The Legitimacy of Global Governance Institutions", *Ethics and International Affairs* 20:4 (2006).
52 Hurd, *After Anarchy*, 32.
53 Thomas Franck, *The Power of Legitimacy among Nations* (Oxford: Oxford University Press, 1990) 16.
54 Ibid.
55 Ibid., 19.
56 Williams, *Legitimacy in International Relations and the Rise and Fall of Yugoslavia*, 13.
57 Thomas Franck, *Fairness in International Law and Institutions* (Oxford: Clarendon Press, 1995).
58 Abram Chayes and Antonia H. Chayes, *The New Sovereignty: Compliance with International Regulatory Agreements* (Cambridge, MA: Harvard University Press, 1995) 128.
59 Christian Reus-Smit, "International Crises of Legitimacy", *International Politics* 44:1 (2007) 160.
60 Hurd, *After Anarchy*, 32.
61 Beetham, *The Legitimation of Power*, 14.
62 See also Breitmeier, *The Legitimacy of International Regimes*; and Buchanan and Keohane, "The Legitimacy of Global Governance Institutions".

63. Hurd, *After Anarchy*, 7.
64. Ibid., 7–8.
65. Nathaniel Berman, "Intervention in a 'Divided World': Axes of Legitimacy", in Hilary Charlesworth and Jean-Marc Coicaud, eds., *Fault Lines of International Legitimacy* (Cambridge: Cambridge University Press, 2010) 143–145.
66. Hurd, *After Anarchy*, 8.
67. The reasons for this will be discussed in detail later in this chapter.
68. Hurd, *After Anarchy*, 30–31.
69. Ibid., 76.
70. Ibid.
71. Wendt, *Social Theory of International Politics*, 224.
72. Hurd, *After Anarchy*, 32.
73. Ibid., 31.
74. Reus-Smit, "International Crises of Legitimacy", 158. Emphasis added.
75. Ibid., 159.
76. Coicaud, *Legitimacy and Politics*, 11.
77. Ognyan Minchev, "The Kosovo Crisis and the International System: Issues of Legitimacy and Actors' Motivation", *Institute for Regional and International Studies Strategic Papers Collection* 5, http://www.iris-bg.org/menu.php?i_id=279.
78. For an example, see Claude, "Collective Legitimization as a Political Function of the United Nations". For a discussion, see Reus-Smit, "International Crises of Legitimacy".
79. Reus-Smit, "International Crises of Legitimacy", 162.
80. Ibid. Reus-Smit draws on Wendt's *Social Theory of International Politics* to make this point.
81. Reus-Smit, "International Crises of Legitimacy", 162.
82. Ibid., 163.
83. Ibid., 167.
84. Ibid., 168. He refers to this, respectively, as "acute" and "chronic".
85. Martin Wight, "International Legitimacy", *International Relations* 4:1 (1972) 1.
86. Daniel Philpott, *Revolutions in Sovereignty: How Ideas Shape Modern International Relations* (Princeton, NJ: Princeton University Press, 2001) 15.
87. Martin Wight, *Systems of States*, Hedley Bull, ed. (Leicester: Leicester University Press, 1977) 158.
88. Clark, *Legitimacy in International Society*, 26.
89. See, for instance, Barry Buzan, *From International to World Society? English School Theory and the Social Structure of Globalization* (Cambridge: Cambridge University Press, 2004); Tim Dunne, "Sociological Investigations: Instrumental, Legitimist and Coercive Interpretations of International Society", *Millennium – Journal of International Studies* 30:1 (2001); and Philpott, *Revolutions in Sovereignty*.
90. Clark, *Legitimacy in International Society*, 2.
91. Ibid., 7
92. Ibid., 5.
93. Ibid.
94. Ibid., 24.
95. Reus-Smit, "International Crises of Legitimacy", 158.
96. Independent International Commission on Kosovo, *The Kosovo Report: Conflict, International Response, Lessons Learned* (Oxford: Oxford University Press, 2000) 4.
97. Allen Buchanan, "Reforming the International Law of Humanitarian Intervention", in J.L. Holzgrefe and Robert O. Keohane, eds., *Humanitarian Intervention: Ethical Legal, and Political Dilemmas* (Cambridge: Cambridge University Press, 2003) 131.

98 For an insightful comparison of the 2003 Iraq invasion with the Kosovo intervention, see Corneliu Bjola, "Legitimating the Use of Force in International Politics: A Communicative Action Perspective", *European Journal of International Relations* 11:2 (2005).
99 Clark, *Legitimacy in International Society*, 221.
100 Ibid., 220.
101 Ibid., 221.
102 Ibid., 225. Emphasis in the original.
103 Ibid., 208.
104 Thomas Franck, *Recourse to Force: State Action against Threats and Armed Attacks* (Cambridge: Cambridge University Press, 2002) 182.
105 Clark, *Legitimacy in International Society*, 226.
106 Ibid., 207.
107 This distinction and this labelling are derived from Pegg's clarification of the two.
108 Silvia von Steinsdorff and Anna Fruhstorfer, "Post-Soviet De Facto States in Search of Internal and External Legitimacy", *Communist and Post-Communist Studies* 45:1 (2012) 117–121.
109 Scott Pegg and Pål Kolstø, "Somaliland: Dynamics of Internal Legitimacy and (Lack of) External Sovereignty", *Geoforum* 66:1 (2015) 193–202.
110 Eiki Berg and Raul Toomla, "Forms of Normalisation in the Quest for De Facto Statehood", *The International Spectator: Italian Journal of International Affairs* 44:4 (2009) 27–45; Eiki Berg and Ene Kuusk, "What Makes Sovereignty a Relative Concept? Empirical Approaches to International Society", *Political Geography* 29:1 (2010) 40–49.
111 Noé Cornago, "Diplomacy and Paradiplomacy in the Redefinition of International Security: Dimensions of Conflict and Co-operation", in Francisco Aldecoa and Michael Keating, eds., *Paradiplomacy in Action: The Foreign Relations of Subnational Governments* (New York: Frank Cass, 1999) 40.
112 James Ker-Lindsay, *The Foreign Policy of Counter-Secession: Preventing the Recognition of Contested States* (Oxford: Oxford University Press, 2012) 14.
113 Nina Caspersen, "Degrees of Legitimacy: Ensuring Internal and External Support in the Absence of Recognition", *Geoforum* 66:1 (2015) 186.
114 Ibid.
115 Ibid.
116 Ian Hurd, "Legitimacy and Authority in International Politics", *International Politics* 53:2 (1999) 388. Coicaud goes so far as to claim that problems of legitimacy and its contestation only take place in a setting where actors are "integrated into a given community, so that they identify with it and are aware of their rights and duties". Coicaud, *Legitimacy and Politics*, 205.
117 Franck, *Fairness in International Law and Institutions*, 26.
118 Coicaud, *Legitimacy and Politics*, 11.
119 Mark C. Suchman, "Managing Legitimacy: Strategic and Institutional Approaches", *Academy of Management Review* 20:3 (1995) 574.
120 Berg and Kuusk, "What Makes Sovereignty a Relative Concept? Empirical Approaches to International Society", 40.
121 This question drills to the very core of Pegg's seminal work, and to the point eloquently raised by Laurence Broers: "De facto states present an existential paradox in their simultaneously transgressive and mimetic qualities: they both challenge the international state order by violating de jure borders, and replicate it by seeing to exhibit the normal appearance of a state". Laurence Broers, "Recognising Politics in Unrecognised States: 20 Years of Enquiry into the De Facto States of the South Caucasus", *Caucasus Survey* 1:1 (2013) 59.

Bibliography

Beetham, David. *The Legitimation of Power* (Atlantic Highlands, NJ: Humanities Press, 1991).

Beetham, David, and Lord, Christopher. *Legitimacy and the EU* (London: Routledge, 1998).

Bellah, Robert N. "Rousseau on Society and the Individual", in Susan Dunn, ed., *Jean-Jacques Rousseau, the Social Contract; and the First and Second Discourses* (New Haven, CT: Yale University Press).

Berg, Eiki, and Kuusk, Ene. "What Makes Sovereignty a Relative Concept? Empirical Approaches to International Society", *Political Geography* 29:1 (2010) 40–49.

Berg, Eiki, and Toomla, Raul. "Forms of Normalisation in the Quest for De Facto Statehood", *The International Spectator: Italian Journal of International Affairs* 44:4 (2009) 27–45.

Berman, Nathaniel. "Intervention in a 'Divided World': Axes of Legitimacy", in Hilary Charlesworth and Jean-Marc Coicaud, eds., *Fault Lines of International Legitimacy* (Cambridge: Cambridge University Press, 2010) 743–769.

Bjola, Corneliu. "Legitimating the Use of Force in International Politics: A Communicative Action Perspective", *European Journal of International Relations* 11:2 (2005) 266–303.

Breitmeier, Helmut. *The Legitimacy of International Regimes* (Farnham, UK: Ashgate, 2008).

Broers, Laurence. "Recognising Politics in Unrecognised States: 20 Years of Enquiry into the De Facto States of the South Caucasus", *Caucasus Survey* 1:1 (2013) 59–74.

Buchanan, Allen. "Political Legitimacy and Democracy", *Ethics* 112:1 (2002) 114–135.

Buchanan, Allen. "Reforming the International Law of Humanitarian Intervention", in J.L. Holzgrefe and Robert O. Keohane, eds., *Humanitarian Intervention: Ethical Legal, and Political Dilemmas* (Cambridge: Cambridge University Press, 2003) 130–174.

Buchanan, Allen. *Justice, Legitimacy, and Self-Determination: Moral Foundations for International Law* (Oxford: Oxford University Press, 2004).

Buchanan, Allen, and Keohane, Robert O. "The Legitimacy of Global Governance Institutions", *Ethics and International Affairs* 20:4 (2006) 405–437.

Buzan, Barry. *From International to World Society? English School Theory and the Social Structure of Globalization* (Cambridge: Cambridge University Press, 2004).

Caspersen, Nina. "Degrees of Legitimacy: Ensuring Internal and External Support in the Absence of Recognition", *Geoforum* 66:1 (2015) 184–192.

Chayes, Abram, and Chayes, Antonia H. *The New Sovereignty: Compliance with International Regulatory Agreements* (Cambridge, MA: Harvard University Press, 1995).

Clark, Ian. *Legitimacy in International Society* (Oxford: Oxford University Press, 2005).

Claude, Inis L. "Collective Legitimization as a Political Function of the United Nations", *International Organization* 20:3 (1966) 367–379.

Coicaud, Jean-Marc. *Legitimacy and Politics: A Contribution to the Study of Political Right and Political Responsibility* (Cambridge: Cambridge University Press, 2002).

Coicaud, Jean-Marc. "Deconstructing International Legitimacy", in Hilary Charlesworth and Jean-Marc Coicaud, eds., *Fault Lines of International Legitimacy* (Cambridge: Cambridge University Press, 2010) 29–86.

Coicaud, Jean-Marc. "Legitimacy, Across Borders and Over Time", in Hilary Charlesworth and Jean-Marc Coicaud, eds., *Fault Lines of International Legitimacy* (Cambridge: Cambridge University Press, 2010) 17–28.

Cornago, Noé. "Diplomacy and Paradiplomacy in the Redefinition of International Security: Dimensions of Conflict and Co-operation", in Francisco Aldecoa and Michael Keating, eds., *Paradiplomacy in Action: The Foreign Relations of Subnational Governments* (New York: Frank Cass, 1999) 40–57.

Dunne, Tim. "Sociological Investigations: Instrumental, Legitimist and Coercive Interpretations of International Society", *Millennium – Journal of International Studies* 30:1 (2001) 67–91.

Dworkin, Ronald. *Law's Empire* (Cambridge, MA: Harvard University Press, 1986).

Edmundson, William. *Three Anarchical Fallacies* (Cambridge: Cambridge University Press, 1998).

Erman, Eva. "Global Political Legitimacy beyond Justice and Democracy?" *International Theory* 8:1 (2016) 29–62.

Flathman, Richard E. "Legitimacy", in Robert E. Goodin and Philip Pettit, eds., *A Companion to Contemporary Political Philosophy* (Oxford: Blackwell, 1993) 527–533.

Franck, Thomas. "Why a Quest for Legitimacy?", *U.C. Davis Law Review* 21:3 (1988) 535–548.

Franck, Thomas. *The Power of Legitimacy among Nations* (Oxford: Oxford University Press, 1990).

Franck, Thomas. *Fairness in International Law and Institutions* (Oxford: Clarendon Press, 1995).

Franck, Thomas. *Recourse to Force: State Action against Threats and Armed Attacks* (Cambridge: Cambridge University Press, 2002).

Friedrich, Carl Joachim. *Man and His Government: An Empirical Theory of Politics* (New York: McGraw-Hill, 1963).

Grafstein, Robert. "The Failure of Weber's Concept of Legitimacy", *Journal of Politics* 43 (1981) 456–472.

Habermas, Jurgen. *Communication and the Evolution of Society* (London: Heinemann, 1979).

Hart, Herbert L.A. "Are There Any Natural Rights?", *The Philosophical Review* 64:2 (1955) 175–191.

Hurd, Ian. "Legitimacy and Authority in International Politics", *International Politics* 53:2 (1999) 379–408.

Hurd, Ian. *After Anarchy* (Princeton, NJ: Princeton University Press, 2007).

Independent International Commission on Kosovo, *The Kosovo Report: Conflict, International Response, Lessons Learned* (Oxford: Oxford University Press, 2000).

Ker-Lindsay, James. *The Foreign Policy of Counter-Secession: Preventing the Recognition of Contested States* (Oxford: Oxford University Press, 2012).

Klosko, George. "Legitimacy, Authority and Political Obligation", in Achim Hurrelmann, *et al.*, eds., *Legitimacy in an Age of Global Politics* (Basingstoke, UK: Palgrave Macmillan, 2007) 57–74.

Kratochwil, Friedrich. "On Legitimacy", *International Relations* 20:3 (2006) 251–272.

Lipset, Seymour Martin. "Some Social Requisites of Democracy: Economic Development and Political Legitimacy", *The American Political Science Review* 53:1 (1959) 69–105.

Locke, John. *Two Treatises on Government*, Peter Laslett, ed. (New York: New American Library, 1965).

Merelman, Richard. "Learning and Legitimacy", *American Political Science Review* 60 (1966) 548–561.
Minchev, Ognyan. "The Kosovo Crisis and the International System: Issues of Legitimacy and Actors' Motivation", *Institute for Regional and International Studies Strategic Papers Collection* 5, http://www.iris-bg.org/menu.php?i_id=279.
Onuf, Nicholas, and Klink, Frank F. "Anarchy, Authority, and Rule", *International Studies Quarterly* 33:2 (1989) 149–173.
Parsons, Talcott. *Structure and Process in Modern Societies* (New York: Free Press, 1960).
Pegg, Scott, and Kolstø, Pål. "Somaliland: Dynamics of Internal Legitimacy and (Lack of) External Sovereignty", *Geoforum* 66:1 (2015) 193–202.
Pitkin, Hanna. *Wittgenstein and Justice* (Berkeley: University of California Press, 1972).
Philpott, Daniel. *Revolutions in Sovereignty: How Ideas Shape Modern International Relations* (Princeton, NJ: Princeton University Press, 2001).
Powell, G. Bingham. *Elections as Instruments of Democracy: Majoritarian and Proportional Visions* (New Haven, CT: Yale University Press, 2000).
Rawls, John. *A Theory of Justice* (Cambridge, MA: Harvard University Press, 1971).
Rawls, John. *Political Liberalism* (New York: Columbia University Press, 1993).
Raz, Joseph. *The Morality of Freedom* (Oxford: Oxford University Press, 1986).
Reus-Smit, Christian. "International Crises of Legitimacy", *International Politics* 44:1 (2007) 157–174.
Ruggie, John. *Constructing the World Polity: Essays on International Institutionalization* (London: Routledge, 1998).
Schaar, John. "Legitimacy in the Modern State", in William Connolly, ed., *Legitimacy and the State* (Oxford: Basil Blackwell, 1984) 104–133.
Scharpf, Fritz W. *Governing in Europe: Effective and Democratic?* (Oxford: Oxford University Press, 1999).
Simmons, A. John. *Moral Principles and Political Obligations* (Princeton, NJ: Princeton University Press, 1979).
Simmons, A. John. *Justification and Legitimacy: Essays on Rights and Obligations* (Cambridge: Cambridge University Press, 2001).
Spencer, Martin E. "Weber on Legitimate Norms and Authority", *British Journal of Sociology* 21:2 (1970) 123–134.
Steffek, Jens. "Legitimacy in International Relations: From State Compliance to Citizen Compliance", in Achim Hurrelmann, *et al.*, eds., *Legitimacy in an Age of Global Politics* (Basingstoke, UK: Palgrave Macmillan, 2007) 175–192.
Steinsdorff, Silvia von, and Fruhstorfer, Anna. "Post-Soviet De Facto States in Search of Internal and External Legitimacy", *Communist and Post-Communist Studies* 45:1–2 (2012) 117–121.
Suchman, Mark C. "Managing Legitimacy: Strategic and Institutional Approaches", *Academy of Management Review* 20:3 (1995) 571–610.
Voeten, Erik. "The Political Origins of the UN Security Council's Ability to Legitimize the Use of Force", *International Organization* 59:3 (2005) 527–557.
Weber, Max. *The Theory of Social and Economic Organization*, Talcott Parsons, ed. (New York: Free Press, 1968).
Weber, Max. *Economy and Society: An Outline of Interpretive Sociology*, Guenther Roth and Claus Wittich, eds. (Berkeley: University of California Press, 1978).

Wendt, Alexander. *Social Theory of International Politics* (Cambridge: Cambridge University Press, 1999).
Wight, Martin. "International Legitimacy", *International Relations* 4:1 (1972) 1–28.
Wight, Martin. *Systems of States*, Hedley Bull, ed. (Leicester: Leicester University Press, 1977).
Williams, John. *Legitimacy in International Relations and the Rise and Fall of Yugoslavia* (London: Macmillan, 1998).
Zelditch, Morris Jr. "Theories of Legitimacy", in John T. Jost and Brenda Major, eds., *The Psychology of Legitimacy: Emerging Perspectives on Ideology, Justice, and Intergroup Relations* (Cambridge: Cambridge University Press, 2001) 33–53.

3 The Nagorno Karabakh Republic

On a Sunday afternoon in September 2016, a group from the Armenian diaspora gathered at the Australian Institute of International Affairs in Sydney. They were attending a conference to commemorate 25 years since Nagorno Karabakh's declaration of independence, which was convened by the Nagorno Karabakh Republic's (NKR) representative office in Australia. Most of the audience shared an unexpected characteristic: while passionate supporters of the NKR, few of them had ever stepped foot in its territory. Such is the significance of Nagorno Karabakh in the narrative of Armenian nationalism. A region whose autonomy was forged through horrific war, that is internationally isolated, whose residents live in economic insecurity and with a constant threat of armed conflict unites members of the Armenian community who live thousands of kilometres from 'the Motherland'. From 1994 to 2020, Nagorno Karabakh was in a state commonly referred to as 'no peace, no war', a phrase that describes the existential threat of conflict that has never left. In that state of discordant ambivalence, statebuilding progressed, infrastructure was erected and institutions of governance slowly evolved. As this chapter will soon demonstrate, the successes of statebuilding played a significant part in strengthening the NKR's symbolic power. These critical, intertwined forces of state identity construction make the NKR an illuminating case study for exploring the analytical utility of state identity as a lens to better understand the relationship between de facto states and international society.

At the time of writing, the dust is settling on the volatile security landscape that is the aftermath of the Second Karabakh War of late 2020. Over a period lasting barely two months, combat drones, rocket attacks, trench warfare and controversial cluster munitions were used with devastating effect. A cease-fire has been declared, documents signed, and perimeters and boundaries adjusted. Two thousand Russian peacekeepers patrol the borders and the one non-militarised access road. Azerbaijan, which is only in control of one-third of Nagorno Karabakh's territory, is victoriously claiming that the conflict is resolved. The shadow of Turkish involvement lingers over the landscape of Russian influence and Azerbaijani ambitions. The future of Nagorno Karabakh as a de facto state is, at best, highly uncertain, and some would say it is perilous.

DOI: 10.4324/9781003178521-4

In staying true to the aim of this research, this chapter focusses on the *development* of the NKR as a de facto state in order to better understand its relationship with international society. While recognising its current state is seriously destabilised, there is little to be currently gained in terms of de facto state knowledge from the folly of premature crystal-ball-gazing.

NKR State Identity: Embodying Armenian Victory

The Origins of Armenian–Azerbaijani Enmity

Initial tensions between Armenians and Azerbaijanis were primarily the result of political dynamics that began brewing during the Tsarist Russian regime. This tension notably began gaining momentum in the late nineteenth century, manifesting as a class division stemming from economic and social inequalities. The Armenians were reaping greater benefits from the booming oil industry centred on Baku,[1] and were favoured among the ruling Russian elite, which was evident in their frequent selection for powerful economic and political positions in the major cities of the South Caucasus.[2] These socio-economic inequalities were fertile ground for anti-Armenian sentiment.[3] Class and ethnicity underpinned the broiling contempt, and the divisive graphics of a fractured urban existence perpetuated and exacerbated differences in culture, religion and language.[4] These cultural differentiations, along with the rise of a self-conscious Azerbaijani intelligentsia from 1880 onwards who sought to improve the lives of Muslims within the Russian Empire,[5] became accentuated and burgeoned with the rise of Pan-Turkism spreading throughout the region.

Pan-Turkism was a secular nationalist movement that grew out of the waning Ottoman Empire in the last decades of the nineteenth century.[6] Pan-Turkism championed a stronger pride in the national, linguistic and historic community of all Turkic peoples throughout Europe, the Middle East, the Caucasus and Asia.[7] The movement gained momentum in the Azerbaijani community of the Caucasus partly as a reaction to the attempted Russification of the area by the Tsarist regime and partly in an attempt to acquire support from Turkey to aid their aspirations for socio-economic and political development.[8] The initial anti-Russification response quickly morphed into anti-Armenian sentiment because Armenia was perceived to be a geographical roadblock dividing the greater Turkic community.[9] The anti-Armenian disposition was reinforced by a similar distrust and dislike that was only partly reactionary. The rise of Pan-Turkism made it very easy for the Armenians to equate the Azerbaijani Turks with the Ottoman Turks, fuelling Armenian antipathy towards the Azerbaijanis. In the aftermath of the anti-Armenian policies of the Ottoman Turks, culminating in the pogroms – known commonly as the Hamidian Massacres – of 1895–1896, Armenian nationalism was potent and incendiary, a force likely to be directed towards any friend or kin of the Ottoman Turks.[10] The nationalist and symbiotic mutual contempt increased in volatility until the Russian Revolution of 1905 provided fertile conditions for the increasing tensions to boil over.

Unrest and disorder spread across the South Caucasus after Baku was engulfed by riots in response to the death of an Azerbaijani at the hands of an Armenian policeman.[11] What began as Azerbaijanis exacting revenge on the Armenian quarters of Baku quickly turned to violent clashes in Tbilisi, Nakhichevan, Gyandzha, Yerevan and Shushi.[12] Thousands were killed, and swathes of property were destroyed, including over a thousand of the region's oil wells.[13] The disintegration of the revolutionary movement in Russia saw order slowly restored to the South Caucasus. By 1907, however, there were two crucial developments that could not be quelled so easily. First, significant bloodshed had taken place between these two ethnic groups, solidifying an underlying hostility that could quickly be galvanised. Second, the laconic response by the Russians made it evident to both the Armenians and the Azerbaijanis that they each needed to develop their own independence and work towards being self-sufficient, given the fact that there was no other party either side could rely on to guarantee their security or prosperity.

The need for each to be increasingly self-reliant, alongside mutual contempt, paved the way for the development of a territorial dynamic to feature in their dispute. As the Armenian Revolutionary Federation – commonly known as the Dashnaktsutiun (and often abbreviated to Dashnaks) – grew in size and strength, it began to focus its efforts on promoting the need for greater Armenian control over territory that it considered to be traditionally Armenian.[14] This included the South Caucasus' territories of Nakhichevan and Nagorno Karabakh, both of which belonged to the Azerbaijani administrative units under the imperial Russian system.[15] Nagorno Karabakh quickly became a generative bed for the Armenian nationalism that was taking root. Unsurprisingly, the Azerbaijanis perceived these claims to be a threat to land they considered rightfully theirs, increasing the intensity with which Azerbaijani nationalism flourished in the wake of the 1905 turmoil. Nagorno Karabakh had soon become the home of two staunch nationalisms, each rising in the heat of the other's claims and intensifying as they simmered in their own sense of injustice.

A defining and unifying event of Armenian nationalism in the twentieth century then took place against this volatile backdrop: the Armenian Genocide. The 1908 Young Turk Revolution saw a fierce Turkish nationalism destroy any hope of a multinational Ottoman identity. In early 1915, barely 20 years after the Hamidian Massacres, the Ottoman government set up a secretive paramilitary body known as the Special Organisation, whose sole purpose was to arrange the deportation of Armenians without being publicly identifiable as a government outfit.[16] This furtive Special Organisation then created killing squads, known as *chetes*, composed largely of convicted criminals who were engaged and organised to systematically slaughter Armenians; many of them were released from incarceration specifically to participate in the massacre.[17] An estimated 30,000 ex-convicts filled the ranks of the *chetes*, who relied on the military and provincial police to arrest and deport Armenians.[18] Using ex-convicts was not only considered to be an efficient means of dispatching the victims, it also equipped the government with a means of diluting or distancing their responsibility, or so it believed.[19] Over 2 million Armenians were deported between April 1915 and July 1916, approximately 1.5 million of whom were slaughtered.[20]

The genocide was catastrophic by any historical measure. It was also inevitably and understandably formative and defining for the Armenian national consciousness. Following the unrelenting and systematic atrocities, their importance was intensified by attempts to cover up, to misrepresent and in effect to deny their occurrence by several nation states. Although the atrocities committed against the Armenians were widely known at the time, in the years that followed the accounts of these events outside the Armenian community were disavowed, sanitised and "subverted".[21] Illustratively, many genocide scholars claim that in 1939, before invading Poland, Adolf Hitler attempted to motivate his generals with the following words: "Who speaks today of the extermination of the Armenians?".[22]

In light of the contemporary contestation over what the Turkish refer to as "the so-called Armenian question" or "the events of 1915",[23] it is important to note that the renowned and widely respected human rights barrister Geoffrey Robertson surveyed what he declared to be a "mass of compelling evidence" that "any forensic investigation would find credible".[24] The prevalence of the human rights discourse over the past 60 years, the "prolonged amnesia" following the genocide,[25] and the widespread reticence, equivocation and denial surrounding the recognition of a severe crime against humanity have all bolstered the centrality of the genocide in the Armenian national consciousness and strengthened the self-perception of Armenians as victimised survivors.[26]

Conflict in Nagorno Karabakh

The Russian retreat from the South Caucasus in 1918 left a vacuum of power that caused regional ethnic tensions to heighten. Azerbaijani forces joined the Turkish troops, who sought to establish a clear passage from Turkey to Azerbaijan at the cost of the Armenians situated in the middle, who fought to prevent their decimation at the hands of the Pan-Turkic "Army of Islam".[27] With this latest conflict taking place then shortly after the Armenian Genocide, the Armenians had every reason to believe that, if they were to fight and lose, they could well be facing the annihilation of their people. In the face of this looming possibility, the Armenians accepted the Treaty of Batum, known officially as the "Treaty of Peace and Friendship between the Imperial Ottoman Government and the Republic of Armenia" in June 1918, ceding the districts of Kars and Ardahan, and relinquishing claims to their "historic heartland of eastern Turkey".[28] Having followed Azerbaijan and Georgia in declaring their independence in May, Armenia by June had been reduced to a shell of its former self, desperate to hold on to the people and territory that had survived.

In the spring of 1918, Ottoman troops invaded Armenia, reaching the perimeter of Nagorno Karabakh by August. The Turks demanded that the Karabakh Armenians submit to the authority of Azerbaijan. By October, the Armenians were clearly going to be overpowered, and appeared to have little choice but to acquiesce to the Turks' request.[29] Following a "terror campaign" of persecution that included public hangings and arbitrary arrests *en masse*, the Armenians reneged on their agreement with the Turks and formed an insurgency.[30] The Armenian guerrillas managed to hold off a Turkish occupation of Nagorno Karabakh until Ottoman Turkey was defeated in October 1918, when the Turks agreed to withdraw their remaining troops from the South Caucasus.[31] To be more precise, the Ottoman government did. Mustafa Kemal Ataturk, the Turkish field marshal who would become Turkey's first President, did not. The issue of disputed territories became paramount in the lead up to the Paris Peace Conference, which had been nominated by the Allied Forces as the forum in which any remaining territorial disputes were to be negotiated,[32] adding a sense of urgency to a volatile region awash with nationalist territorial struggles.

Britain then marched assertively into this powder keg. The British adopted a policy in favour of the Azerbaijanis, but one they hoped would also maintain positive relations between the two hostile parties. Britain's strategy was two-fold: develop a stable and prosperous Azerbaijan that could ally with Britain to form a safety buffer, and develop positive relations that would help them gain access to the extensive oil reserves near Baku.[33] In order to achieve this, the British sought to cultivate warm relations with Azerbaijan by coaxing it with the prospect of confirming Nagorno Karabakh as a part of the Republic of Azerbaijan.[34] The Armenians felt betrayed by Britain's move. The Armenians had fought with the Allies in the First World War, and were subsequently dismayed that their valuable and costly loyalty had then been cast aside in favour of geopolitical opportunism.[35]

With their security and perceived homeland under threat once again, the Armenians of Karabakh formed an armed resistance, declaring that they would defend against any attempts to consolidate Azerbaijani sovereignty of Karabakh. The British and Azerbaijanis responded by effectively blockading Nagorno Karabakh and terrorising the surrounding Armenian villages.[36] After the British forces retreated from the Karabakh mountains, open conflict spread across the region once more. The Karabakh Armenians believed the British had played a part in restraining the Azerbaijani forces up until that point.[37] So when the British declared their withdrawal from the South Caucasus prior to the anticipated territorial settlement, which was to take place at the Paris Peace Conference, the Karabakh Armenians, outnumbered and overpowered, agreed to partake in negotiations with their enemy.[38] In August 1919, they signed an agreement that established a temporary authority of Azerbaijan over Nagorno Karabakh, allowing it limited autonomy, all of which was provisional in the lead up to the Paris Peace Conference, where a final settlement of the territorial dispute was supposed to take place.[39]

One of the heaviest emotional blows for the Armenians in the Nagorno Karabakh narrative prior to the escalation of the 1980s was another perceived betrayal, this time by Stalin. By the end of 1920, the Bolsheviks had captured Azerbaijan, Nagorno Karabakh and Armenia. In 1921, the Armenian Soviet Socialist Republic (SSR) was given authority over Zangezur but lost authority over the territory of Nakhichevan to Azerbaijan at the signing of the Treaty of Kars.[40] This was a heavy blow, for upon the creation of the Armenian SSR, Stalin had disingenuously stated that:

> The age-old enmity between Armenia and the surrounding Moslem peoples has been dispelled at one stroke by the establishment of fraternal solidarity between the working people of Armenia, Turkey and Azerbaijan.[41]

On 4 July 1921, the Caucasian Bureau of the Communist Party met in the presence of Stalin, who was the Soviet Commissar for Nationalities at the time, and after taking a vote the Bureau decided that Nagorno Karabakh should be incorporated into the Armenian SSR.[42] The following day, however, the Bureau officially released a statement to the contrary, declaring that the territory from then onwards was to remain as an autonomous region within the Azerbaijan SSR, a decision that was justified because of the "economic" and "permanent" ties with Azerbaijan.[43] There are multiple sources that accuse Stalin of intervening and ultimately effecting this policy reversal, although there are varying accounts as to why he did so. It is important to note that the sources sympathetic to Armenia are united in their claims about Stalin's role, demonstrating one of the key injustices that Armenians, especially Karabakh Armenians, *perceive* themselves to have been subjected to.

Before the Caucasian Bureau of the Communist Party officially incorporated Nagorno Karabakh into the Azerbaijan SSR, the Armenian people already perceived themselves as having suffered grievous injustices at the hands of the Ottoman Turks, the Azerbaijani Turks and the British Empire. Nagorno Karabakh was already of historical significance to the Armenian national consciousness. Following the Armenians' persecution in the heat of the Pan-Turkic wildfire and the genocide at the hands of the Ottoman Turks, Nagorno Karabakh began to symbolise Armenian determination in the face of a truly existential threat. The opportunism of the geopolitically expedient British in trying to gift Nagorno Karabakh to the Azerbaijanis solidified the Armenians' perception of the territory as a fervent stronghold of the Armenian cause. After indicating that the territory may at long last be returned to its people, the Bureau's decision to act against their original vote and declare Nagorno Karabakh as belonging to the Azerbaijan SSR endowed the mountainous district with unshakeable meaning, representing the pathology of cumulative injustice endured by the battered yet defiant and ever tenacious Armenian nation.

For most of the Soviet era, strong centralised rule from Moscow managed to keep the simmering Armenian–Azerbaijani tensions at bay. During the 'thaw' of the Khrushchev years, multiple petitions signed by Karabakh Armenians were lodged to little effect; otherwise the issue of Nagorno Karabakh was kept beneath the surface until after Mikhail Gorbachev became the General Secretary of the Communist Party of the Soviet Union (CPSU) in 1985. Gorbachev famously introduced the policy of *glasnost*, meaning "openness", with the intention of allowing public discussion of issues that had previously been forbidden, incidentally opening the door to issues of nationality and ethnicity that had been lying dormant since Stalin's iron fist. As Gorbachev's agenda incited – directly or indirectly – a wave of national movements,[44] the question of Karabakh predictably resurfaced once again.

The first serious conflict came in the wake of a reinvigorated debate about who was the rightful inheritor of Caucasian Albania, heightening tensions throughout the South Caucasus.[45] Violence erupted in February 1988 after a council representing the Armenians of Karabakh petitioned the Azerbaijan SSR, Armenian SSR and USSR governments to support the reintegration of Nagorno Karabakh into the Armenian SSR.[46] This was a revolutionary move, which was described insightfully by Thomas de Waal as "making politics from below for the first time in the Soviet Union since the 1920s".[47] This gave rise to protests throughout Armenia, and elicited a passionate nationalist fervour across Azerbaijan.[48]

It is important to note that many of the Armenian people at this time had sparse prior knowledge let alone awareness of Karabakh's history. Nora Dudwick, a sociologist who witnessed the protests first-hand, provides a telling depiction of how Karabakh's rich history was revisited and revitalised for the narrative construction of collective Armenian memory:

> Before the demonstrations, I rarely heard references to Karabagh ... By the end of February, most people in Yerevan had absorbed some version of this history and "knew" that Karabagh was part of Armenia's primordial homeland, that Armenians had been the majority population there for nearly two millennia, that it was the birthplace of the historical Armenian liberation struggle against the "Turkish-Persian yoke", and that only due to Stalin's machinations in 1920 had it become part of Azerbaijan. In short, the history of Karabagh had become as fully incorporated into collective memory as the genocide.[49]

Nagorno Karabakh had quickly become a powerful symbol of Armenian nationalism and the cumulative injustices suffered by the Armenian people throughout the twentieth century.

The ferment peaked on 28 February in the Azerbaijani town of Sumgait, where an angry mob of hundreds of Azerbaijani locals and refugees who had fled Karabakh took to the Armenian quarter.[50] A pogrom ensued. Acts of savage barbarism, including rape, immolation and murder, were inflicted on the local Armenian community.[51] Some victims, axed to death, were hacked so brutally that their remains were unidentifiable.[52] The official death toll was

32,[53] with hundreds more injured; however, there is some debate surrounding the accuracy of the numbers, given that the Azerbaijan SSR police did not intervene and the Soviet official press attempted to cover up the details.[54] The protests by Karabakh Armenians had included vicious acts sufficient enough for Karabakh Azerbaijanis to flee. The events of Sumgait were a severe escalation of hostilities and a whole new level of brutality. For the Armenians, the pogrom evoked spectres of the 1915 genocide and the sheer ruthlessness associated with the Turks in the narrative of Armenian nationalism.

Hostilities continued to spread across Karabakh itself, and by 1989 an "undeclared war" between Armenia and Azerbaijan was underway.[55] By February 1989, a further 90 people had been killed, over 1,600 were wounded and more than 500,000 people had become refugees; Armenians fleeing Azerbaijan and Azerbaijanis fleeing Armenia and Nagorno Karabakh.[56] Anti-Armenian pogroms broke out in January of 1990, causing the deaths of approximately 90 people and resulting in an exodus of all remaining Armenians from Baku.[57]

On 30 August 1991, the Supreme Council of the Azerbaijani SSR declared independence from the USSR. This created a predicament for the Karabakh Armenians; an independent Azerbaijan could mean that the question of Nagorno Karabakh would technically no longer be a question for the Soviet Union. Subsequently, three days later the Nagorno Karabakh Autonomous Oblast (NKAO) declared its independence from the Azerbaijani SSR in accordance with the legislation of the USSR that regulated the secession of Soviet Republics.[58] The 2 September 1991 declaration, according to the Karabakh Armenians and their supporters, legally located Nagorno Karabakh as a direct subject of the USSR according to the 1990 USSR Law on Secession.[59] After the Supreme Council of the Azerbaijani SSR confirmed their independence from the Soviet Union with a constitutional act on 18 October, it responded to the NKAO's declaration by revoking the autonomous status of Nagorno Karabakh within the Azerbaijani legislation, announcing its relegation to a regular region of the newly independent state of Azerbaijan on 26 November. On 10 December, Nagorno Karabakh held a referendum, which in its view was according to the legal provision of the Soviet Constitution. On 28 December, it held Parliamentary elections; the next day, Azerbaijan's independence was confirmed by a country-wide referendum. This was, of course, taking place simultaneously with the dissolution of the Soviet Union: the Soviet flag was lowered for the last time at the Kremlin on 25 December, and by 31 December Russia's succession of the Soviet Union at the United Nations Security Council had been confirmed.

In the wake of this cascading political disintegration and rapid repositioning, the recently elected Parliament of Nagorno Karabakh adopted the Declaration on the State Independence of the Nagorno Karabakh Republic on 6 January 1992. Resultantly, full-scale war broke out in January between Armenia and Azerbaijan, as well as in Nagorno Karabakh. One of the first major battles was for the town of Khojaly, which contained the region's airport and had been the focus of a major Azerbaijani resettlement programme. On the night of 25 February, Armenian armoured vehicles surrounded the town, securing it for the Armenian troops to execute what was to be the single bloodiest attack of the war. The town was guarded by approximately 160–200 militiamen, yet the official Azerbaijani Parliamentary investigation stated the death toll was 485,[60] and human rights groups estimated the toll to be between 300 and 800.[61] Not only were there severe civilian casualties, it is now accepted by both sides that many of the civilians were killed as they were fleeing.[62] The exact events and statistics are heavily contested; however, the fact that it was an atrocity causing civilian casualties is indisputable. The events at Khojaly fuelled the two "pathological" nationalisms to heighten the conflict to new levels of violence.[63]

Open warfare continued for another two years until the Bishkek Ceasefire was signed on 12 May 1994. Over 20,000 people were killed and more than 1 million people from both sides became refugees or were internally displaced.[64] The Bishkek Ceasefire, facilitated by Russia and signed by Armenia, Azerbaijan and Nagorno Karabakh, oversaw a state in which full-scale battle was avoided, though regular violations occurred by both sides trading fire across the line of contact. This situation has frequently been described as "no peace, no war".[65] Over the next 26 years, Nagorno Karabakh undertook gradual yet constant state-building, despite Azerbaijan's steadfast rejection of its right to exist. In this state of "no peace, no war", the development of Nagorno Karabakh as a state-like entity came to be a powerful symbol of defiance and victory for the Armenian nation.

From Victim to Victor

> "The whole Armenian nation realised … apart from being victims, we can be victors. That is what Karabakh showed them."[66]

When open warfare commenced, Nagorno Karabakh symbolised the struggle and injustices in the consciousness of the Armenian nation. Maintaining control of its territory was seen to defy the continuation of Armenians as victims, and to deny their oppressors the power that had shaped their national consciousness over the past 100 years. Although 'no peace and no recognition' is not the ideal or desired situation for the Karabakh Armenians, 'no war and retaining territorial control' was viewed as a historic victory. The birth of the Nagorno Karabakh Republic (NKR) was a turning point in the Armenian narrative, bestowing on the de facto state a nationalist significance that transcends its borders. To comprehend the recognition narrative of the NKR, the symbolic power of the de facto state's existence to the wider Armenian nation needs to be considered.

In the eyes of many Armenian people, the construction of the NKR embodies a transition from victim to victor; it is the story of a nation that has risen like a phoenix from the ashes of sustained, accumulated and disastrous oppression. This embodiment has become a vital thread woven into the NKR's state-level narrative. A spokesperson for the NKR's Prime Minister described how the citizens of the NKR "now perceive Karabakh as, first of all, independent domestically, and secondly, as a part of the Armenian homeland and nation. These are the two main pillars of Karabakh identity".[67] This sentiment was reinforced by the Chairman of the National Assembly, who claimed that "whereby Karabakh has a role to play, and did play the role of reviving, and sending a positive signal for the diaspora to be more Armenian, to preserve its Armenianness",[68] and echoed by the Deputy Foreign Minister, who stated that "Karabakh's present statehood, the success of Karabakh, is the reason for the second wave of diaspora to feel their Armenianness; the revival of their Armenian roots".[69]

As referenced at the start of this chapter, the symbolic power of Nagorno Karabakh was on full display at a conference in Sydney during September 2016. The conference was convened by the NKR Representative Office in Australia to commemorate 25 years of Nagorno Karabakh's independence. Many of the local Armenian diaspora gathered to celebrate the 'successful' quarter century of independence, and to discuss the future of the de facto state. The telling characteristic of the audience that had gathered was the fact that, although they were passionately Armenian and devoted to supporting the heartland of Nagorno Karabakh, barely any of the attendees had ever actually visited Karabakh itself.[70] This was directly in line with how one NKR government representative had described the relationship: "The perception of the diaspora of Karabakh is more of an emotional feel than anything else".[71] While verifying this sentiment is beyond the scope of this book's objectives, what is important is acknowledging the extent to which it has become a central and consistent theme in the narrative of Armenian nationalism and in turn the narrative of the NKR.

The centrality of the NKR is reflected in Armenian politics as well. Political careers of Armenian leaders have been made and broken based on their approach to and relationship with the de facto state. The first President of Armenia, Levon Ter-Petrosyan, disagreed with the leadership of the NKR on how to approach the conflict in Karabakh in the late 1990s. Ter-Petrosyan pushed for a phased approach whereas Robert Kocharyan, the President of NKR, insisted on a package solution. This dispute led to Ter-Petrosyan resigning from the position of President and Robert Kocharyan resigning his leadership of the NKR to replace Ter-Petrosyan as President of Armenia. This was a remarkable and telling turn of events. As Nina Caspersen aptly describes: "The periphery had taken over the centre"; the patron–client relationship had almost been reversed.[72] Serzh Sargsyan, the President of Armenia from 2008 to 2018, was the Chairman of Nagorno Karabakh's Self-Defence Forces Committee from 1989 to 1993. Sargsyan was perceived as one of the key leaders in the Karabakh conflict and was awarded the Hero of Artsakh Medal. This reputation contributed significantly to his success in Armenian politics, further demonstrating the powerful symbol of Karabakh to Armenian nationalism.[73] To any dispassionate external observer, it seems incontrovertible to acknowledge that the 'victory' of the NKR's existence; its survival, progress and advancement in the face of adversity; and its perceived multiple betrayals, together with increasing international awareness of its history and determined endurance, have come to represent an important emblematic victory for the entire Armenian nation.

The power of this emblematic victory is evident, even in the aftermath of the recent historic loss to Azerbaijan, which completely shifted the balance of power between these warring foes. In the years following the Bishkek Ceasefire, minimal progress was made in relations between Armenia and Azerbaijan. Tensions increased markedly from 2014 as breaches of the ceasefire escalated, boiling over into the so-called 'Four-Day War' of 2016 in which hundreds more were killed. The precarious state of 'no peace, no war' was maintained until July 2020, when clashes along the Armenia–Azerbaijan border became constant, eventually leading to open, full-scale war in late September along the line of contact demarcating Nagorno Karabakh. A return to devastating, bloody conflict ensued. The Second Karabakh War claimed the lives of at least 5,700 combatants and more than 170 civilians, while an estimated 130,000 were displaced.[74] Azerbaijan, bolstered by substantial Turkish support, recaptured approximately one-third of the Nagorno Karabakh territory including the strategically crucial town of Shushi. On 10 November, Russia brokered a ceasefire agreement that stipulated Azerbaijan's control over recaptured territories, and over the seven districts surrounding Nagorno Karabakh that Armenia had captured in the conflict of 1991–1994.[75] The ceasefire also mandated the deployment of Russian peacekeepers along the line of contact and the Lachin Corridor (the single access point to Nagorno Karabakh from Armenia). Azerbaijan rejoiced in a decisive victory.

Once Azerbaijan forces took control of Shushi – strategically located in an elevated position above the capital of Stepanakert – it is highly likely that the ceasefire prevented Azerbaijan's otherwise seemingly inevitable capture of the capital. Even NKR President at the time, Arayik Harutyunyan, admitted that the ceasefire was inevitable and that, had the conflict continued, all of Karabakh would have been captured by Azerbaijan.[76] However, the clamour in Yerevan appeared to be ignorant of the harsh reality facing Stepanakert, as protesters opposing the terms of the ceasefire arose, broke into the Parliament building and government buildings, and looted the Prime Ministerial residence of Nikol Pashinyan, calling for his resignation. Although the violence was quelled, staunch resistance to the ceasefire remained constant in the following months, plunging the domestic political sphere into dysfunctional turmoil. By February 2021, several senior military officers had united in their call for Pashinyan's resignation, including the Chief of General Staff Onik Gasparyan, who was consequently dismissed by Pashinyan in response to the demands for his resignation.[77] The constant pressure on Pashinyan's leadership in response to the losses in the 2020 war finally led to Pashinyan's resignation and his call for snap elections, which were to be held in June 2021.[78]

The 2020 war and subsequent loss of territory and of control of critical infrastructure means that the future of Nagorno Karabakh is deeply uncertain and likely to be highly restricted compared to the inter-war years. With Azerbaijan in control of the strategically critical village of Shushi and Russian peacekeepers controlling access through the Lachin Corridor, it is hard to envision the de facto state growing quite as it did in the 20 years following the Bishkek Ceasefire. Azerbaijan arose from the Second Karabakh War as the indisputable victor. While at present Azerbaijan is the perceived victor and Armenia the defeated, the domestic response within Armenia has further demonstrated the symbolic power of Nagorno Karabakh. It came to represent a great victory and powerful uplift in the narrative of Armenian nationalism. The immediate response of Armenians in the early days of the Second Karabakh War's aftermath demonstrates this symbolic power holding firm.

NKR State Identity: Self-Determined State

Nagorno Karabakh was formed and began to advocate its independence and promote its distinctive identity at a time when the discourse of self-determination was at the forefront of international relations, and it has continued to build on those foundations by striving to construct a democratic, functioning and recognisable state. That journey, however, has not been without significant challenges, and part of that attempt to development an identity and grow democracy has been the need to balance tensions between the world of those who were procedurally used to the standardised Soviet system of authoritarian decision-making and imposed autocracy for many years, and those, mostly a younger generation, who harbour expectations and a vision for participative democratic change.

Democratic credentials

The NKR embodies a type identity of an incipient democracy. The development of democracy in de facto states has been a central analytical theme in the de facto state literature.[79] The claims made by de facto state governments to be increasingly democratic have frequently been perceived as attempts to demonstrate their suitability to be recognised as fully fledged members of international society, a concept known as "earned sovereignty".[80] Put simply, the de facto state claims to display democratic credentials as a "central part of the legitimising narrative"[81] are described by Laurence Broers as "competitive democratization".[82] The NKR's democratisation efforts have been perceived in some quarters as primarily an image-building exercise aimed at improving the international perception of the territory from that of a warring secessionist movement to a democratic self-determined state, but a state that nonetheless lacks the tangible qualities of genuine democratisation. The strength of the NKR's democracy was emphasised by all of the government officials interviewed during my fieldwork; therefore, the function of this type identity requires a closer examination. The role of elections was frequently specified as a key indicator of the NKR's robust democracy.[83] This view of elections as a central democratic credential is aligned with the logic of Western liberal democracies, where elections are seen as a partial guarantor of the legitimacy of the government.[84] In Weberian terms, elections are essential for fulfilling the legal-rational pillar of legitimacy.

The history of the NKR's Parliamentary elections presents an evolving image of an increasingly purposeful democratic system of government. The first Parliamentary elections in the post-Bishkek Ceasefire period took place in 1995. This was a key first step towards stability and order in the newly born de facto state. Unfortunately, significant tension and hostility between the Dashnaktsutiun and Armenian President Ter-Petrosyan led to the Dashnak Party being banned in Armenia, and then it subsequently decided not to participate in the 1995 NKR Parliamentary elections.[85] Given that the Dashnaktsutiun was a driving force behind the Karabakh movement throughout the twentieth century, its absence led many to question the ability of the elected Parliament to represent the people of Nagorno Karabakh. Robert Kocharyan became the Armenian President and removed the ban on the Dashnaks in 1998, encouraging them to participate in the NKR's 2000 Parliamentary elections, which, for this reason, are seen by many as the first genuinely democratic Parliamentary elections to be held in Karabakh.

In the lead up to the 2000 Parliamentary elections, the domestic political sphere was filled with tension. Considerable military autonomy was a hangover from the conflict, pervading the domestic political landscape. Revered Armenian war hero Samvel Babayan was appointed Minister of Defence in 1995, a position that he was eventually seen to exploit for personal financial gain. Through nepotistic appointments, he eventually gained control of the NKR's security apparatus.[86] Babayan was dismissed in 1999; however, the threat from the military strongman to political stability only abated when he was eventually jailed for an assassination attempt on President Arkadi Ghukasyan in 2000, typifying the frailty of the budding democracy.[87] The 2000 Parliamentary elections were the first to be contested through a political party format and were considered by international observers to be free and fair.[88] The formation of the NKR's first coalition government between the Dashnaks and President Arkadi Ghukasyan's party, the Democratic Party of Artsakh, which won 9 seats and 13 seats, respectively, was perceived as an encouraging signal of stability and democratic progress at a time when NKR domestic politics had been fraught with tension. Observers and NKR elites therefore both perceived the 2000 Parliamentary elections as a turning point in the NKR's democratisation.[89]

In 2004, Nagorno Karabakh's democratisation continued on its positive trajectory of incremental development, reforming the electoral legislation with the aim of bolstering the party system. The National Assembly would from then onwards reserve one-third of its seats for proportional representation based on party lists. This provided for the most widely contested Parliamentary election yet in 2005, with the 33 seats being contested by 127 candidates, including members of the newly formed parties of Free Motherland and Movement 88, the latter forming an alliance with the Dashnaks.[90] The pro-government parties of Free Motherland and the Democratic Party of Artsakh won 22 seats between them, which was perceived as a resounding victory for Ghukasyan's incumbent government.[91] The opposition alliance of Movement 88 and the Dashnaks, having only received a total of 3 seats, complained that the election was not conducted or contested fairly. However, the majority of the 130 non-governmental, largely international observers agreed that the elections were predominantly free and fair.[92] The opposition may have suffered a loss, but the state of electoral democracy in Nagorno Karabakh had taken a progressive step forward.

The electoral system was tweaked over the following five years, with adjustments made to make the party representation in the National Assembly stronger by lowering the base threshold and increasing the number of candidates from party lists. The 2010 Parliamentary elections were held using this refined system. The Dashnaks increased their representation from 3 members to 6, and the Free Motherland party increased its holding to 14 seats, winning 44.2 per cent of the vote.[93] The increase in opposition representation, especially the Dashnaks, alongside the increase in the representation of Free Motherland Party, which continued to support the Democratic Party of Artsakh, ensured that the result was not plagued by the controversy of the 2005 elections. Furthermore, international observers declared the elections had been conducted fairly. The 2010 elections demonstrated that a baseline of Parliamentary democracy had been established in Nagorno Karabakh. This baseline continued on an even keel from 2010, with 2015 seeing another successful Parliamentary election in which Movement 88, the Dashnaks, and Free Motherland all gained an extra seat, while the Democratic Party of Artsakh lost one seat, resulting in a similar balance of power to the preceding period.

While Parliamentary elections in Nagorno Karabakh progressed positively, presidential elections paint a picture of a less pluralist democracy. After being appointed to the position of President in 1994 by the parliament, Robert Kocharyan won the first contested presidential elections in 1996. In 1998, Kocharyan stood down from the Nagorno Karabakh presidency so that he could take the helm of the Armenian government as Prime Minister (until 1998) and then as President. Elections were held to replace Kocharyan, and the Foreign Minister, Arkadi Ghukasyan, was elected President with 89.3 per cent of the vote. Kocharyan backed Ghukasyan, significantly increasing Ghukasyan's image as a likely provider of security; close relations between Yerevan and Stepanakert were perceived to increase the chances of stability. Ghukasyan won the 2002 presidential elections with a similar margin, albeit against four opponents this time instead of two. In 2006, Nagorno Karabakh's Constitution was adopted by referendum. The Constitution included an article preventing the President from being re-elected more than once. Ghukasyan initially planned to run for President a third time in 2006, claiming that, because the Constitution had been introduced after his first appointment, there were no legal grounds upon which to prevent him from running. Ghukasyan faced strong opposition from within the government, some of members of which claimed that his candidature would run contrary to the spirit of the Constitution that had only just been adopted and therefore put the nascent democratic process of Nagorno Karabakh at risk. Ghukasyan chose not to run, a decision that strengthened the perception of an increasingly influential democratic progression.

While Ghukasyan's respect for the Constitution may have been considered a victory for democracy at the time, the role of the President in Karabakh has raised questions about the extent of democratisation in the de facto state. Following Ghukasyan's decision not to contest the 2007 elections, Bako Sahakyan was elected with an overwhelming majority vote of 85 per cent. Sahakyan was the Head of the National Security Service and a widely respected military leader in the war, so the popular mandate was unsurprising. However, Sahakyan was re-elected in 2012, in what was arguably the most contested Presidential election in Nagorno Karabakh history, receiving 67 per cent of the vote. Sahakyan was still in power after a referendum was held in 2017 that reformed the Constitution to shift Nagorno Karabakh from a semi-Presidential system into a centralised, fully Presidential system. As a part of this transition, Sahakyan was able to retain power until the next Presidential elections, which were held in 2020, after which the conditions of the President and Parliament were be concurrent.[94] Although the 2020 Presidential elections were marred by the coronavirus pandemic, power was successfully transferred. In the vote on 31 March, previous Prime Minister Arayik Harutyunian won 49 per cent of the vote, and former Foreign Minister Masis Mayilian won 26 per cent, neither surpassing the 50 per cent required to secure victory. A run-off vote was held on 14 April; however, Mayilian urged people not to vote given the increasing risk posed by the coronavirus, and only 45 per cent of eligible voters turned out, compared to 72 per cent in the first round, handing Harutyunian a victory of 88 per cent.

While the successful transition of power in 2020 was a positive indication of democratic progress, Sahakyan's tenure prior to the 2020 election, although legal according to the laws of Karabakh, encourages questions to be asked about the extent of democratisation. A widely held view in Karabakh is that the volatile security situation necessitates a strong leadership, so much so that genuine contestation could be too destabilising to risk. Pål Kolstø and Helge Blakkisrud recount a Karabakhi observer's perspective: "Presidential elections are too serious for the de facto state to be openly contested".[95] The fallout from the 2020 conflict has followed in this vein. Following the defeat to Azerbaijan, Harutyunian announced that new elections would be held in which he would not partake. Vitaly Balasanyan, a veteran of the First Karabakh War, was appointed National Security Advisor, and is considered by many to be a likely frontrunner in the elections.[96]

State-building amidst the constant existential threat of invasion by Azerbaijan is undoubtedly challenging; the perceived condition of 'no peace, no war' provides even greater challenges to democratic state-building. Further to guaranteeing the security of the people – a fundamental objective interest for any state in the international system – is the challenge of adopting a new type identity when the corporate identity consists of leaders, people and institutions that were born of a Soviet yoke. As the NKR's Deputy Foreign Minister put it:

> Many people are used to the Soviet system and they are used to the Soviet style. They are used to working by standards that were set by the Soviet Union. Now you have to convince them that no, now you have to actually have more options than that one single standard. That is where we have problems.[97]

For those who survived the war and were raised in the Soviet era, having a pluralist National Assembly and genuine Parliamentary elections is a significant democratic change. Furthermore, having a 'strongman' leader is not unfamiliar, and is considered by some to be the suitable form of government in a hostile security situation. This was the perception put forward by several of the government's representatives.[98]

Nagorno Karabakh faces many challenges to its state-building process. As one of the most isolated de facto states, with Azerbaijan effective in ensuring that there is minimal international engagement, the government has not had the benefit of international advisors or consultants throughout the process. "We rely on the Armenian laws and we see what they have, change [them] to meet the necessary criteria and tailor them to our own needs ... Otherwise we just do it the way we see it".[99] The process of using Armenia as a leading example can be seen in the recent constitutional changes of Nagorno Karabakh. The shift towards a more centralised system of government mirrored the Armenian constitutional reforms of 2015.

The role of civil society in Nagorno Karabakh is another feature that government representatives use to strengthen their claims to the status of a democratising state. At the local level, organisations such as the NK Helsinki Initiative-92, the Stepanakert Press Club, and the Centre for Civic Initiatives have continuously pushed to ensure that government representation is not the only means by which people in Nagorno Karabakh can have their voices heard[100] or indeed to be accurately or at least dispassionately informed about national developments. Again, the development of civil society is hampered by the severe isolation of Nagorno Karabakh, which limits the ability of organisations to seek funding outside of the Armenian diaspora. While several academics have sketched theoretical roles that civil society could play, including transforming the conflict resolution process,[101] local initiatives to give the people a voice have taken innovative forms.

One local journalist described to me how social media has provided a platform upon which these local initiatives have been able to flourish. One of the projects the journalist was working on at the time was a media project

94 *The Nagorno Karabakh Republic*

called 'Unheard Voice', which aims to reveal the voices of the lives of people living in the villages near the front line, and record their opinions on the NKR conflict.[102] It has been a tripartite project, with journalists from Armenia, Azerbaijan and the NKR participating, communicating through Facebook and publishing in their respective newspaper pieces.

Assessments of civil society mirror the perspectives forwarded about the NKR's democratic process more generally. Some observers claim that civil society has strengthened significantly since 2005, when civil society organisations were provided with a legal basis within which to operate.[103] Since then, organisations have been able to register with the government, and many of them have been able to receive partial government funding for specific initiatives on a competitive basis. The coordinating body, the Council of NGOs, has at times adopted an activist role in its posture towards the international community. In this sense, many of the civil society initiatives are semi-independent supporters of government initiatives. This trend can be seen in the media sector as well, where organisations such as the Stepanakert Press Club have overseen the development of independent local newspapers that, at times, may be critical of government perspectives but only on minor issues; the NKR's international relations and its approach to conflict resolution are not openly criticised. So long as funding is limited to government coffers or to sources in the diaspora, which are criticised for lacking strategic vision in their approach to funding and which provide money for building monuments or rebuilding churches, efforts that do little to develop the local community,[104] civil society is likely to exist but in a form that largely conforms to and reinforces the views of the government.[105]

The electoral history and development of civil society in Nagorno Karabakh portray a de facto state that has made progress in developing democratic credentials but that remains immature. The autocratic Soviet institutions in which the leadership were trained, in combination with the lasting effects of the illiberal Soviet society in which many of the people were raised, are significant influences that form core components of Nagorno Karabakh's corporate identity. To instil the practices and values required to successfully adopt the type identity of a democratic state within these corporate-level constraints is a huge challenge. To successfully develop democracy whilst under the existential threat of invasion and to exist in a constant state of 'no peace, no war' is an even greater challenge. Hence, it is understandable that some observers perceive this attempt at democratisation as a calculated move to frame the de facto state for the instrumental purpose of appealing to the international community by seeking legal recognition. Yet, while this view has merit, it overlooks a key subjective interest of the NKR. This is the crucial role that the democratic image plays in securing diaspora investment: it serves the objective interest of economic development.

The image of a burgeoning democracy can have significant benefits beyond the idea of appealing to members of international society. According to government representatives, progressing the democratic project has helped to secure the Armenian Diasporic support that is a crucial pillar of Nagorno Karabakh's economy. As the Chairman of the National Assembly put it:

> When we talk about Karabakh democracy and the diaspora's part especially, I think that because most of the diaspora lives in democratic societies, be it in France, be it in the United States, be it in Australia or elsewhere, they look at it [Karabakh] as something natural; they look at Karabakh through the prism of their own democracy.[106]

This view was reinforced by several members of government, who attested to the important function of maintaining democratic credentials to maximise the engagement of the diaspora.[107] While there are no reliable official numbers to quantify the precise amount of money that flows from the diaspora into Karabakh,[108] it is estimated to be in the tens of millions of dollars, and is one of two main sources of funding for the government; the other source is direct funding from Armenia. Meeting the baseline economic needs required to provide for the people of Karabakh is an objective interest for the NKR. Building and maintaining a strong relationship with the diaspora is the subjective interest required to achieve this primary objective interest. Democratisation – albeit slow and imperfect – is deemed by the NKR authorities to enable the realisation of this subjective interest. This key finding provides a deeper understanding of the democratisation process in Karabakh. This process reinforces the perception that the state-building efforts are aligned with international society's norms, which increases the NKR's perceived normative standing, and it contributes to achieving one of the state's most basic objective interests.

Para-Diplomatic Relations and Symbolic Recognition

The NKR's ability to build para-diplomatic relations has become a key feature in its recognition narrative. Para-diplomacy is an important area of consideration for two reasons. First, it plays a significant part in facilitating forms of symbolic recognition that have strengthened the NKR's perceived moral appeal to international society. Second, as discussed in earlier chapters, international engagement through para-diplomatic relations has been widely perceived as a fixed interest for de facto states. Analysing it in the context of the NKR's normative standing enables a deeper understanding: the moral value of symbolic recognition reinforces the NKR's perception of its moral and constitutional standing.

The NKR stresses the limiting effects of its severe isolation, yet it also stresses how successful it has been at building para-diplomatic relations given the severity of its currently inescapable remoteness. The main barrier to building international relations is Azerbaijan's staunch stance against international entities engaging the NKR government. Despite this, the NKR Ministry of Foreign Affairs considers itself to have made significant progress in forming and maintaining para-diplomatic relations. As formal, 'Track 1' diplomatic relations are unobtainable, the focus of their para-diplomacy has been through the establishment of foreign representative offices in foreign countries, through relationship-building with international NGOs and through informal networks such as the European Friends of Armenia.

The NKR Ministry of Foreign Affairs claims that the foreign representative offices that have been set up abroad are about much more than image-building; the offices have been utilised for specific purposes that have enabled the NKR to survive in its current de facto state. The first foreign offices to be established abroad were – other than those in Yerevan – in France, the United States and Russia.[109] These were strategically placed in the three countries that chair the OSCE Minsk Group to best place the NKR to maximise its voice in future negotiations.[110] Subsequent offices have also been opened in Australia, Germany and Lebanon. Germany was deemed to be the most appropriate avenue for accessing Europe, and all three of these countries have a substantial Armenian diaspora.[111]

The diaspora has been a key focus for the development of the NKR's international engagement. The worldwide Armenian population is estimated to be approximately ten million people strong, of which only three million live in Armenia or Nagorno Karabakh. The other seven million have been a key source of funding for the NKR through family remittances, official project funding and an array of other initiatives. For instance, there is an annual telethon broadcast by the Armenia Fund in the United States on Thanksgiving, which across 2013 and 2014 raised over $35 million to build infrastructure connecting Armenia and Karabakh.[112] Further to funding, such a large diaspora has resulted in many ethnic Armenians being found in powerful positions around the world, increasing the reach and power of pro-Armenian lobbyists.

Charles Tannock is a Member of the European Parliament, the foreign affairs and human rights spokesperson for the UK Conservative delegation, and a member of the Foreign Affairs Committee, in which he is a member of the Human Rights Sub-Committee.[113] Tannock has written about several de facto states including Somaliland, the Kurdistan Region of Iraq (KRI), Taiwan, South Ossetia, Abkhazia and Nagorno Karabakh. Tannock often prefaces these pieces with disclaimers expressing that the "opinions are entirely personal to the author and do not necessarily reflect the views of his political party, European Parliamentary group or the Conservative-led UK coalition government".[114] However, Tannock's active role in championing causes such as Nagorno Karabakh ensures that the discourse is continued in parliaments around the world.[115] While the European Friends of Armenia association does not have an official role in the European Union, it has ensured that any opportunity to turn the European Union's attention to Armenian- and Nagorno Karabakh-related issues is utilised.[116]

The NKR government's innovative international engagement includes a strong focus on building personal relations with influential individuals. When asked about the government's strategy towards building international relations, one of the key points made by NKR's Deputy Foreign Minister was precisely this:

> I truly believe that people-to-people relations are the strongest, as opposed to nominal official relations with a country. If you have ties with people, they will always be stronger and in ways that you can rely on them and those stronger connections.[117]

At face value, it is easy to perceive this as a mere justification for the limited forms of external relations that the government is able to develop. When official diplomatic channels are unavailable, there are few options beyond using the diaspora to form a web of people-to-people relations. However, further investigation reveals the considerable benefits that this tactic can have if it bears fruit: gaining the support of powerful political figures.

The diaspora has been a powerful force in the NKR's successful para-diplomatic relations building, but the perception of the other enablers provides an important insight into the role that increased international engagement plays. The Spokesperson for the Prime Minister confirmed that the Armenian diaspora was the greatest enabler, but that the NKR's democratic and governing institutions were fundamental to the state's success as well.[118] Echoing other government representatives' perspectives on democratisation, he claimed that major diaspora donors were not moved simply by their Armenian ties; investing in a functioning democracy is a crucial quality when it comes to securing their investment. The Spokesperson added that the adversarial role played by Azerbaijan helped to shine a positive light on the NKR. Azerbaijan's democratic credentials are significantly weaker than the NKR's, consistently falling behind the de facto state in Freedom House ratings. While the NKR's democracy is imperfect, the fact that Azerbaijan is labelled as illiberal and authoritarian increases the perception of Karabakh as deserving of support.

The sustained success of the NKR's para-diplomatic relations, in combination with the perception of this success being partly due to the strength of its state institutions, has bolstered the perceived alter-casting of the de facto state as an international actor:

> It is not a full subject of international law, but it is an international actor of 'Track 1.5'. Para-diplomacy is not full diplomacy, but it is a way, a necessary way, to 'Track 1' diplomacy ... it [NKR] is an actor, primarily in the region, and due to our role in the [sic] regional security.[119]

This view is aligned with the notion of the self-determined state: "If we are not an actor, we do not decide our future as a country, we do not decide the situation on the border with Azerbaijan".[120] The NKR recognises that para-diplomacy does not give it the social sanctioning of full diplomatic relations and therefore that it has limited agency in the international system. The quote above does, however, demonstrate that the NKR believes that building para-diplomatic relations is a

98 The Nagorno Karabakh Republic

necessary step towards building more official diplomatic ties. Alongside enabling the economic interests of the NKR by leveraging the former's relationship with the diaspora, para-diplomacy is also perceived to be a positive step towards building the relations that will eventually help it increase its agency within the international system.

One of the important outcomes of the para-diplomatic relations that the NKR has built consists in the forms of recognition that they have given rise to. For instance, in 2012 the Legislative Council of the state of New South Wales in Australia adopted a resolution to recognise the right of the people of Nagorno Karabakh to self-determination.[121] Similarly, in 2014 the state of California in the United States adopted a similar motion.[122] These are forms of symbolic recognition that do not empower the NKR in any way. However, they carry significant moral value, as described by the Chairman of the National Assembly:

> For us, this is first of all an attention that the largest state in Australia, the same way as California is the largest state in the US, at the level of the legislation, encourages other people's aspirations for freedom, for human rights, for democracy, and it would be surprising if those states, be it California or NSW, had acted differently, or if they condemned for example, those processes, because we should not forget that all of them at some stage of their history were standing where we stand now ... Not that it does recognise Karabakh internationally, but, at least for the people of Karabakh it is an encouragement that they are not alone, that they are on the right path, and that they should continue on this path that they have taken.[123]

This perspective was echoed by many government representatives and civil society members, suggesting that the moral value of this symbolic recognition has genuine benefits. This moral value is especially important because strong diaspora support and symbolic recognition do not in and of themselves equate to strengthening or improving the official stance of recognised states towards the NKR.[124] The people whose collective beliefs and actions constitute the agency of the NKR, however, perceive the moral support they receive as an affirmation that their mode of self-determination is normatively right.

In summary, the role identity of 'victor' has been strongly underpinned and reinforced by a kind of democratic state-building which serves to promulgate the image of the self-determined state. This has thereby increased the moral standing of the NKR because it is perceived to be self-determining, and it has achieved this perception by building effective para-diplomatic relations that provide symbolic recognition and associated moral validation that the NKR is on the normative path to at least acknowledged if not formally recognised statehood. The fact that this state has achieved all this while under the constant threat of invasion reinforces the role identity of persistent victor. Continuing to survive as an incipient state under challenge while receiving external validation affirms the notion that quotidian nominal statehood is a victory for the whole Armenian nation.

Nagorno Karabakh's International Legitimation

The volatile security situation following the Second Karabakh War has clearly taken the question of recognition off the table for the foreseeable future. However, prior to that Nagorno Karabakh had already deprioritised seeking formal international recognition.[125] The view espoused by government representatives was that, although the empowerment of recognition would have instrumental value, the entity had achieved effective statehood regardless of whether or not it would ever be internationally recognised, and that it refused to be defined by the lack of recognition:

> Even international recognition cannot seriously affect our identity because ... the citizens of Karabakh live here without seriously caring for international recognition or non-recognition; it is a technical part for our country. If the independence is recognised, Karabakh can build more relationships with other states, Karabakh can invite more investments, more credit, loans, but these are only technical.[126]

This sentiment was consistently promoted, and was echoed by the Deputy Foreign Minister:

> We were attacked, we defended ourselves, we created our statehood and we are now developing that statehood. In that sense, we say that our problem is solved. The lack of recognition does create obstacles, but, for Karabakhis, they are not obstacles that cannot be overcome. It creates additional hardships, and more costs, but it does not make our life impossible.[127]

The Chairman of the National Assembly reinforced the notion that this view is not just held by members of the government: "On the level of public perception in Karabakh, people don't consider the recognition as the number one problem".[128] It is important to note here that there is a strong desire held by many to unite with Armenia, which may also contribute to this sentiment towards recognition.[129] However the NKR's stated goal and declaration is – although an unlikely prospect – independence and recognition by international society.

The approach of Nagorno Karabakh to recognition is likely heavily influenced by its position as a severely isolated de facto state. With no formal recognition, not even by its patron state, and a hostile parent state relationship, Nagorno Karabakh is condemned to a level of social isolation that is not conducive to hope for gaining international recognition. As such, it is unsurprising that Karabakh has adopted an approach of living with its condition of non-recognition. Such isolation is in itself a form of alter-casting by the international community; the lack of inter-state engagement and the clarity with which confirmed states have made their posture towards Nagorno Karabakh clear have socially conditioned the NKR. The reality of isolation is stark and clear. It is in the context of this reality that considering Nagorno Karabakh's normative standing proves to be insightful.

Nagorno Karabakh's Legal Standing

Nagorno Karabakh is in a precarious legal position. The main legal argument used by the NKR is that, when it made the 2 September 1991 declaration, it legally located Nagorno Karabakh as a direct subject of the USSR according to the 1990 USSR Law on Secession. This is based on the USSR's April 1990 response to the Armenian SSR's announcement of reunification with the NKAO, which was shortly after the Azerbaijan SSR rejected the NKAO's request. Lacking the military appetite or means to intervene, the USSR released the *Law on Procedure for Resolving Questions Connected with a Union Republic's Secession from the USSR*. Supporters of Nagorno Karabakh's independence position this statute as overruling the Soviet Constitution, which only provided the SSRs with the right to secede from the Soviet Union; this right was not extended to their *oblasts*. Under the new 1990 law, however, Article 3 states the following:

> In a Union republic which includes within its structure autonomous republics, autonomous oblasts, or autonomous okrugs, the referendum is held separately for each autonomous formation. The people of autonomous republics and autonomous formations retain the right to decide independently the question of remaining within the USSR or within the seceding Union republic, and also to raise the question of their own state-legal status.[130]

Armenia and Karabakh supporters interpret Article 3 to empower the NKAO with the right to determine its own legal status, whereas Azerbaijan interprets this same article to mean that the *oblasts* had one of two choices: to join the republic that was seceding or to remain as part of the USSR.[131] Ultimately, Nagorno Karabakh's legal case ensures that it can make claim to having an international legal basis for its statehood, but, because the laws to which it appeals were made by an entity that no longer exists, there can be no definitive acceptance or rejection of its legal position.

Nagorno Karabakh's Moral Standing

Nagorno Karabakh's type identity of a budding democracy is intrinsic to its moral standing. State-building whilst under the ever-present existential threat of invasion is inherently challenging, but developing democratic institutions with a corporate identity of Soviet origins whilst under constant threat is even more difficult. Nagorno Karabakh government representatives claim that democracy is what the people of Karabakh fought for, and that this forms part of their mandate. The democratic type identity has become fundamental to their perceived moral pillar, in part, because of the lack of democracy in their parent state of Azerbaijan. Karabakh, having fought for its perceived right to self-determination, has made a concerted attempt to adopt principles of democratic good governance that align with international society's discourse of good governance. Meanwhile, the parent state of Azerbaijan has continued to administer an illiberal authoritarianism. For the leaders of Karabakh, establishing the foundations of democratic institutions in a post-conflict society while the state that the international community declares it must remain a part of is practising governance that many in the international community condemn enables a sense of injustice and associated perception of moral standing. Nagorno Karabakh perceives its own statehood to align with the norms of international society more closely than Azerbaijan's statehood. Furthermore, the fact that it has fought for this democratic statehood has bolstered the NKR's perception that it is deserving of recognition. Put simply:

> Karabakh has managed to survive, to withstand the attack of a neighbour. After overcoming this problem, we have managed to create a democratic statehood. We have deserved the right to be a legitimate state. Many states in the world haven't really struggled that much to get what they now take for granted.[132]

The moral value brought by the symbolic recognition of Nagorno Karabakh's right to self-determination by sub-state actors in foreign countries, discussed above in this chapter, bolsters this perceived moral high ground.

Nagorno Karabakh's Constitutional Standing

Building para-diplomatic relations is perceived and actioned by the NKR as a necessary step towards building diplomatic relations. Therefore, while successful para-diplomacy does not increase the state's normative standing, it is a calculated move that the NKR believes will assist it in developing the practices and behaviours that can eventually increase its normative standing. Increased international engagement does not by default lead to an immediate increase in normative standing. However, it is the type of engagement that matters. The severe international isolation of Nagorno Karabakh is a clear indicator of the lack of constitutional standing it currently holds. The expectations within the current international society clearly prohibit states from engaging Nagorno Karabakh: even the NKR's patron state of Armenia has chosen not to recognise its sovereignty. So long as the condition of 'no peace, no war' prevails, and so long as Azerbaijan is successful in nullifying the attempts of the NKR to participate in international forums, Nagorno

Karabakh's constitutional standing is likely to be the weakest of its normative appeals. Furthermore, the stability that it has been able to achieve has further complicated its constitutional standing, as is demonstrated by the status quo bias that currently exists.

Prior to the so-called 'Four-Day War' of 2016, Nagorno Karabakh was widely referred to as a "frozen conflict".[133] Although this is a telling appellation for discerning the relationship between de facto states and international society, it is a misleading and erroneous phrase that disregards the skirmishes and sniper attacks that consistently violated the Bishkek Ceasefire. While the OSCE Minsk Group is the official avenue for resolving the conflict, it has not managed to make meaningful progress. In the eyes of the NKR, the Minsk Group has no levers with which it can influence the peace process.[134] This was demonstrated in April 2016, when the worst conflict since the Bishkek Ceasefire – prior to 2020 – erupted; four days of bloody war saw the deployment of helicopters, tanks and assault drones in a conflict that claimed approximately 350 lives.[135] The Minsk Group has been attributed by some as having brokered the cessation of this conflict, but the conflict itself was seen as a big step in reverse for the peace process. By comparison, the Second Karabakh War of 2020 can only be considered as a giant leap backwards. Given that Russia brokered the ceasefire without other members of the Minsk Group, the Group's power to affect any future peace process has almost certainly been severely diminished. The stability of the Caucasus is now dangling delicately in the balance of power between rivals Russia and Turkey. While Armenia's defence alliance with Russia has been central to Armenia's defence posture and ability to maintain an asymmetrical rivalry,[136] Russia has demonstrated that it will not exert overt support against Azerbaijan in the conflict. Turkey's support for Azerbaijan, however, is not only explicit, it was critical to Azerbaijan's success in the Second Karabakh War. It is too early to surmise how Nagorno Karabakh's role identities will evolve now that 2,000 Russian peacekeepers patrol its perimeters, though some degree of transmutation is to be expected.

Prior to 2020, while the peace process had stagnated and a peaceful resolution was seemingly unobtainable, the NKR was successfully state-building, progressing democratic practices – even if they were arguably inchoate – and slowly but surely furthering economic development. That quotidian statehood, although perceived by some as increasing the palatability of NKR as a prospective member of international society, was in fact (somewhat ironically) removing many of the incentives for the international community to have pushed for peace. The stalemate came about in the first instance because of the irreconcilability of Nagorno Karabakh's and Azerbaijan's demands. However, in that condition of stalemate, the prospering statehood of the NKR contributed to a status quo bias. A fundamental principle of international society is the maintenance of order.[137] While it has been argued that de facto states perceive effective state-building and attempts at democratisation as a means of 'earning' their sovereignty – a perception propagated by the 'standards before status' discourse – the potential unintended consequence of demonstrating effective statehood is that by providing stability in the international system it removes the incentives from the members of international society to act to change the status quo.

The proposition of a status quo bias in the international system further develops the relationship between international society and international system presented here. Where scholars of international society have proclaimed the fundamental purpose of an international society to be maintaining order in that society, by positioning the system and society as coalescing, this work, drawing on the case study evidence, proposes that the order that international society seeks to maintain is in fact order in the international system. This is not a revolutionary suggestion; it is a theoretical refinement and conceptual extension that enables a deeper understanding of the relationship between de facto states and international society. Nagorno Karabakh has proven its ability to maintain its position in the international system while developing a statehood that was slowly aligning with some of the norms of international society. In doing so, it created stability in the system and contributed to a status quo bias that was a significant driver of the stasis in its relationship with international society. The bloody conflict of 2020 and the volatile security situation left in its aftermath are likely to bolster international society's bias for a new status quo that all but eliminates any hope the NKR may have harboured for achieving international recognition in a foreseeable time frame.

Conclusion

The contours of constitutionality are continuously being refined and redefined, and can therefore be difficult to set in print or stone at any given point in time. Nagorno Karabakh declared independence in the midst of the Soviet dissolution, a period of turmoil when the international discourse of self-determination was strong. The NKR developed its corporate identity in the midst of that turmoil. The establishment of the ceasefire, followed by the steady state-building in the face of Azerbaijan's overt rejection of its right to exist, has formed the role identity of victor. The historical antecedents of this de facto state mean that this role identity takes on a greater meaning: this is a de facto state embodying a nationalism and symbolising a victory for an entire nation, the vast majority of which happen to thrive elsewhere.

A crucial pillar of Karabakh's perceived victory is the successful state-building and nascent democratisation. A closer examination of this type identity reveals that the discourse of democratisation in Nagorno Karabakh is more than just a legitimation strategy and is in fact a key component that contributes to the role identity of victor. This type identity is a pillar in this de facto state's normative standing and is an important component of its state identity, both of which contribute to the status quo that has, in part, solidified the stasis of its relationship with international society. The analytical lens of identity allows us to form a better understanding of the forces driving the behaviour that can be erroneously perceived as purely attempted legitimation. Identity enables us to see that the international persona and para-diplomatic strategy of Nagorno Karabakh are not only tools for seeking international recognition. Actively trying to project the image of a democratising polity may be perceived as a precursor to achieving recognition, but this is not the only purpose it serves. On the contrary, democratisation has also been a subjective means of achieving the fundamental objective interest of economic development.

Interviews Cited

Armine Alexanyan, NKR Deputy Minister of Foreign Affairs, Interview with the author, Stepanakert, 13 November 2015.

Artak Beglaryan, Spokesperson for the Prime Minster of the NKR (now Human Rights Ombudsman), Interview with the author, Stepanakert, 10 November 2015.

Anahit Danielyan, Editor-in-Chief of Nagorno Karabakh Open Society, Interview with the author, Stepanakert, 10 November 2015.

Dashnak Youth Members, Interview with the author, Stepanakert, 13 November 2015.

Ashot Ghoulian, Chairman of the NKR National Assembly and Former Foreign Minister, Interview with the author, Stepanakert, 11 November 2015.

Davit Ishkhanyan, Member of the NKR National Assembly, Interview with the author, Stepanakert, 13 November 2015.

Masis Mayilyan, NKR Former Deputy Minister of Foreign Affairs (Minister of Foreign Affairs at the time of writing), Interview with the author, Stepanakert, 9 November 2015.

Members of the Armenian Revolutionary Federation Youth Party, Interview with the author, Stepanakert, 13 November 2015.

Karen Ohanjanyan, Head of the Helsinki Initiativ-92, Interview with the author, Stepanakert, 12 November 2015.

Notes

1. Audrey L. Altstadt, "The Azerbaijani Turks' Response to Russian Conquest", *Studies in Comparative Communism* 19:3 (1986) 270.
2. Michael P. Croissant, *The Armenia–Azerbaijan Conflict: Causes and Implications* (Westport, CT: Praeger, 1998) 8.
3. Ronald G. Suny, *Looking toward Ararat: Armenia in Modern History* (Bloomington: Indiana University Press, 1993) 199.
4. Suzanne Goldenberg, *Pride of Small Nations: The Caucasus and Post-Soviet Disorder* (London: Zed, 1994) 28.
5. Goldenberg, *Pride of Small Nations: The Caucasus and Post-Soviet Disorder*, 28.
6. Croissant, *The Armenia–Azerbaijan Conflict*, 8.
7. Ibid.
8. Suha Bolukbasi, *Azerbaijan: A Political History* (London: I.B. Tauris, 2011) 27.

9   Christopher J. Walker, *Armenia and Karabagh: The Struggle for Unity* (London: Minority Rights Publications, 1991) 84.
10 Croissant, *The Armenia–Azerbaijan Conflict*, 9.
11 Ibid. Goldenberg claims that it was specifically a Dashnak unit responsible for the death (see explanation of Dashnak in the accompanying text).
12 Goldenberg, *Pride of Small Nations: The Caucasus and Post-Soviet Disorder*, 29.
13 Christopher J. Walker, *Armenia: The Survival of a Nation* (New York: St. Martin's Press, 1980) 77.
14 Croissant, *The Armenia–Azerbaijan Conflict*, 9.
15 Ibid.
16 Geoffrey Robertson, *An Inconvenient Genocide: Who Now Remembers the Armenians?* (London: Biteback, 2014) 46.
17 Richard G. Hovannisian, "Intervention and Shades of Altruism during the Armenian Genocide", in Richard G. Hovannisian, ed., *The Armenian Genocide* (Basingstoke, UK: Palgrave, 1992) 174.
18 Peter Balakian, *The Burning Tigris* (New York: HarperCollins, 2003) 183. Balakian draws on evidence from an American historian, a German historian and a Swiss historian, whose estimates range from 30,000 to 34,000.
19 Ibid.
20 Robertson, *An Inconvenient Genocide*, 46–56.
21 Roger W. Smith, "The Armenian Genocide: Memory, Politics, and the Future", in Richard G. Hovannisian, ed., *The Armenian Genocide: History, Politics, Ethics* (Basingstoke, UK: Palgrave, 1992) 2–3.
22 Adolf Hitler, quoted in Hannibal Travis, "Did the Armenian Genocide Inspire Hitler?", *Middle East Quarterly* 20:1 (2013) 27. Travis acknowledges the "hot debate" about the authenticity of this quote, which, as stated, is widely accepted by genocide scholars, including Geoffrey Robertson.
23 Jennifer M. Dixon, "Norms, Narratives, and Scholarship on the Armenian Genocide", *International Journal of Middle East Studies* 47:4 (2015) 796.
24 Robertson, *An Inconvenient Genocide*, 59.
25 Richard G. Hovannisian, "Introduction", in Richard G. Hovannisian, ed., *The Armenian Genocide: History, Politics, Ethics* (Basingstoke, UK: Palgrave, 1992) xvii.
26 For a detailed analysis of this in diasporic context, see Gayle R. Simidian, "Constructing Armenian Identity: The Influences of Historical Legacy on Succeeding Generations of the Armenian Genocide" (Doctoral Dissertation, Harvard University, 2007).
27 Caroline Cox and John Eibner, *Ethnic Cleansing in Progress: War in Nagorno Karabakh* (London: Institute for Religious Minorities in the Islamic World, 1993) 27.
28 Croissant, *The Armenia–Azerbaijan Conflict*, 14.
29 Richard G. Hovannisian, *The Republic of Armenia, Volume 1: The First Year, 1918–1919* (Berkeley: University of California Press, 1971) 85.
30 Croissant, *The Armenia–Azerbaijan Conflict*, 15.
31 Cox and Eibner, *Ethnic Cleansing in Progress*, 29.
32 Croissant, *The Armenia–Azerbaijan Conflict*, 15.
33 Hovannisian, *The Republic of Armenia*, 157.
34 Croissant, *The Armenia–Azerbaijan Conflict*, 15.
35 Artin H. Arslanian, "Britain and the Question of Mountainous Karabagh", *Middle Eastern Studies* 16:1 (1980) 93.
36 Walker, *Armenia and Karabagh*, 95.
37 Croissant, *The Armenia–Azerbaijan Conflict*, 16.
38 Ibid.
39 Walker, *Armenia and Karabagh*, 95.

106 *The Nagorno Karabakh Republic*

40 Claude Mutafian, "Karabagh in the Twentieth Century", in Levon Chorbajian, Patrick Donabedian and Claude Mutafian, eds., *The Caucasian Knot: The History and Geo-Politics of Nagorno-Karabagh* (London: Zed, 1994) 134–135.
41 Joseph Stalin, quoted in James Forsyth, *The Caucasus: A History* (Cambridge: Cambridge University Press, 2013) 426.
42 Ibid.; Michael Kambeck and Sargis Ghazaryan, "Timeline 1918–2011", in Michael Kambeck and Sargis Ghazaryan, eds., *Europe's Next Avoidable War: Nagorno Karabakh* (Basingstoke, UK: Palgrave Macmillan, 2013) 24.
43 Ibid.
44 Croissant, *The Armenia–Azerbaijan Conflict*, 26.
45 Audrey A. Altstadt, *The Azerbaijani Turks: Power and Identity under Russian Rule* (Stanford, CA: Stanford University Press, 1992) 195.
46 Forsyth, *The Caucasus*, 650.
47 Thomas de Waal, *Black Garden* (New York: New York University Press, 2003) 12.
48 For a detailed account, see De Waal, *Black Garden*.
49 Nora Dudwick, "Memory, Identity, and Politics in Armenia" (Doctoral Dissertation, University of Pennsylvania, 1994) 28.
50 Forsyth, *The Caucasus*, 650.
51 De Waal, *Black Garden*, 35.
52 Ibid.
53 Croissant, *The Armenia–Azerbaijan Conflict*, 68.
54 Forsyth, *The Caucasus*, 650, footnote 8.
55 Ibid., 654.
56 Ibid.
57 Kambeck and Ghazaryan, "Timeline 1918–2011", 24–25.
58 Ibid., 25.
59 The legal debate will be explored in detail below in this chapter.
60 De Waal, *Black Garden*, 170–171.
61 Human Rights Watch, "Bloodshed in the Caucasus: Escalation of the conflict in Nagorno Karabakh", https://www.hrw.org/sites/default/files/reports/1992%20Bloodshed%20in%20Cauc%20-%20Escalation%20in%20NK.pdf (1992).
62 Ibid.
63 Svante Cornell, *Small Nations and Great Powers* (London: RoutledgeCurzon, 2005) 80.
64 Thomas de Waal, "Remaking the Nagorno Karabakh Peace Process", *Survival* 52:4 (2010) 159.
65 See, for example, the numerous uses of the phrase by various authors in Laurence Broers, ed., *The Limits of Leadership: Elites and Societies in the Nagorny Karabakh Peace Process* (London: Conciliation Resources, 2006).
66 Armine Alexanyan, NKR Deputy Minister of Foreign Affairs, Interview with the author, Stepanakert, 13 November 2015.
67 Artak Beglaryan, Spokesperson for the Prime Minster of the NKR (now Human Rights Ombudsman), Interview with the author, Stepanakert, 10 November 2015.
68 Ashot Ghoulian, Chairman of the NKR National Assembly and Former Foreign Minister, Interview with the author, Stepanakert, 11 November 2015.
69 Ashot Ghoulian, Interview with the author.
70 The author attended this conference.
71 Ashot Ghoulian, Interview with the author.
72 Nina Caspersen, "Playing the Recognition Game: External Actors and De Facto States", *The International Spectator: Italian Journal of International Affairs* 44:4 (2010) 53.

73　Sargsyan stepped down from political office in 2018, after protests some refer to as the "Velvet Revolution" were held opposing Sargsyan's new position as Prime Minister, seeing it as an extension of his decade of power as President.
74　The number of deaths does not account for soldiers who are still missing. See Crisis Group, "The Nagorno-Karabakh Conflict: A Visual Explainer", *Crisis Group*, https://www.crisisgroup.org/content/nagorno-karabakh-conflict-visual-explainer#1 (2021).
75　Russian Presidential Office, "Statement by President of the Republic of Azerbaijan, Prime Minister of the Republic of Armenia and President of the Russian Federation", *Russian Presidential Office*, http://en.kremlin.ru/acts/news/64384 (10 November 2020).
76　BBC, "Armenia, Azerbaijan and Russia Sign Nagorno-Karabakh Peace Deal", *BBC News Online*, https://www.bbc.com/news/world-europe-54882564 (10 November 2020).
77　Al-Jazeera, "Armenia: Tensions Reignite between PM Pashinyan, Army", *Al-Jazeera News Online*, https://www.aljazeera.com/news/2021/3/10/armenian-pm-says-army-chief-of-staff-dismissed (10 March 2021).
78　Ann M. Simmons, "Armenia's Prime Minister Calls Snap Election after Nagorno-Karabakh Losses", *The Wall Street Journal*, https://www.wsj.com/articles/armenias-prime-minister-calls-snap-election-after-nagorno-karabakh-losses-11616080451 (18 March 2021).
79　Nina Caspersen, "Separatism and Democracy in the Caucasus", *Survival: Global Politics and Strategy* 50:4 (2008) 113–136; Anne-Marie Gardner, "Beyond Standards Before Status: Democratic Governance and Non-State Actors", *Review of International Studies* 34:3 (2008) 531–552; Laurence Broers, "Mirrors to the World: The Claims to Legitimacy and International Recognition of De Facto States in the South Caucasus", *Brown Journal of World Affairs* 20:11 (2014) 145–159; Nina Caspersen, *Unrecognized States: The Struggle for Sovereignty in the Modern International System* (Cambridge: Polity, 2012) 77–101; Eiki Berg and Martin Mölder, "Who Is Entitled to 'Earn Sovereignty'? Legitimacy and Regime Support in Abkhazia and Nagorno Karabakh", *Nations and Nationalism* 18:3 (2012) 527–545.
80　Michael Scharf, "Earned Sovereignty: Juridical Underpinnings," *Denver Journal of International Law and Policy* 31:5 (2004) 373–387.
81　Nina Caspersen, "Democracy, Nationalism and (Lack of) Sovereignty: The Complex Dynamics of Democratisation in Unrecognised States", *Nations and Nationalism* 17:2 (2011) 337.
82　Laurence Broers, "The Politics of Non-Recognition and Democratization", *Accord* 17:1 (2005) 68.
83　Ashot Ghoulian, Interview with the author; Artak Beglaryan, Interview with the author; Davit Ishkhanyan, Member of the NKR National Assembly, Interview with the author, Stepanakert, 13 November 2015.
84　Joseph A. Schumpeter, *Capitalism, Socialism, and Democracy* (New York: Routledge, 2010).
85　Pål Kolstø and Helge Blakkisrud, "De Facto States and Democracy: The Case of Nagorno-Karabakh", *Communist and Post-Communist Studies* 45 (2012) 145.
86　Ibid., 146.
87　De Waal, *Black Garden*, 242.
88　British Helsinki Human Rights Group, *Nagorno Karabakh Parliamentary Election, 18th June 2000*, http://www.bhhrgarchive.org/Countries/Nagorno%20Karabakh/Nagorno%20Karabakh%20parliamentary%20election%202000.pdf.
89　Ibid.; Razmik Panossian, "The Irony of Nagorno Karabakh: Formal Institutions versus Informal Politics", *Regional and Federal Studies* 11:3 (2001) 149; Caspersen, *Unrecognized States*, 88; Davit Ishkhanyan, Interview with the author.

90 Karine Ohanian, "Opposition Angry at Karabakh Poll", *Global Voices CRS* 292, https://iwpr.net/global-voices/opposition-angry-karabakh-poll (June 2005).
91 Ibid.
92 Ibid.
93 Kolstø and Blakkisrud, "De Facto States and Democracy", 145.
94 The changes to the Constitution also included changing the official name of the de facto state from the Nagorno Karabakh Republic to the Republic of Artsakh, a move that predictably drew heavy criticism from Azerbaijan.
95 Kolstø and Blakkisrud, "De Facto States and Democracy," 146.
96 Neil Hauer, "Bitter Military Losses Lead to Power Struggle in Nagorno-Karabakh", Radio-Free Europe / Radio Liberty, https://www.rferl.org/a/karabakh-power-struggle-haratiunian-balasanian-russia-armenia-azerbaijan/31196526.html (10 April 2021).
97 Armine Alexanyan, Interview with the author.
98 Armine Alexanyan, Interview with the author; Davit Ishkhanyan, Interview with the author.
99 Armine Alexanyan, Interview with the author.
100 Masis Mayilyan, Former NKR Deputy Minister of Foreign Affairs (Minister of Foreign Affairs at the time of writing), Interview with the author, Stepanakert, 9 November 2015.
101 For a detailed analysis of this point, see Vincec Kopecek, Tomas Hoch and Vladimir Baar, "Conflict Transformation and Civil Society: The Case of Nagorno-Karabakh", *Europe-Asia Studies* 68:3 (2016) 441–459.
102 Anahit Danielyan, Editor-in-Chief of Nagorno Karabakh Open Society, Interview with the author, Stepanakert, 10 November 2015.
103 Nona Shahnazarian, "Nagorny Karabakh's *De facto* Non-Governmental Organization Domain: Political Society vs. Civil Society?", *Caucasus Analytical Digest* 65:1 (2014) 10–11.
104 Anahit Danielyan, Interview with the author; Dashnak Youth Members, Interview with the author, Stepanakert, 13 November 2015.
105 Kopecek et al., "Conflict Transformation and Civil Society", 442.
106 Ashot Ghoulian, Interview with the author.
107 Davit Ishkhanyan, Interview with the author; Masis Mayilyan, Interview with the author.
108 Armine Alexanyan, Interview with the author.
109 Masis Mayilyan, Interview with the author.
110 Ibid.
111 Ibid.
112 Rik Adriaans, "The Humanitarian Road to Nagorno Karabakh: Media, Morality and Infrastructural Promise in the Armenian Diaspora", *Identities: Global Studies in Culture and Power* 26: 1 (2017), 2.
113 Charles Tannock, *Dr Charles Tannock: Member for European Parliament for London Biography*, http://www.charlestannock.com/biography.asp (2018).
114 Charles Tannock, "The EU's Commitment in the Nagorno Karabakh and the Required Steps Ahead", in Michael Kambeck and Sargis Ghazaryan, eds., *Europe's Next Avoidable War* (London: Palgrave Macmillan, 2013) 185.
115 See, for example, European Friends of Armenia, "European Parliament Commemorates the Centennial of the Armenian Genocide", http://eufoa.org/european-parliament-commemorates-the-centennial-of-the-armenian-genocide/ (April 2015); European Friends of Armenia, "MEP Charles Tannock Asks Federica Mogherini About Ceasefire Violations", http://eufoa.org/mep-charles-tannock-asks-federica-mogherini-about-ceasefire-violations/ (September 2015).
116 Ibid.
117 Armine Alexanyan, Interview with the author.

118 Artak Beglaryan, Interview with the author.
119 Ibid.
120 Ibid.
121 Armenian National Committee of Australia, "Australia's Largest State of NSW Recognises the Republic of Nagorno Karabakh", http://www.anc.org.au/news/Media-Releases/Australia's-largest-state-of-NSW-recognises-the-Republic-of-Nagorno Karabakh (October 2012).
122 News.am, "California State Resolution Recognising Karabakh Independence", https://news.am/eng/news/208466.html (May 2014).
123 Ashot Ghoulian, Interview with the author.
124 This is supported by Eiki Berg and Scott Pegg's study. See Eiki Berg and Scott Pegg, "Lost and Found: The WikiLeaks of De Facto State – Great Power Relations", *International Studies Perspectives* 17:3 (2016).
125 Armine Alexanyan, Interview with the author; Ashot Ghoulian, Interview with the author; Caspersen demonstrates that this shift in strategy took place following the partial international recognition of Kosovo in 2008. Nina Caspersen, "The Pursuit of International Recognition after Kosovo", *Global Governance* 21:3 (2015).
126 Artak Beglaryan, Interview with the author.
127 Armine Alexanyan, Interview with the author.
128 Ashot Ghoulian, Interview with the author.
129 Nina Caspersen, "Recognition, Status Quo or Reintegration: Engagement with de facto States", *Ethnopolitics* 17:4 (2018) 378. See also Laurence Broers, *Anatomy of a Rivalry* (Edinburgh: Edinburgh University Press, 2019).
130 Edward E. Walker, *Dissolution: Sovereignty and the Breakup of the Soviet Union* (Lanham, MD: Rowman and Littlefield, 2003) 73.
131 William Slomanson, "Nagorno Karabakh: An Alternative Legal Approach to Its Quest for Legitimacy", *Miskolc Journal of International Law* 9:1 (2012) 74.
132 Armine Alexanyan, Interview with the author.
133 The Economist, "A Frozen Conflict Explodes", *The Economist*, https://www.economist.com/europe/2016/04/09/a-frozen-conflict-explodes (9 April 2016).
134 Masis Mayilyan, Interview with the author.
135 Carey Cavanaugh, "Renewed Conflict over Nagorno Karabakh: Contingency Planning Memorandum 30", *Council on Foreign Relations* (21 February 2017) 1. https://www.cfr.org/report/renewed-conflict-over-nagorno-karabakh.
136 For a detailed and authoritative examination of this relationship, see Broers, *Anatomy of a Rivalry*.
137 See Chapter Two.

Bibliography

Adriaans, Rik. "The Humanitarian Road to Nagorno Karabakh: Media, Morality and Infrastructural Promise in the Armenian Diaspora", *Identities: Global Studies in Culture and Power* 26:1 (2017) 1–19.

Al-Jazeera. "Armenia: Tensions Reignite between PM Pashinyan, Army", *Al-Jazeera News Online*, https://www.aljazeera.com/news/2021/3/10/armenian-pm-says-army-chief-of-staff-dismissed (10 March 2021).

Altstadt, Audrey L. "The Azerbaijani Turks' Response to Russian Conquest", *Studies in Comparative Communism* 19:3 (1986) 161–326.

Altstadt, Audrey L. *The Azerbaijani Turks: Power and Identity under Russian Rule* (Stanford, CA: Stanford University Press, 1992).

Armenian National Committee of Australia. "Australia's Largest State of NSW Recognises the Republic of Nagorno Karabakh", http://www.anc.org.au/news/Media-Relea

ses/Australia's-largest-state-of-NSW-recognises-the-Republic-of-Nagorno Karabakh (October 2012).
Arslanian, Artin H. "Britain and the Question of Mountainous Karabagh", *Middle Eastern Studies* 16:1 (1980) 92–104.
Balakian, Peter. *The Burning Tigris* (New York: HarperCollins, 2003).
BBC. "Armenia, Azerbaijan and Russia Sign Nagorno-Karabakh Peace Deal", *BBC News Online*, https://www.bbc.com/news/world-europe-54882564 (10 November 2020).
Berg, Eiki, and Mölder, Martin. "Who Is Entitled to 'Earn Sovereignty'? Legitimacy and Regime Support in Abkhazia and Nagorno Karabakh", *Nations and Nationalism* 18:3 (2012) 527–545.
Berg, Eiki and Pegg, Scott. "Lost and Found: The WikiLeaks of De Facto State – Great Power Relations", *International Studies Perspectives* 17:3 (2016) 267–286.
Bolukbasi, Suha. *Azerbaijan: A Political History* (London: I.B. Tauris, 2011).
British Helsinki Human Rights Group. *Nagorno Karabakh Parliamentary Election, 18th June 2000*, http://www.bhhrgarchive.org/Countries/Nagorno%20Karabakh/Nagorno%20Karabakh%20parliamentary%20election%202000.pdf.
Broers, Laurence. "The Politics of Non-Recognition and Democratization", *Accord* 17:1 (2005) 68–71.
Broers, Laurence, ed. *The Limits of Leadership: Elites and Societies in the Nagorny Karabakh Peace Process* (London: Conciliation Resources, 2006).
Broers, Laurence. "Mirrors to the World: The Claims to Legitimacy and International Recognition of De Facto States in the South Caucasus", *Brown Journal of World Affairs* 20:11 (2014) 145–159.
Broers, Laurence. *Anatomy of a Rivalry* (Edinburgh: Edinburgh University Press, 2019).
Caspersen, Nina. "Separatism and Democracy in the Caucasus", *Survival: Global Politics and Strategy* 50:4 (2008) 113–136.
Caspersen, Nina. "Playing the Recognition Game: External Actors and De Facto States", *The International Spectator: Italian Journal of International Affairs* 44:4 (2010) 47–60.
Caspersen, Nina. "Democracy, Nationalism and (Lack of) Sovereignty: The Complex Dynamics of Democratisation in Unrecognised States", *Nations and Nationalism* 17:2 (2011) 337–356.
Caspersen, Nina. *Unrecognized States: The Struggle for Sovereignty in the Modern International System* (Cambridge: Polity, 2012).
Caspersen, Nina. "The Pursuit of International Recognition after Kosovo". *Global Governance* 21:3 (2015) 393–412.
Caspersen, Nina. "Recognition, Status Quo or Reintegration: Engagement with De Facto States", *Ethnopolitics* 17:4 (2018) 373–398.
Cavanaugh, Carey "Renewed Conflict over Nagorno Karabakh: Contingency Planning Memorandum 30", *Council on Foreign Relations*, https://www.cfr.org/report/renewed-conflict-over-nagorno-karabakh (21 February 2017).
Cornell, Svante. *Small Nations and Great Powers* (London: Routledge Curzon, 2005).
Cox, Caroline, and Eibner, John. *Ethnic Cleansing in Progress: War in Nagorno Karabakh* (London: Institute for Religious Minorities in the Islamic World, 1993).
Crisis Group. "The Nagorno-Karabakh Conflict: A Visual Explainer", *Crisis Group* https://www.crisisgroup.org/content/nagorno-karabakh-conflict-visual-explainer#1 (2021).
Croissant, Michael P. *The Armenia–Azerbaijan Conflict: Causes and Implications* (Westport, CT: Praeger, 1998).

De Waal, Thomas. *Black Garden* (New York: New York University Press, 2003).
De Waal, Thomas. "Remaking the Nagorno Karabakh Peace Process", *Survival* 52:4 (2010) 159–176.
Dudwick, Nora. "Memory, Identity, and Politics in Armenia" (Doctoral Dissertation, University of Pennsylvania, 1994).
Economist, The. "A Frozen Conflict Explodes", *The Economist*, https://www.economist.com/europe/2016/04/09/a-frozen-conflict-explodes (9 April 2016).
European Friends of Armenia. "European Parliament Commemorates the Centennial of the Armenian Genocide", http://eufoa.org/european-parliament-commemorates-the-centennial-of-the-armenian-genocide/ (April 2015).
European Friends of Armenia. "MEP Charles Tannock Asks Federica Mogherini about Ceasefire Violations", http://eufoa.org/mep-charles-tannock-asks-federica-mogherini-about-ceasefire-violations/ (September 2015).
Forsyth, James. *The Caucasus: A History* (Cambridge: Cambridge University Press, 2013).
Gardner, Anne-Marie. "Beyond Standards Before Status: Democratic Governance and Non-State Actors," *Review of International Studies* 34:3 (2008) 531–552.
Goldenberg, Suzanne. *Pride of Small Nations: The Caucasus and Post-Soviet Disorder* (London: Zed, 1994).
Hauer, Neil. "Bitter Military Losses Lead to Power Struggle in Nagorno-Karabakh", *Radio-Free Europe / Radio Liberty*, https://www.rferl.org/a/karabakh-power-struggle-haratiunian-balasanian-russia-armenia-azerbaijan/31196526.html (10 April 2021).
Hovannisian, Richard G. *The Republic of Armenia, Volume 1: The First Year, 1918–1919* (Berkeley: University of California Press, 1971).
Hovannisian, Richard G. "Intervention and Shades of Altruism during the Armenian Genocide", in Richard G. Hovannisian, ed. *The Armenian Genocide: History, Politics, Ethics* (Basingstoke, UK: Palgrave, 1992) 1–25.
Hovannisian, Richard G. "Introduction", in Richard G. Hovannisian, ed. *The Armenian Genocide:History, Politics, Ethics* (Basingstoke, UK: Palgrave, 1992) xiv–xxii.
Human Rights Watch. *Bloodshed in the Caucasus: Escalation of the Conflict in Nagorno Karabakh*, https://www.hrw.org/sites/default/files/reports/1992%20Bloodshed%20in%20Cauc%20-%20Escalation%20in%20NK.pdf (September 1992).
Kambeck, Michael, and Ghazaryan, Sargis. "Timeline 1918–2011", in Michael Kambeck and Sargis Ghazaryan, eds., *Europe's Next Avoidable War: Nagorno Karabakh* (Basingstoke, UK: Palgrave Macmillan, 2013) 24–32.
Kolstø, Pål, and Blakkisrud, Helge. "De Facto States and Democracy: The Case of Nagorno-Karabakh", *Communist and Post-Communist Studies* 45 (2012) 141–151.
Kopecek, Vincec, Hoch, Tomas and Baar, Vladimir. "Conflict Transformation and Civil Society: The Case of Nagorno-Karabakh", *Europe-Asia Studies* 68:3 (2016) 441–459.
Mutafian, Claude. "Karabagh in the Twentieth Century", in Levon Chorbajian, Patrick Donabedian and Claude Mutafian, eds., *The Caucasian Knot: The History and Geo-Politics of Nagorno-Karabagh* (London: Zed, 1994) 109–170.
News.am. "California State Resolution Recognising Karabakh Independence", https://news.am/eng/news/208466.html (May 2014).
Ohanian, Karine. "Opposition Angry at Karabakh Poll", *Global Voices CRS* 292, https://iwpr.net/global-voices/opposition-angry-karabakh-poll (June 2005).
Panossian, Razmik. "The Irony of Nagorno Karabakh: Formal Institutions versus Informal Politics", *Regional and Federal Studies* 11:3 (2001) 143–164.

Robertson, Geoffrey. *An Inconvenient Genocide: Who Now Remembers the Armenians?* (London: Biteback, 2014).

Russian Presidential Office. "Statement by President of the Republic of Azerbaijan, Prime Minister of the Republic of Armenia and President of the Russian Federation", *Russian Presidential Office*, http://en.kremlin.ru/acts/news/64384 (10 November 2020).

Scharf, Michael. "Earned Sovereignty: Juridical Underpinnings," *Denver Journal of International Law and Policy* 31:5 (2004) 373–387.

Schumpeter, Joseph A. *Capitalism, Socialism, and Democracy* (New York: Routledge, 2010).

Shahnazarian, Nona. "Nagorny Karabakh's *De facto* Non-Governmental Organization Domain: Political Society vs. Civil Society?", *Caucasus Analytical Digest* 65:1 (2014) 9–14.

Simidian, Gayle R. "Constructing Armenian Identity: The Influences of Historical Legacy on Succeeding Generations of the Armenian Genocide" (Doctoral Dissertation, Harvard University, 2007).

Simmons, Ann M. "Armenia's Prime Minister Calls Snap Election after Nagorno-Karabakh Losses", *The Wall Street Journal*, https://www.wsj.com/articles/armenias-prime-minister-calls-snap-election-after-nagorno-karabakh-losses-11616080451 (18 March 2021).

Slomanson, William. "Nagorno Karabakh: An Alternative Legal Approach to Its Quest for Legitimacy", *Miskolc Journal of International Law* 9:1 (2012) 69–77.

Smith, Roger W. "The Armenian Genocide: Memory, Politics, and the Future", in Richard G. Hovannisian, ed. *The Armenian Genocide: History, Politics, Ethics* (Basingstoke, UK: Palgrave, 1992) 1–20.

Suny, Ronald G. *Looking toward Ararat: Armenia in Modern History* (Bloomington: Indiana University Press, 1993).

Tannock, Charles. "The EU's Commitment in the Nagorno Karabakh and the Required Steps Ahead", in Michael Kambeck and Sargis Ghazaryan, eds., *Europe's Next Avoidable War* (London: Palgrave Macmillan, 2013) 185–198.

Tannock, Charles. *Dr Charles Tannock: Member for European Parliament for London Homepage*, http://www.charlestannock.com/biography.asp.

Travis, Hannibal. "Did the Armenian Genocide Inspire Hitler?", *Middle East Quarterly* 20:1 (2013) 27–35.

Walker, Christopher J. *Armenia: The Survival of a Nation* (New York: St. Martin's Press, 1980).

Walker, Christopher J. *Armenia and Karabagh: The Struggle for Unity* (London: Minority Rights Publications, 1991).

Walker, Edward E. *Dissolution: Sovereignty and the Breakup of the Soviet Union* (Lanham, MD: Rowman and Littlefield, 2003).

4 The Republic of Somaliland

"We have demonstrated that recognition is in the best interests of other countries, the region, and the world as whole."[1]

When I was fortunate enough to visit Somaliland in 2015, I had managed to go about my days in the capital with little need to be fearful, and to talk to people and make friends with ease. Yet as we approached the checkpoint to go beyond the city limits of Hargeisa, the challenges of the security environment were front of mind. Western government travel advice had warned of the stringent security measures I must adhere to if I was serious about self-preservation, and journeying beyond Hargeisa required hiring a government-sanctioned guard in order to be allowed past the perimeter checkpoint. This was a volatile security environment. Approaching the checkpoint, it became abundantly clear that, if there was now peace and stability in Somaliland, it might derive from something other than the appearance and capability of their security services. The 'checkpoint' was a single guard controlling a 'barrier' comprising a solitary length of rope pulled taut across the road. I was accustomed to the questioning, probing, vehicle-searching and disciplined inquisitions by Peshmerga at checkpoints in the Kurdistan Region of Iraq; there was, however, a striking lack of rigour as we drove through the checkpoint at speed. It was cause to register the sincerity of Somalilanders' claims to enjoy peace and stability in a de facto state that came into existence in the aftermath of a bloody and devastating war, the kind that so often only perpetuates a vicious cycle of further conflict. The qualities of Somaliland's corporate identity formation that underpin its unique political environment are part of what makes it an insightful case study for better understanding the relationship between de facto states and international society.

Formation of the Somaliland Republic's Corporate Identity

Overview of the Somali Clans

An outline of the Somali clan structure is necessary to understand the societal dynamics of Somaliland and, in this case, the peace-making and state-building processes that formed the corporate identity of the Republic of Somaliland.

DOI: 10.4324/9781003178521-5

Somalis are an ethnically homogenous group that have much diversity in their kin groupings. The four main clan families are the Isaq, Dir, Darod and Hawiye. In Somaliland, the predominant clan family is the Isaq, which makes up over 70 per cent of the population[2] and which consists of four clans: the Habar Awal, Habar Jalo, Garhajis, and Arap. The Habar Awal clan has two major sub-clans, the Iisa Muse and Saad Muse, while the Garhajis have two major sub-clans, the Habar Yoris and Eidagalle. Somaliland also has sizeable populations of Gadabursi (clans belonging to the Dir family) as well as the Harti clans of Dhulbahante and Warsangeli (the Harti clans belong to the Darod family). Somaliland's majority population of Isaq means that it does not have the same degree of conflict between clan families as south-central Somalia, where the Darod and Hawiye clan families compete; however, as will be discussed throughout this and later sections, sub-clan divisions have been the source of both conflict as well as positive community cohesion.

The Union of Somalia

Like many states in Africa, the state of Somalia is the result of colonial centralisation and boundary creation. The governance structures that were put in place by the colonising powers had lasting effects that shaped the state-building trajectory of the Republic of Somalia in the 1960s, and arguably the state-building of Somaliland in the 1990s.[3] In the Italian Trust Territory of Somalia, the Italians imposed an authoritarian bureaucracy, enforcing imported political structures they perceived necessary to control the colony. Conversely, the British took a much lighter approach to managing the Protectorate of Somaliland. The political organisation through the community structures formed by the clans was left largely intact.[4] As one observer commented: "Interested only in getting cheap meat to feed its Aden garrison and in keeping the French out, England treated its Somali colony with benign neglect".[5] This benign neglect, however, enabled traditional cultural structures to be maintained, a unique feature that marked a distinct difference in the colonies of Somaliland and Somalia.

The global appetite for colonialism waned in the middle of the twentieth century, and nationalist agitation in the British Protectorate of Somaliland began to take root. As the strategic benefits of the protectorate to the British diminished, the British began preparing the way for local self-governance.[6] Somaliland locals began to take over key administrative positions from 1957 with the formation of the Legislative Council of Somaliland. In February 1960, the Legislative Assembly had its first elections, and in May 1960 the British and the Somaliland Council of Elders agreed to a succession plan and to establish independence.[7] The British declared the Protectorate of Somaliland an independent state on 26 June 1960. Five days later, the Italians granted the independence of the Italian Trust Territory of Somalia on 1 July 1960, and on the same day the two newly independent states voluntarily unified to form the Somali Republic. While Somalilanders are commonly thought to harbour retrospective acrimony about the unification, the benefits at the time were clear, for as Mark Bradbury describes, "colonialism bequeathed Somalia the political accoutrements of a modern state, but not an economy to sustain it".[8] Today, there is a prominent view amongst many Somalilanders that the union with Somalia was never properly consummated, and I will address this issue below.

The newly independent state of Somalia was a short-lived attempt at democracy. The National Assembly was an amalgamation of the two parliaments, with 90 representatives from Somalia and 33 from Somaliland. The parties and politicians that led the country quickly became fragmented along clan lines. State resources became the focus of competition and contest, often with "scant regard for the interests of their constituents".[9] Disadvantaged by the allocation of parliamentary seats and comparatively inexperienced in the context of politics, Somalilanders in the Somali Republic were virtually "second-class citizens".[10] The façade of democracy crumbled in October 1969, when President Abdirashid Ali Sharmake was killed; before a vote could be held to elect his successor, the military seized control of the state under the leadership of Major General Mohammed Siyad Barre.

As soon as Barre's government was in power, it enacted administrative and legislative reforms designed to contain the people's civil and political rights. The regime legally sanctioned the removal of any perceived potential opposition to its rule through an anti-subversion law, which it justified as protecting the country's national security. It complemented the legal means of suppressing the people with extra-legal measures such as the deployment of a para-military force to act as neighbourhood monitor with powers allowing it to arrest people at will and the establishment of the National Security Service (NSS), an omnipresent secret police force.[11] Barre's regime grew increasingly oppressive, attracting proponents of resistance internally and abroad.

The Somali Civil War

The Somali National Movement (SNM) was formed by a diaspora community in London in 1981. The SNM's members were predominantly from the Isaq clan and they formed their organisation with the central objective of overthrowing the Barre regime.[12] However, the SNM was not originally designed to be an Isaq-oriented group, and numerous attempts were made to expand the leadership beyond the Isaq clan. The SNM was successful in incorporating some clan diversity within its ranks; however, it also actively sought the endorsement of the Isaq clan elders on the ground in Somalia.[13] The movement became Isaq-led for an important strategic reason: many of the planned military operations were to take place in traditionally Isaq territories. Without Isaq elders, the SNM could not establish the required network or popular support required to launch a military offensive in the Isaq lands. The endorsement by the Isaq clan elders was accompanied by the establishment of an advisory body made up of clan elders to consult with the SNM administration known as the *gurti*.[14] The SNM's Constitution outlined the importance of maintaining the territorial integrity of Somalia; however, right from its conception there was a secessionist faction that desired independence for Somaliland.[15]

Barre's government saw all Isaqs as prospective supporters of the SNM, and actively opposed and suppressed the SNM from 1981. It used the emergence of the SNM, and any suspected presence of the SNM, as a pretence for the violent persecution of individuals or groups who were known or suspected critics of the government. This persecution was constant throughout the 1980s. The methodical persecution is evident in a leaked 1987 report written by Somali Major General Mohamed Saeed Hirsi, in which he specifically outlines his intention to destroy the inhabitability of the northern Isaq regions and acknowledges the targeted obliteration of many Isaq-dominated villages.[16] Full-scale war broke out on 27 May 1988, when the SNM tried to capture Burao. On 31 May, its troops attacked the government forces in Hargeisa. This led to systematic arrests of Isaq men across the north in towns such as Berbera, Burao and Erigavo. Isaq members of the armed forces in these towns were systematically executed,[17] presumably because they were perceived to have the greatest capacity to actively advance the SNM cause. The violence and bloodshed spiralled rapidly, and by 1990 an estimated 50,000–60,000 people had been killed, with a further 400,000 refugees fleeing to neighbouring countries and an estimated 400,000 fleeing to points elsewhere within the country.[18] The government's reaction to the SNM's military campaign was to wage genocidal destruction in the north. The turning point in the war arrived when the SNM successfully captured all the major northern towns in a sweeping initiative in January 1991, paving the way for the former British protectorate to seek peace in the form of statehood.

1991–1997: Somaliland Adjusts from Peace-Building to State-Building

Two core features of the subsequent peace-building era in Somaliland were the national inter-clan peace conferences and the local reconciliation processes.[19] The national conferences of Burao and Borama were pivotal in shepherding Somaliland from a war-torn land towards a more peaceful, comparatively stable de facto state. These conferences were focussed primarily on governance at the systemic, constitutional level. Complementing the national conferences were a number of smaller regional and district meetings that focussed on more common or civil matters such as managing pastoral lands, facilitating trade and enabling local arrangements for the implementation of security. The national conferences and the local meetings were both inspired by the traditional cultural practices of Somali society, whereby clan elders mediated meetings between conflicted entities.[20] The first years of the post-Barre period illustrate the unique and fundamental role that the leadership of the clan elders played in guiding the incipient republic through a formative and at times bloody period in which the eventual pillars of Somaliland's unique democracy were constructed.

The elders of Somaliland's clans met in Berbera in early 1991, where they discussed the path to peace and planned for the first reconciliatory conference in Burao. The declaration of the independent Republic of Somaliland came after leaders of the Dir, Harti and Isaq met at the reconciliatory Grand Conference of the Northern Peoples[21] in Burao. The SNM leadership was not initially in favour of secession, but the groundswell from Somalilanders demanding independence – hardened by the atrocities committed against them – was strong. The SNM was sanctioned by the *gurti* to govern for two years; it was to be guided by a swiftly compiled charter and govern with the intention of preparing the polity for elections in two years' time.[22] While this marked the beginning of the intent to resume independent statehood, the practical realities of state-building were far from purposefully planned, and in that ad hoc stage regression to familiar local practices and procedures understandably became the norm.

In fact, Somaliland's first years after the overthrow of the Barre regime were a tumultuous start to the state-building process. In January 1991, after Barre was dislodged, the SNM's territorial control spread beyond its traditional stronghold of the north-western region of Somalia. Militias from the clans that had previously aligned with Barre during the civil war, namely the Dhulbahante, Gadabursi and Warsangeli, were forced to negotiate peace with the SNM.[23] The truce and reconciliation conference in Burao was largely deemed to be successful, and the announcement of independence injected a wave of optimism for the future. It is important to note here that the commitment to independence was made by the Dhulbahante, Gadabursi and Warsangeli clans' representatives, not just the representatives of the Isaq clan.[24] The interim government was assembled hastily, which, given the minimal design consideration, defaulted to governance structures that closely resembled those already in place within the SNM.

The lack of design forethought and the newly acquired power contributed to a rise in tensions between internal factions of the SNM. As each of the clans began establishing their own militia,[25] distribution of economic, military and political resources increased tensions between the clan militias, mainly between those who supported President Abdirahman Ahmed Ali Tur and those who opposed him. Fighting between the clans broke out in Burao in January 1992, killing approximately 300 people. While the government had officially established its administration in Hargeisa, it was yet to establish control over the means of force.[26] When President Tur attempted to obtain control of Berbera in March 1992, a key economic resource for the country because of its valuable shipping port, further violence erupted as the Isaq sub-clan of Iisa Muse, which controlled the port city, opposed Tur's regime, which mostly consisted of Garhajis.[27] Such intra-Somaliland violence continued across the region for eight months and claimed an estimated 1,000 lives.[28]

The disputes underpinning the widespread violence were first addressed at the *tawfiq* conference in Sheikh from 28 October to 11 November 1992. Elders from the Gadabursi, Dhulbahante and Isaq clans assembled in Sheikh and established a ceasefire between the Habar Yunis and the Iisa Muse. The meeting achieved political agreements to oversee co-operative security relations and the allocation of resources, in particular the Berbera port, which would become an important asset for the Somaliland governments in the years to come. The Sheikh meeting was the first time that the collective *gurti* of Somaliland clan elders had formed, with all clans except for the Warsangeli represented. That meeting was the initial turning point in the establishment of agreed peace under the collective leadership of the clans.[29] The *gurti* that had advised the SNM leadership throughout the war was expanded to include all of Somaliland's clans and pave the way for them to become an official force in the establishment of the Republic of Somaliland.[30]

The Borama conference of January 1993 built on the success of the Sheikh assembly and made a giant leap forward in the formation of the Republic of Somaliland's corporate identity. Means for disarming and managing the militias were agreed upon, underpinned by the writing of a national peace charter. To support these peace-making efforts, the elders recognised the need for a formal administration.[31] This gave birth to the design of the executive interim government and a national charter detailing the system of government that combined the strengths of traditional socio-political structures with institutions inspired by Western-style democracy.[32] The importance of power-sharing amongst the clans was incorporated into the bicameral Parliament, which was composed of an Upper House of Elders, also referred to as the *gurti*,[33] and a Lower House of Representatives that comprised members nominated by a designated group of elders on a clan basis. The allocation of seats in the House of Representatives was based on principles of pluralism and proportional representation.[34] This ensured that the smaller clans were given a voice in the Parliament.

The conference also resulted in a judiciary intended to be independent and the installation of an executive President to complement the bicameral Parliament.[35] At the conference, Muhummad Haji Ibrahim Egal was appointed to the position of President in place of Tur. Bradbury positions this transition as Egal being chosen by the *gurti* in a straightforward process, emphasising the supreme powers of the *gurti*.[36] However, Dominik Balthasar proposes that it was the support of the militarised hard-line *Alan As* faction in a "prolonged tug-of-war" that was crucial to the establishment of Egal as President. While the process of appointment is debated, there is consensus that the *gurti* played a key role in facilitating the conference and the subsequent transition from Tur to Egal. The elementary principles and framework of Somaliland's unique democracy had been established.

Egal was initially successful in progressing the economic and military pillars of the state-building project. On the security front, he demobilised some of the militias and created a national army for Somaliland, supported by a state administration. In an attempt to satisfy the demobilised fighters, he provided many of them with jobs in the administration. This contributed to a burgeoning public service that, becoming increasingly oversized, required a sound economic base to support it. With the support of the Iisa Muse in Berbera, Egal was able to build a steady stream of tax revenue from the Berbera port. Furthermore, he established customs offices along the Ethiopian border to tax the vast quantities of the narcotic *khat* that were being imported on a daily basis. During this time, Egal also introduced a new currency, the Somaliland shilling, which is still in use throughout the Republic today.[37] The introduction of the Republic's own currency was not only perceived as a significant symbol of state-building, but it also purposely injected a substantial financial contribution into the newly established state coffers.[38]

While the initial stages of Egal's state-building project were successful, there remained strong opposition to his leadership that soon challenged the stability of the state. Ex-President Tur and other prominent leaders of the Garhajis openly stated their rejection of the Egal government's legitimacy. They claimed that the centralisation at the heart of Egal's state-building violated the National Charter, but they were also averse to the lack of Garhaji representation in the administration and the empowerment of ministers who had been violent opponents of the Tur government.[39] The Eidagalle – one of the two Isaq clans that constitute the Garhajis – retaliated by capturing control of the Hargeisa airport in March 1994. The airport was within their traditional clan boundaries, allowing them to claim that their actions were within the scope of the National Charter, which allowed for some local administration of security. This defiant act stood to not only endanger the stability of the government, but also served to undermine it economically by taking control of a major revenue stream.

Somaliland then endured the bloodiest conflict of the post-Barre period with a reported 4,000 people killed.[40] The catalyst for the conflict that began in November 1994 is contested. A widely accepted version is that the government deemed it necessary to purge the Garhajis' opposition in order to consolidate its control and establish a stable authority in the name of state-building.[41] While this may have been an initial motivation, Balthasar points out the subsequent benefits that Egal stood to gain, positing that Egal "willingly entertained" the following civil wars in order to shore up his political control.[42] Egal did indeed resist calls for another national conference,[43] and the war that ensued bolstered his power by not only weakening the Garhajis, but weakening the *Alan As*, whose support for the President at the Borama conference had forced Egal to comply with their interests, further destabilising the emerging republic. Egal managed to weaken both factions by framing the Garhajis as the subversive initiators of the conflict and then positioning the *Alan As* as the reactionary force, diminishing his responsibility for the loss of life while weakening the Garhajis and delegitimising the *Alan As*.[44]

While the war had a devastating effect on the immediate conditions of Somaliland, it allowed Egal to consolidate his power, laying a stable foundation upon which an effective state-building process could possibly begin again. Egal had removed the opposition posed by the Garhajis. Having positioned the *Alan As* as a liability, during the conflict he removed it from positions of authority and incorporated many of its followers into the state's forces. Furthermore, Egal portrayed the opposition as not only being anti-government, but also as being in favour of reunion with Somalia. This enabled him to portray himself as a reliable nationalist leader, strengthening his popular appeal at a time of turbulence and instability. By incorporating key economic and military powerbrokers into his administration and by weakening the opposition, all the while depicting himself as a strong leader of an independent Somaliland with the support of the *gurti*, Egal made astute political manoeuvres that established the conditions in which a previously turbulent Republic of Somaliland could focus on building a more stable state.

The civil war was concluded by another successful reconciliation conference in Hargeisa between October 1996 and February 1997. The five-month assembly brought the conflict to an end through the same traditional approach to conflict resolution, resulting in the opposition being granted greater representation in both houses of Parliament. Further to securing peace, the conference was another crucial step in the development of Somaliland's emerging democracy, producing a new constitution that replaced the Borama conference charters, outlining a vision and procedure for establishing a multi-party political system and new criteria for selecting the President. Although Egal had, before the conference, stated his intention to step down from the Presidency at the end of that term, he was re-elected in February 1997 by clan elders for another five-year term. Where Egal's first Presidential term had resulted in devastating conflict and a consequent halt in state-building, his second term was a productive period of economic development and stabilisation for the newly formed de facto state. Somaliland's corporate identity was constructed in the aftermath of a bloody war, the likes of which in Africa has rarely been conducive to stability or the realisation of democratic aspirations.

Somaliland State Identity: State-Building in a Society of Divisions

> "Somalia failed because it was not designed and owned by the people. Our people came together".[45]

State-Building on the Foundations of a Unique Democracy

A central theme in the recognition narrative of Somaliland is the de facto state's perceived and promoted successful democratisation. Government representatives consistently refer to the unique democracy and effective institutions that have been constructed. The lack of external assistance or intervention throughout the state-building process[46] is a point of pride for the government.[47] The unique state-building process explored in the first section of this chapter has given birth to a type identity that, according to government representatives, underpins the establishment of peace and stability. This in turn is the foundation of other core threads in Somaliland's recognition narrative and is the basis of a role identity that is central to its normative standing: a self-determined state involuntarily embraced by a failed state. This section of the chapter will therefore explore this type identity in greater detail.

After the collapse of the Barre regime and the success of the SNM, the dearth of state institutions in Somaliland was effectively filled by clan institutions in what has widely been referred to in the literature as a "hybrid political system".[48] The clan elders were pivotal in guiding the peace and consolidation process, as discussed above. While the period between 1991 and 1997 had its bloody conflicts, the *gurti* played a crucial role in guiding the eventual resolutions, using traditional Somali cultural approaches to dispute resolution at the national level for the first time. Marleen Renders goes so far as to say that, when the conflict began under President Tur, the Isaq *gurti* stepped in and took ownership of the conflict as an intra-Isaq conflict.[49] Clan elders enabled Egal's success. His adept political manoeuvring was only successful with their support, and his bolder moves, such as ridding his administration of the *Alan As* and dissolving its political agency, were only executed when he established favour and legitimacy with the *gurti*.

There is a consensus view that a foundation for the stability in post-1991 Somaliland is the successful hybrid political system that was built. Integrating traditional authorities into these earlier stages of state-building was intrinsic to the political stabilisation process. This does not mean that the hybrid system has continued to be the most effective at embedding democracy. While the role of the *gurti* is widely acknowledged as important to successful stabilisation in the 1990s, the hybrid model has been criticised for inhibiting democratisation in more recent years. Markus Hoehne criticises the way in which the *gurti* came to be "co-opted and manipulated" by Somaliland's presidents, supporting presidential decrees that prevented due democratic processes.[50] Rebecca Richards highlights how the *gurti* evolved from the community-serving council of the early 1990s, into a politicised apparatus of the state by the early 2000s.[51] Hybrid governments have inevitable tensions between the components of the system which can lead to shortcomings in their governance.[52] Somaliland is no exception. In subsequent years, the relationship between the *gurti*, the President and the House of Representatives evolved throughout Somaliland's state-building trajectory, and some developments in this evolution reflect a system challenged by democratic ideals. However, the relative stability and the purported responsiveness of the political system, in which the *gurti* have played a critical part, represent a central thread in Somaliland's recognition narrative.

In 2001, Somaliland began the transition away from appointed representation towards elected representation, a potentially significant progression for its democratic aspirations and credentials. A draft constitution had been put forward at the 1996 Hargeisa conference; however, it was subject to scrutiny and contestation that lasted until 2000, when Egal and the government finally indicated approval of the proposed draft. The Constitution, outlining a partially electoral political system, was passed by plebiscite in May 2001. While the shift to a representative system of government was a positive indicator of democratic progress, the integrity of the plebiscite's execution has been questioned. There are claims that ballot boxes were distributed and labelled in a manner that made a participant's vote identifiable by elections officials; police and government administrative staff were mobilised to campaign in favour of voting to approve the Constitution; and counting and registration lacked robust oversight.[53] The result of 97 per cent in favour of approving the Constitution suggests that it is unlikely the process closely adhered to the norms of free, fair and open voting.

The new approved system provided for the establishment of political parties, but prohibited parties from constructing platforms based on religious or tribal dispositions.[54] Elections for 23 district councils were held in December 2002, and major political parties were formed in the lead up to the April 2003 presidential elections. The presidential elections took place amidst heightened tensions and uncertainty stemming from the unexpected death of Egal while undergoing surgery in May 2002. The immediate proceedings following Egal's death were an encouraging display of the state institutions at work. In accordance with the Constitution, the two houses of Parliament installed the Vice-President, Dahir Riyale Kahin, to the position of President. As Bradbury notes, the "peaceful manner in which power was transferred proved that the state was now stronger than one individual".[55] The 2003 presidential elections would test the strength of the state and the commitment to democratic procedure. The preliminary results gave the United People's Democratic Party (UDUB) (Egal's party) a tight victory over the Peace, Unity and Development Party (known as Kulmiye in Somali) by a margin of 80 votes (205,595 to 205,515).[56] Ahmed Mohamoud Silanyo, the Chairman of Kulmiye, contested the results through the constitutionally outlined process of pursuing his challenge in the Supreme Court. When the Supreme Court upheld the outcome, Kulmiye initially continued to reject the outcome of the elections, casting clouds of doubt over the possibility of a peaceful and democratic outcome. However, three weeks after UDUB's Riyale had been sworn in as President, Silanyo and Kulmiye conceded. This was a defining moment in the maturation of Somaliland's electoral history. The positive trajectory of electoral democracy continued with the first parliamentary elections being held in 2005. Whereas the democratic development of Somaliland in the 1990s resulted in violent fluctuations, the stability of the early 2000s indicated that the principles of democracy had indeed become better accepted and were taking root in practice.

Since the first elections were held under the new Constitution, the strengths of Somaliland's electoral democracy have been weakened by repeated delays in holding elections. Similar to other de facto states such as Nagorno Karabakh, free and fair elections are heralded as a hallmark of a successful democracy and successful state-building. This view is expressed by senior government representatives of Somaliland,[57] and has permeated Somalilander society as well: "Our statehood depends on how we manage our elections".[58] However, delays to elections have become more common than elections themselves. The presidential elections due in April 2008 were delayed by President Riyale until June 2010. Local council elections due in December 2007 were delayed until November 2012. Parliamentary elections that were due in 2010 are still yet to be held at the time of writing. Initially scheduled for 2013, they were delayed until 2015 to align with presidential elections. President Silanyo delayed the combined elections until 2017 but then only the presidential elections were held. The continuous irregularity of elections in Somaliland distorts the image of the state as a predictable electoral democracy.

A major contributing factor to the weaknesses of the electoral system is the "lack of institutionalisation" in the electoral process.[59] The 2015 elections were initially delayed because the Somaliland National Electoral Commission was insufficiently prepared to conduct the elections.[60] A local think tank director pointed to the volatility of the process due to a lack of sustainable funding.[61] Aly Verjee et al. outline the reliance on donor funding, ranging from a low of 2.16:1 (donor to local funding) for the local council elections of 2002, through to a high of 4.01:1 for the local council elections of 2012.[62] Furthermore, there is a lack of democratic capacity-building. The endogenous design of Somaliland's government draws on traditional local institutions and Western-inspired democratic models, the strength of which has been intrinsic to stability, but the complexity of a hybrid governance model lies in the constant tension between the two poles. Put simply: "We don't have the expertise".[63] The idiosyncratic nature of the peace-building and state-building in Somaliland may have been critical to its success; however, the isolation that accompanied it may have had detrimental effects on the system's practicable efficacy. Democratic capacity-building could have strengthened these institutions. Sarah Phillips has convincingly argued that the absence of international actors in Somaliland's formational period, specifically the absence of "institutional endpoints" prescribed by international donor organisations, enabled local incentives to underpin decision-making; elites driving the formation process could pick and choose components of local and international models that were most likely to work in Somaliland.[64] While it can be argued that Somaliland's electoral institutions could be strengthened, the cost of weaker institutions as a result of an endogenous corporate-identity formation process that has been a pillar of post-conflict stability is arguably a price worth paying.

Somaliland may have challenges in adhering to election timelines; however, there have been reasonably peaceful transitions and transfers of power through election processes, a relatively rare phenomenon in incipient democracies. In 2010, incumbent presidential candidate Riyale of UDUB was defeated by Silanyo of Kulmiye, a reverse outcome to the razor-thin victory for Riyale in 2003. Riyale conceded defeat, and the presidency not only changed leaders but changed political parties as well. The 2017 presidential elections, although delayed for two years, saw Somaliland's fifth President inaugurated when Musa Bihi Abdi, Silanyo's successor in leading Kulmiye (Silanyo chose not to seek re-election), was elected as President. As Scott

Pegg and Michael Walls highlight, Somaliland's first four Presidents all departed the presidential office through what Daniel Posner and Daniel Young refer to as "regular" means (natural death, voluntary resignation or losing an election).[65] It is worthy of note, however, that Riyale was the only President of Somaliland who was not a leader of the SNM, suggesting that, while there have been transfers of power, pluralism may not be as embedded as these transfers of power often suggest.

Democratic Responsiveness Strengthening Nationalism

There are four main components that contributed to the distinctly northern Somali identity of the Somalilander that were crucial in their initial identification as a community distinct from south-central Somalia.[66] The first is the fact that they have a dominant clan family in the Isaq clan, which, although it has suffered infighting along sub-clan lines, still provides an overarching sense of "clanship" compared to the south-central region, where the Hawiye and Darod compete.[67] The second component is the colonial experience that differed so greatly from the Italian Trust Territory in Somalia. The autonomy granted by the British to the people of the north was markedly different from the authoritarian experience of the south, which left many elements of the traditional institutions in place, and this was key to enabling the negotiation processes of the 1990s.[68] The third component is the experience of marginalisation under the Union of Somalia, which in turn led to the oppression under the Barre regime from 1969 onwards. This discrimination reinforced the sense of unity – albeit limited – that came from being Isaq. This leads to the fourth component: the preferential treatment of the ethnically Somali refugees that fled Ethiopia after the Ogaden War. After Somalia's defeat at the hands of Ethiopian forces, the ethnically Somali refugees that fled to Somalia from Ethiopia were given greater access to aid, employment and social services, galvanising the acrimony of the northern Isaqs towards the central government in Mogadishu.

The four components outlined by Asterias Huliaras form a strong foundation upon which a distinct Somalilander identity has taken form. This is only a foundation. This book makes no claims about nationalism in Somaliland prior to the declaration of independence; however, the development of nationalism since that declaration has become distinctly relevant because of the pressure it has applied on the state and the consequent effect it has had on the recognition-seeking efforts of its governments. Having declared independence in 1991, Somaliland is now home to many adults who have grown up in the Republic of Somaliland, living amidst the discourse of recognition and the de facto state's recognition narrative. Several civil society members described the effects of having a generation that has grown up in a society of perceived independence.[69] The Somaliland Youth Development Association (SOYDA) specifically focusses on empowering Somaliland youth by trying to increase the levels of engagement between the youth and the government.[70] The Director of SOYDA claimed that there is a big divide between the perspectives of the youth, who are increasingly disenfranchised and nationalist, and the older generations who are in power: between those who fought and those who have grown up in Somaliland.[71] It is widely perceived that, while non-recognition has had an impact on all Somalilanders, it has had a distinct impact on the identity of the youth, who have been raised to know and feel the condition of non-recognition as an injustice. The increasing disenfranchisement is partly driven by the government's inability to progress the quest for recognition. This has led to increasing amounts of pressure being applied by the youth on the government, which in turn has revealed a strength in Somaliland's democracy: civil society providing forums in which the people's voices are expressed. This has been particularly evident recently in expressions of frustration about the lack of progress and in the perceived lack of strategic direction by the government in seeking recognition.

In December 2015, the Ministry of Foreign Affairs and International Cooperation (MFAIC) held a conference focussing on the direction of Somaliland's foreign policy.[72] Somaliland's overseas representatives had been recalled for the conference, and prominent members of the local community, from NGO representatives to journalists and clan elders, were invited to participate. According to the Foreign Minister, the conference had three main aims that were centred on training their representatives: sharing experiences between representatives; capacity-building specifically around conducting diplomatic communication; and discussing the direction of Somaliland's foreign policy.[73] The conference finished with a commitment by the attendees from the Ministry to intensify their recognition-seeking efforts. Several conference attendees claimed that the invitee list had included so many members from the community because of the consensus-based, consultative approach that exists within the culture of Somaliland.[74]

Some NGO leaders and local think-tank specialists claimed that the open nature of the conference was designed to conjure an image of the Ministry taking action to animate its ambassadors in a renewed push for independence.[75] The Centre for Policy Analysis (CPA) in Hargeisa held a conference in the preceding August to discuss recognition-seeking and what tangible steps the government was taking to turn the rhetoric about recognition into action. A view shared by many locals is that the August conference was organised because of the widely held opinion that the government was not doing enough to seek recognition, despite it featuring so heavily in the political discourse of Hargeisa. There is clearly widespread discontent with the government's lack of a recognition strategy – or at least with its inability to demonstrate to the populace that it has a plan of action – demonstrating the importance of recognition to a significant portion of the populace.

Somaliland's International Legitimation

There are four major components to Somaliland's recognition strategy: legal, historical, political and moral.[76] Political advisors supporting the MFAIC's claim that these four components have always been present in Somaliland's case for recognition, but historically the emphasis placed on any one component has changed without any clear strategic reasoning.[77] One advisor stated: "They are looking for a silver bullet".[78] Public rhetoric makes clear that recognition is the highest priority for the MFAIC; however, the focus of the Ministry away from the public eye in recent years has been on building and using diplomatic relations to develop a stronger economic future. This is not to suggest that the government has abandoned their recognition-seeking efforts; rather, it is simply not prioritising it as highly as it states publicly.

In recent years, the diplomatic efforts at recognition-seeking have centred on the strategy of trying to secure the support of other African states.[79] The logic behind this strategy is that the support of African states will help it to build stronger relations with the African Union.[80] While this strategy is logical at an abstract level, the Somaliland government is realistic about the obstacles it faces. The African Union will only recognise an independent Somaliland if Somalia does.[81] As highlighted above in previous chapters, the recognition of the parent state remains a steadfast roadblock to gaining rightful membership in international society.

While there has been a clearer strategy in recent years, historically the government's foreign policy has not been so strategic. The relationships that were built were much more dependent on the abilities of the diaspora.[82] The initial para-diplomacy relied on individuals within the diaspora who were well connected, independently wealthy and motivated to further Somaliland's recognition-seeking cause. One advisor to the MFAIC claimed that there is very little benefit coming from the para-diplomacy initiatives.[83] Where this was once a strength demonstrated by the diaspora, it appears to have now largely transferred that responsibility to the government, which has struggled to execute this task due to a lack of resources and a lack of strategic foresight.[84]

The MFAIC has also struggled to have a consistent strategic approach to recognition because it is hard to get agreement on a coherent approach to recognition within the wider government. Put simply, "it is hard to get a unity of purpose within the government".[85] The Kulmiye, Waddani and Justice and Development political parties promulgate and parry rhetoric about recognition; however, there have not been coherent policies presented by any of them.[86] The parties use the subject of recognition in an attempt to build a favourable image, positioning themselves as having greater ability to obtain it; however, there have not been policies or actions sufficient to substantiate these claims.[87] One consistent element within this discourse is the appeal to the people of Somaliland, suggesting that the topic of recognition is a high priority for the general public.[88]

Somaliland's Legal Standing

Somaliland's main claim to legal standing is based on historical title, which can be broken down into multiple parts. The first is the significance of the existence of Somaliland as a geopolitical entity that existed as the British Protectorate from 1897 until its independence in 1960. Somaliland argues that, because the territorial borders of the Republic – as of the dissolution of the Union in 1991 – are the same borders as the British Protectorate, it therefore aligns with the principle of *uti possidetis juris*.[89] Somaliland interprets this principle – which is not directly referred to – as being enshrined in the Constitutive Act of the African Union, which in Article 4(b) declares the "respect of borders existing on achievement of independence".[90] Independence in Somaliland's interpretation, in this case, refers to the independence achieved in 1960, when it was granted independence by Britain. Its independence at this time followed the norms of the acceptable realisation of independence for colonised countries as discussed in Chapter Two. Somaliland explicitly makes this case, maintaining that "former colonial boundaries should be maintained upon independence",[91] pointing out that the borders upon the 1991 declaration are the same borders as when it was an independent state in 1960.

Somaliland hence does not consider itself to be a case of secession; rather, it is the dissolution of the union with Somalia, a union that it unilaterally chose to exit as the sovereign state that had entered the union. Somaliland also argues that there is precedent for the dissolution of unions within Africa. The Somaliland MFAIC gives the examples of Egypt and Syria dissolving the United Arab Republic (1958–1971); Senegal and Mali disbanding the Fédération du Mali (1959–1960); Senegal and Gambia devolving from the Sénégambia Confederation (1982–1989); and the separation of Eritrea from Ethiopia in 1993.[92] While this is a compelling compilation of examples, it fails to consider the role of the states dissolving and whether or not the dissolution was mutually approved. For, although Somaliland can directly reference the Constitutive Act of the African Union and can draw on the concept of *uti possidetis juris*, these legal arguments will not be sufficient grounds for recognition in the eyes of the international community so long as Somalia does not recognise its sovereignty; Somaliland's legal case simply has not been able to overcome this constitutional hurdle.

The final pillar of Somaliland's legal argument is that the 1960 Act of Union was not properly ratified. Somaliland argues that the parties representing Somalia and Somaliland signed different Acts of Union, agreeing to different terms of unification, which is made more questionable by the fact that the union was passed retrospectively in January 1961 and by the fact that in the June 1961 referendum held on the Constitution of the Somali state, less than 17 per cent of Somalilanders voted and the majority of those who did vote rejected the Constitution.[93] This attempts to paint a convincing picture that there was widespread disapproval of the union throughout Somaliland at the time of the referendum. Although Somaliland positions this as part of its legal argument, it is a less convincing component, especially alongside arguments that give de facto state experts such as Pegg and Kolstø reason to conclude that "it is hard to imagine any other would-be sovereign state putting together a better case than the one Somaliland has both been blessed with and earned for itself".[94]

Somaliland's Moral Standing

A central component of Somaliland's moral argument is that, by denying Somaliland recognition, the international community is condemning the people of Somaliland to endure the costs of non-recognition. The perceived costs of non-recognition are substantial. In the opinion of the government ministers and NGO representatives that I interviewed, the main costs are lack of access to adequate healthcare; lack of access to training, health and education; and underemployment, which could be partially remedied by attracting foreign direct investment.[95]

In the opinion of local think tank directors, one of the benefits of non-recognition has been the growth of civil society, which they believe has grown significantly for two reasons. First, noting that they consider NGOs to be within the definition of civil society, their perception is that, because funding cannot go to the government directly, NGOs instead receive funding that allows them to partake in developmental work that could otherwise be undertaken by the government were it able to attract the direct international aid contributions. As many of the members pointed out, this is a very ineffective and inefficient way to develop Somaliland. The inability for Somaliland to receive direct funding increases the need for intermediaries. Introducing intermediaries significantly increases costs along the value chain, meaning that the end return on investment is lower. This is not sustainable, and it minimises the impact of the money that is nominally going towards Somaliland but in actuality is "covering the operational costs of organisations that are based in Nairobi".[96] The greater the number of links in the chain, the smaller the sum of money that actually gets invested in Somaliland.

A widely shared perspective was that there has been a significant positive trajectory in the abilities of the government. A World Bank report estimated that the Government of Somaliland's budget increased from US$45 million in to 2009 to US$130 million in 2012.[97] That figure had risen to US$295million for 2016.[98]

Second, several local businesspeople asserted the ease with which non-recognition is too easily blamed for everything, and how inaccurate this blaming can be.[99] Non-recognition has become a scapegoat. Another local businessperson pointed to how this idea of victimisation is propagated, giving the example of the discourse surrounding the drought that was present in the region at the time.[100] He proclaimed that, although the drought had been damaging, the problem in Somaliland was not the absence of regular rainfall but the lack of effective water management strategies. There is a lack of foresight and investment in this area, which is a significant impediment to further development across the region.[101]

It is important to acknowledge the degree to which this discourse of victimisation can be perpetuated. Some of the proponents of this view claimed that the victimisation within the recognition narrative must be continued to justify the squalid conditions of Somaliland. The government must be seen to be trying to gain recognition, so that it can use the cost of non-recognition as an explanation for why there is not greater development. However, all of the businesspeople that I interviewed did recognise one key element that underpins many of Somaliland's developmental woes. As one businessperson put it: "The lack of appropriate investment in the agriculture industry could be partially because the government has to prioritise security".[102]

In the eyes of many of those interviewed, there appears to be an increasing awareness of the way in which the condition of non-recognition was used to justify as many government administration short-comings as possible. There was uniformity of opinion from members of the NGO community and local businesspeople that, regardless of the condition of non-recognition, the government had significant capacity to have achieved more progress in the development of fiscal policy; tax reform; revenue collection; and capacity-building (for example, the lack of capacity to collect taxes has a significant negative impact on the budget).[103] Public financial management was frequently cited as the number one area for improvement by local businesspeople and diaspora investors, as well as some government representatives. It is important to acknowledge these areas as in need of betterment; however, it should not be at the cost of glossing over the genuine cost of non-recognition. Direct access to international aid could provide significant means by which to address many of these challenges. The cost of non-recognition is further amplified by the constant lack of a security guarantee that it bestows, a situation illustrated in full colour by the bloody war in 2020 between Armenia and Azerbaijan, where Nagorno Karabakh became perilously close to being recaptured in full by Azerbaijan, and by the forcible eradication seen in Krajina in 1995, Chechnya in 1999 and Tamil Eelam in 2009.

The final component to the moral pillar for Somaliland is an appeal to the concept of remedial secession. As discussed above, the concept of remedial secession has existed since the recognition of Bangladesh as a sovereign state; Pakistan was deemed to have forfeited its sovereignty by committing gross human rights violations. The Somaliland government's appeal to this principle is based on atrocities committed by the Barre regime.[104] James Ker-Lindsay has rightly pointed out that remedial secession lacks the legal grounding that would enable de facto states to use it as a means of achieving recognition.[105] Pegg and Kolstø have highlighted Somaliland's claims to remedial secession as weakened by this lack of legal gravitas.[106] This work agrees that Somaliland's claims to remedial secession do indeed have no legal weight; however, it proposes that the relevance of these claims is better understood through the pillar of morality. As earlier chapters have demonstrated, the standards of legitimate membership of international society are rarely determined by just moral, legal or constitutional claims. Somaliland's evidenced claim that its people have been subjected to gross human rights violations provides a moral argument that complements its claims to have strong legal grounding. The second component of Somaliland's moral argument, which is based on the perception that "Somaliland is being held hostage to a failed state",[107] will be addressed in the following section because it pertains to both morality and constitutionality.

Somaliland's Constitutional Standing

The Government of Somaliland perceives the recognition of Somaliland's sovereignty to be in the interests of international society. In 2015, the Foreign Minister of Somaliland, Dr Saad Ali Shire, described seeking international recognition as the highest priority of the MFAIC. In fact, he said it was the highest priority for everyone in the government. Dr Saad explicitly stated that, while there are legal, historical and moral reasons that the international community should recognise Somaliland, what his Ministry finds confounding is the fact that, from Somaliland's perspective, it has demonstrated that it is in the best interests of the region and the international community for Somaliland to be recognised as a sovereign state. From the perspective of the government, not only does Somaliland have a right to self-determination, not only has it satisfied the legal criteria for statehood, and not only has it demonstrated that it can abide by international norms of good governance, it has shown that it is in the *interests* of international society for Somaliland to be recognised.[108] The main rationale underpinning this assertion was the role that Somaliland could play as a positive force for security in the Horn of Africa.[109]

The terrorist group al-Shabaab is well established in Somalia, and is one of the most destructive groups in the Horn of Africa. With a fighting force of between 7,000 and 9,000, al-Shabaab is responsible for thousands of deaths in Somalia and is present across vast swathes of the country.[110] While al-Shabaab has been a consistent force for destabilisation and destruction in Somalia since its inception in 2006, Somaliland has suffered far fewer terrorist attacks; the last major al-Shabaab-related bombing in Somaliland was in 2008.[111] This is considered remarkable, given that many of al-Shabaab's powerful figures originate from Somaliland, including Ahmed Abdi Godane, who led al-Shabaab until his death in a US drone strike in 2014. Godane was born in Hargeisa and was Isaq. It is therefore fair to assume that the leaders of al-Shabaab have strong networks in Somaliland. This, combined with the levels of poverty and the drastic increase in the spread of Salafism, could make Somaliland a target breeding ground to recruit and indoctrinate young men into their organisation, and thereby help the group gain a strong foothold there. The growth of Salafism is a growing concern for the stability of Somaliland. As Somaliland expert Dr Bulhan claims, "Salafism is a very serious threat. It is not obvious or openly organised as a political wing, as it is in most Muslim societies. Somaliland is not an immediate hotspot. But it will become one if the democratic system is not seen to work".[112] In light of this, the image of stability of Somaliland is seemingly remarkable. Somaliland points to its current stability and the lack of extremist violence in the Republic as evidence to suggest that, with the international funding opportunities that recognition would provide, it could play a leading role in the fight against

De Facto State Identity and International Legitimation   131

terrorism in the Horn of Africa. The comparative peace and stability in Somaliland compared to Somalia allows the government to paint a compelling picture to this effect.

Somaliland's capacity to fight extremists is, however, yet to be proven. While Somaliland enjoys relative security compared to Somalia, there is evidence to suggest that it is the strength of the communities and clan institutions in Somaliland that have prevented the growth of Islamic extremism. Government ministers and civil society members both attest to the strength of the community as an effective means of preventing Islamic extremism. They claim that there is a strong awareness amongst the adult population of the fact that young men are targets, and the community is attuned to those at risk.[113] Imams and village elders alike take note of those who show signs of harbouring extremist beliefs, or those who display concerning changes in behaviours that indicate they may be at risk. Early identification allows for both prominent members of the clan as well as their religious leaders to help "guide these boys back to the path of good, the path of Allah, not the path of violence".[114]

The image of Somaliland as a force for stability in the region has been reinforced by influential international voices. After a visit to the region, the European Union Commissioner Andris Piebalgs stated in a press release announcing financial support for Somalia, including Somaliland, that "the European Union welcomes the contribution that Somaliland is making to peace and good governance in the region. It is an encouraging example of peace, democracy and stability".[115] The government has since featured this quote on its webpage dedicated to detailing Somaliland's case for recognition.[116]

A key component of the perceived constitutional pillar is that Somaliland has demonstrated that it is a developing, stable, self-determined state that is making concerted attempts to respect and practise norms of good governance. Somaliland's type identity of a unique democracy has also partly constituted a formative role identity relative to Somalia. The volatile security situation in Somalia, and the government's inability to control the use of force, protect its people or provide basic social services, has qualified Somalia to regularly be categorised as one of the world's most fragile states.[117] Yet, it maintains internationally recognised sovereignty while Somaliland, with predominantly free and fair elections, stability and the beginnings of economic development, is denied international recognition. This role identity of a successful self-determined state held captive by a failed state is a core component of Somaliland's recognition narrative and the basis of both its moral and constitutional claims. Morally, as described above, Somaliland perceives international society as inflicting harm on its 3 million nationals by denying it the developmental benefits of international recognition. Constitutionally, Somaliland perceives the success of state-building to align with the prevalent expectations espoused by international society of state conduct. The central function of successful democratic state-building for the perceived moral and constitutional standing of Somaliland demonstrates the continuing impact

132 *The Republic of Somaliland*

that the discourse of democratisation is having on the development of de facto states, and the extent to which they perceive it as intrinsic to the normative fabric of international society. This is apparent even when Somaliland's MFAIC recognises that international society functions with higher priorities.

The MFAIC recognises that the international community's priorities are clearly ordered as security first, stability second and good governance third.[118] This is a telling revelation, for it suggests that the function of international society as a guardian of order – this book argues order in the international system – is recognised by government officials, not just by scholarly observers. Advisors to the MFAIC stated that one of the problems the Ministry faces is a dilemma that exists by virtue of Somaliland being a stable democratising entity: members of the international community are incentivised to maintain the status quo.[119] The condition of non-recognition has given rise to a stable, developing – albeit slowly – entity on a course of democratisation. This view was echoed by local civil society members, one of whom claimed that the condition of non-recognition has "developed resilience", claiming that "Somalia failed because it was not designed and owned by the people. Our people came together".[120]

One of the advisors recounted a story in 2015 of a former Minister of Foreign Affairs and International Cooperation saying in jest that in order to engage the international community Somaliland should start a war.[121] In a public interview, the current Minister was asked about comments he had made threatening conflict with Somalia, to which he replied: "They [Somalia] are claiming Somaliland as part of Somalia. And if they want to exert what they may call their right to rule Somaliland from Mogadishu, then we will fight them and you will have a war".[122] On one hand, these inflammatory remarks could be perceived as an extension of the jesting rhetoric previously voiced designed to highlight a perceived absurdity in the non-recognition of their state. On the other hand, this could indicate a shift in thinking about potential strategic measures to engage the international community. This work does not have sufficient evidence to definitively state this claim, but what can be discerned is the clear status quo bias of international society. That bias is a core contributor to the stasis that currently exists between de facto states and international society.

This need to find new ways to engage the international community is further evidenced in the Somalia–Somaliland dialogue that started in 2012. Somaliland recognised the significant roadblock posed by the stance of Somalia in rejecting Somaliland's claims to recognition. There was seemingly initial progress in improving relations between the two governments, when, in 2012, an official dialogue was facilitated by international intermediaries. One of the key roadblocks to such a dialogue had recently been removed: there was now the Federal Government of Somalia to negotiate with. The Presidents of the respective governments met in the United Arab Emirates (UAE) in June 2012, and again in Turkey in April 2013. This was initially perceived as significant progress; however, by 2015 the talks had collapsed. One of the main reasons that the talks were suspended was the alleged lack of credibility of the group representing Somalia.[123] There was significant disagreement after it was revealed that some of the members of Somalia's party had Somaliland roots.[124] At this time, Turkey was leading the mediation. Given also Turkey's strong anti-secessionist position against the independence aspirations of the Kurdish populations in Turkey and across the Middle East, this raised questions about how fruitful the talks could be for the Somaliland delegation. The MFAIC claimed that Somaliland was realistic about the potential outcome of the talks; Somaliland's main goal in entering these talks was to engage the international community. While Turkey was perceived to be a biased intermediary, simply conducting the talks put the issue in the international news and provided a forum in which other international community members could potentially be invited. After a five-year hiatus from mediation, Somalia and Somaliland re-engaged in 2020, when Ethiopia's Prime Minister Abiy Ahmed hosted Somaliland President Muse Bihi and Somalia's President Abdullahi Mohamed Farmajo in Addis Ababa in February 2020, and after being cajoled by representatives of the United States and the European Union they met again in Djibouti in June 2020.[125]

A key concern that complicates the progress of discussions is that the leaders of Somaliland may not realise how important the non-humiliation of Somalia is.[126] The tunnel vision of Somaliland's leadership on what they have achieved, what they have fought for, how they perceive themselves to have been wronged, and therefore what they perceive they deserve may have blinded them from realising the political importance to their parent state, and to the international community, of the potential humiliation of Somalia. There has been constant international investment in peace-building and state-building efforts in Somalia, with minimal success. A successful Somaliland state, built endogenously, not only risks humiliating the Government of Somalia, it would cast a damning light on the international efforts to stabilise and support Somalia's efforts at state-building.[127] The extent to which the leadership of Somaliland may not be fully cognisant of the negative implications of their independence bid on their externally perceived, and recognised, parent state demonstrates the importance of understanding the role identity of stabiliser that has developed in unison with the type identity of a unique democracy.

Conclusion

Somaliland's legal claim to historical title gives it a stronger legal standing compared with other de facto states; however, in light of the legal grounding proving to be an insufficient means to obtain legitimate membership, Somaliland's legitimation has lacked strategic direction. Its normative standing, however, has developed to represent what some expert observers claim to be a most favourable case for recognition. Somaliland's corporate identity was built on traditional Somali cultural practices that enabled it to establish peace in a time and place of turmoil and bloodshed. The corporate identity-formation process gave birth to a type identity of a unique democracy, a type identity that forms the foundation of its role as a regional stabiliser. Furthermore, this type identity has reinforced international society's status quo bias. Stability in the region provides a degree of order in the international system, which inadvertently serves the interest of the international society that excludes it, the international society which it seeks to join. As Somaliland's normative standing develops further, its unique democracy is contributing to the stasis in its relationship with international society.

Interviews Cited

Ali Husein Ismail, Somaliland's Minister of National Planning and Development (now Former Minister), Interview with the author, Hargeisa, 14 December 2015.

Ambassador for Somaliland's Ministry of Foreign Affairs and International Cooperation, Interview with the author, Hargeisa, 15 December 2015.

Entrepreneur, Interview with the author, Hargeisa, 6 December 2015.

Former Political Advisor to Somaliland's Ministry of Foreign Affairs and International Cooperation, Interview with the author, Hargeisa, 9 December 2015.

Hibak Gamute, Director of the Centre for Policy Analysis, Interview with the author, Hargeisa, 14 December 2015.

Hussein Ismail, Executive Director, Somaliland Youth Development Association, Interview with the author, Hargeisa, 10 December 2015.

Local Businessperson (1), Interview with the author, Hargeisa, 13 December 2015.

Local Businessperson (2), Interview with the author, Hargeisa, 13 December 2015.

Local Businessperson (3), Interview with the author, Hargeisa, 13 December 2015.

Member of the High Judiciary, Interview with the author, Hargeisa, 14 December 2015.

Political Advisor to Somaliland's Ministry of Foreign Affairs and International Cooperation, Interview with the author, Hargeisa, 9 December 2015.

Mohamed Farah Herso, Executive Director of the Academy for Peace and Development, Interview with the author, Hargeisa, 13 December 2015.

Saad Ali Shire, Somaliland's Minister of Foreign Affairs and International Cooperation (current Minister of Finance), Interview with the author, Hargeisa, 15 December 2015.

Notes

1 Dr Saad Ali Shire, Minister of Foreign Affairs for the Republic of Somaliland (current Minister of Finance), Interview with the author, Hargeisa, 15 December 2015.

2. Asteris Huliaras, "The Viability of Somaliland: Internal Constraints and Regional Geopolitics", *Journal of Contemporary African Studies* 20:2 (2002) 158.
3. Dominik Balthasar, "Thinking beyond Roadmaps in Somalia: Expanding Policy Options for State Building", A Report of the CSIS Africa Programme, Centre for Strategic and International Studies, https://www.csis.org/analysis/thinking-beyond-roadmaps-somalia (November 2014), 6.
4. Huliaras, "The Viability of Somaliland", 158.
5. Gerard Prunier, "Somaliland Goes It Alone", *Current History* 97:619 (1998) 225–228.
6. Mark Bradbury, *Becoming Somaliland* (London: Progression, 2008) 32.
7. Ibid.
8. Bradbury, *Becoming Somaliland*, 34.
9. Ioan Lewis, "The Politics of the 1969 Somali Coup", *Journal of Modern African Studies* 10:3 (1972) 399.
10. Dr Saad Ali Shire, Interview with the author.
11. Africa Watch, *Somalia: A Government at War with Its Own People*, https://www.hrw.org/sites/default/files/reports/somalia_1990.pdf (1990), 7.
12. Huliaras, "The Viability of Somaliland", 159; Mark Bradbury et al., "Somaliland: Choosing Politics over Violence", *Review of African Political Economy* 30:97 (2003) 457.
13. Gerard Prunier, "A Candid View of the Somali National Movement", *Horn of Africa* 13:3–4 (1990) 113.
14. Marleen Renders, "Appropriate 'Governance Technology'? – Somali Clan Elders and Institutions in the Making of the 'Republic of Somaliland'", *Africa Spectrum* 42:3 (2007) 444.
15. Matthew Bryden, "Somaliland: Fiercely Independent", *Africa Report* 35:5 (1994) 35–40.
16. Brad Poore, "Somaliland: Shackled to a Failed State", *Stanford Journal of International Law* 45 (2009) 129.
17. Africa Watch, *Somalia: A Government at War with Its Own People*, 9.
18. Ibid., 10–11.
19. Bradbury, *Becoming Somaliland*, 96.
20. Ibid.
21. Ibid., 80.
22. Stig Jarle Hansen and Mark Bradbury, "Somaliland: A New Democracy in the Horn of Africa?", *Review of African Political Economy* 34:13 (2007) 461–476.
23. Balthasar, "Thinking beyond Roadmaps in Somalia: Expanding Policy Options for State Building", 6.
24. Daniel Compagnon, "Somali Armed Movements" in Christopher Clapham, ed., *African Guerrillas* (Oxford: James Currey, 1998) 82; Bradbury et al. "Somaliland: Choosing Politics over Violence", 457.
25. Dominik Balthasar, "The Wars in the North and the Creation of Somaliland", *World Peace Foundation*, https://sites.tufts.edu/reinventingpeace/2013/10/28/the-wars-in-the-north-and-the-creation-of-somaliland/ (October 2013).
26. Ian S. Spears, *Civil War in African States: The Search for Security* (London: First Forum Press, 2010)120.
27. Balthasar, "Thinking beyond Roadmaps in Somalia: Expanding Policy Options for State Building", 6.
28. Bradbury, *Becoming Somaliland*, 96.
29. Lewis, *Making and Breaking States in Africa*, 176.
30. Bradbury, *Becoming Somaliland*, 97.
31. Lewis, *Making and Breaking States in Africa*, 176.
32. Hansen and Bradbury, "Somaliland: A New Democracy", 464.
33. Bradbury, *Becoming Somaliland*, xiii.

34 Dominik Balthasar, "State-Making in Somalia and Somaliland: Understanding War, Nationalism and State Trajectories as Process of Institutional and Socio-Cognitive Standardization" (Doctoral Dissertation, London School of Economics, 2012) 169.
35 Academy for Peace and Development, "The Judicial System in Somaliland", *Workshop Report*, https://apd-somaliland.org/wp-content/uploads/2014/12/JUDICIARY-REPORT-FINAL.pdf (April 2002).
36 Bradbury, *Becoming Somaliland*, 100.
37 USD is used side-by-side.
38 Bradbury, *Becoming Somaliland*, 112.
39 Spears, *Civil War in African States*, 156.
40 Bradbury, *Becoming Somaliland*, 117.
41 Ibid.
42 Dominik Balthasar, "Somaliland's Best Kept Secret: Shrewd Politics and War Projects as Means of State-Making", *Journal of Eastern African Studies* 7:2 (2013) 228.
43 Bradbury, *Becoming Somaliland*, 117
44 Balthasar, "Somaliland's Best Kept Secret", 228.
45 Mohamed Farah Herso, Executive Director of the Somaliland Academy for Peace and Development (APD), Interview with the author, Hargeisa, 13 December 2015.
46 Sarah Phillips, "When Less Was More: External Assistance and the Political Settlement in Somaliland", *International Affairs* 92:3 (2016) 629–645.
47 Dr Saad Ali Shire, Interview with the author; Member of the High Judiciary, Interview with the author, Hargeisa, 14 December 2015.
48 See, for example, Michael Walls and Steve Kibble, "Beyond Polarity: Negotiating a Hybrid State in Somaliland", *Africa Spectrum* 45:1 (2010) 31–56.
49 Marleen Renders, *Consider Somaliland: State-Building with Traditional Leaders and Institutions* (Leiden: Brill, 2012) 96.
50 Markus Virgil Hoehne, "Limits of Hybrid Political Orders: The Case of Somaliland", *Journal of Eastern African Studies* 7:2 (2013) 212.
51 Rebecca Richards, *Understanding Statebuilding: Traditional Governance and the Modern State in Somaliland* (Farnham, UK: Ashgate, 2014) 174.
52 For a succinct overview, see Ken Menkhaus "State Failure, State Building, and Prospects for a 'Functional Failed State' in Somalia", *The Annals of the American Academy of Political and Social Science* 656:1 (2014) 154–172.
53 Anonymous, "Government Recognition in Somalia and Regional Political Stability in the Horn of Africa", *Journal of Modern African Studies* 40:2 (2002) 263.
54 Walls and Kibble, "Beyond Polarity", 41.
55 Bradbury, *Becoming Somaliland*, 136.
56 Bradbury et al., "Somaliland: Choosing Politics over Violence", 470.
57 Ali Husein Ismail, Somaliland's Minister of National Planning and Development (now former Minister), Interview with the author, Hargeisa, 14 December 2015; Dr Saad Ali Sire, Interview with the author.
58 Mohamed Farah Herso, Interview with the author.
59 Ibid.
60 Ibid
61 Ibid
62 Aly Verjee et al., *The Economics of Elections in Somaliland: The Financing of Political Parties and Candidates* (London: Rift Valley Institute, 2015) 14.
63 Ibid.
64 Sarah Phillips, *When There Was No Aid: War and Peace in Somaliland* (Ithaca, NY: Cornell University Press, 2020) 20.

65 Scott Pegg and Michael Walls, "Back on Track? Somaliland after its 2017 Presidential Election", *African Affairs* 117:467 (2018) 327; Daniel N. Posner and Daniel J. Young, "The Institutionalization of Political Power in Africa", *Journal of Democracy* 18:3 (2007) 128.
66 This Somalilander identity structure is proffered by Huliaris. See Huliaris, "The Viability of Somaliland", 157.
67 Ibid., 158.
68 This point is widely accepted. See Balthasar, "Thinking Beyond Roadmaps in Somalia: Expanding Policy Options for State Building"; Bradbury, *Becoming Somaliland*; and Sarah Phillips, "Political Settlements and State Formation: The Case of Somaliland", DLP Research Paper 23, Developmental Leadership Programme, http://www.dlprog.org/news/political-settlements-and-state-formation-the-case-of-somaliland.php (2013).
69 Mohammed Farah Herso, Interview with the author; Hussein Ismail, Executive Director, Somaliland Youth Development Association, Interview with the author, Hargeisa, 10 December 2015; Hibak Gamute, Director of Centre for Policy Analysis, Interview with the author, Hargeisa, 14 December 2015.
70 Hussein Ismail, Interview with the author.
71 Ibid.
72 The author was present for part of this conference.
73 Dr Saad Ali Shire, Interview with the author.
74 Ambassador for Somaliland's Ministry of Foreign Affairs and International Co-operation, Interview with the author, Hargeisa, 15 December 2015.
75 Hibak Gamute, Interview with the author.
76 These will each be discussed in turn later in this section.
77 Political Advisor to Somaliland's Ministry of Foreign Affairs and International Co-operation, Interview with the author, Hargeisa, 9 December 2015; Former Political Advisor to Somaliland's Ministry of Foreign Affairs and International Co-operation, Interview with the author, Hargeisa, 9 December 2015.
78 Political Advisor to the Ministry of Foreign Affairs and International Co-operation, Interview with the author.
79 Ibid.
80 Ibid.
81 Ibid.
82 Former Political Advisor to Somaliland's Ministry of Foreign Affairs and International Co-operation, Interview with the author.
83 Ibid.
84 Ibid.
85 Political Advisor to Somaliland's Ministry of Foreign Affairs and International Co-operation, Interview with the author.
86 Political Advisor to Somaliland's Ministry of Foreign Affairs and International Co-operation, Interview with the author; Former Political Advisor to Somaliland's Ministry of Foreign Affairs and International Co-operation, Interview with the author.
87 Ibid.
88 I recognise that a portion of the population does not support independence, and acknowledge a reputable estimate to be approximately 20 per cent of the population that does not support it. See Phillips, *When There Was No Aid*, 20–21.
89 Dr Saad Ali Shire, Interview with the author.
90 African Union, "Constitutive Act of the African Union", https://au.int/sites/default/files/pages/32020-file-constitutiveact_en.pdf.
91 Somaliland Government, "Why Recognition: The Legal Case", http://recognition.somalilandgov.com/legal/.

138 *The Republic of Somaliland*

92 Ibid.; Seth Kaplan, "The Remarkable Story of Somaliland", *Journal of Democracy* 19:3 (2008) 143–157.
93 Somaliland Government, "Why Recognition: The Legal Case".
94 Scott Pegg and Pål Kolstø, "Somaliland: Dynamics of Internal Legitimacy and (Lack of) External Sovereignty", *Geoforum* 66:1 (2015) 197.
95 Hussein Ismail, Interview with the author.
96 Mohamed Farah Herso, Interview with the author.
97 World Bank, *Transitioning from State Building to Development*, The Somaliland Economic Conference, https://www.slministryofplanning.org/images/HHSurvey/Budget-Policy-2014.pdf (January 2014).
98 The Economist, "Somaliland Sets 2016 Budget", *The Economist*, http://country.eiu.com/article.aspx?articleid=1173782501&Country=Somalia&topic=Economy&subtopic=Forecast&subsubtopic=Fiscal+policy+outlook&u=1&pid=1076744091&oid=1076744091&uid=1 (17 December 2015).
99 Local Businessperson (2), Interview with the author, Hargeisa, 13 December 2015; Local Businessperson (3), Interview with the author, Hargeisa, 13 December 2015; Entrepreneur, Interview with the author, Hargeisa, 6 December 2015.
100 Local Businessperson (1), Interview with the author, Hargeisa, 13 December 2015.
101 Entrepreneur, Interview with the author.
102 Ibid.
103 Ali Husein Ismail, Interview with the author.
104 For a full account of the atrocities, see Robert Gersony, "Why Somalis Flee: Synthesis of Accounts of Conflict Experience in Northern Somalia by Somali Refugees, Displaced Persons and Others", https://www.cja.org/downloads/Why%20Somalis%20Flee.pdf (August 1989).
105 James Ker-Lindsay, *The Foreign Policy of Counter-Secession: Preventing the Recognition of Contested States* (Oxford: Oxford University Press, 2012) 37.
106 Pegg and Kolstø, "Somaliland: Dynamics of Internal Legitimacy", 197.
107 Political Advisor to Somaliland's Ministry of Foreign Affairs and International Co-operation, Interview with the author.
108 Dr Saad Ali Shire, Interview with the author.
109 This has been highlighted be Pegg and Kolstø, "Somaliland: Dynamics of Internal Legitimacy"; and Nina Caspersen, "The Pursuit of International Recognition after Kosovo", *Global Governance* 21:1 (2015) 401.
110 BBC News, "Who Are Somalia's al-Shabab?", https://www.bbc.com/news/world-africa-15336689 (22 December 2017).
111 The attack killed 30 people; al-Shabaab is believed to be the perpetrator, although no organisation took responsibility for the attack.
112 Dr Bulhan, quoted in Simon Allison, "Somaliland: Losing Patience in the World's Most Unlikely Democracy", *Daily Maverick*, https://www.dailymaverick.co.za/article/2015-04-07-somaliland-losing-patience-in-the-worlds-most-unlikely-democracy/ (April 2015).
113 Member of the High Judiciary, Interview with the author; Ali Husein Ismail, Interview with the author; Hussein Ismail, Interview with the author.
114 Member of the High Judiciary, Interview with the author.
115 European Commission, "Somaliland: EU Commissioner Andris Piebalgs Announces More Support for Stability and Regional Cooperation", Press Release, http://europa.eu/rapid/press-release_IP-11-837_en.htm (19 February 2018).
116 Somaliland Government, "Recognition of Somaliland", http://recognition.somalilandgov.com/.
117 J.J. Messner et al., *Fragile States Index 2017 Annual Report*, Fund for Peace, http://fundforpeace.org/fsi/2017/05/14/fragile-states-index-2017-annual-report/

(2017); J.J. Messner et al., *Fragile States Index 2018 Annual Report*, Fund for Peace, http://fundforpeace.org/fsi/2018/04/24/fragile-states-index-2018-annual-report/ (2018).
118 Political Advisor to Somaliland's Ministry of Foreign Affairs and International Co-operation, Interview with the author; Former Political Advisor to Somaliland's Ministry of Foreign Affairs and International Co-operation, Interview with the author.
119 Ibid.
120 Mohamed Farah Herso, Interview with the author.
121 Political Advisor to Somaliland's Ministry of Foreign Affairs and International Co-operation, Interview with the author.
122 Dr Saad Ali Shire in James Wan, "'Otherwise We'll Have to Go to War': Somaliland Demands Recognition 26 Years on", *African Arguments*, http://africanarguments.org/2017/05/22/otherwise-well-have-to-go-to-war-somaliland-demands-recognition-26-years-on/ (22 May 2017).
123 Political Advisor to Somaliland's Ministry of Foreign Affairs and International Co-operation, Interview with the author; Former Political Advisor to Somaliland's Ministry of Foreign Affairs and International Co-operation, Interview with the author.
124 Former Political Advisor to Somaliland's Ministry of Foreign Affairs and International Co-operation, Interview with the author.
125 Omar Mahmood and Zakaria Yusuf, "Somalia–Somaliland: A Halting Embrace of Dialogue", *International Crisis Group*, https://www.crisisgroup.org/africa/horn-africa/somalia/somalia-somaliland-halting-embrace-dialogue (August 2020).
126 Former Political Advisor to Somaliland's Ministry of Foreign Affairs and International Co-operation, Interview with the author.
127 Ibid.

Bibliography

Academy for Peace and Development. "The Judicial System in Somaliland", *Workshop Report*, https://apd-somaliland.org/wp-content/uploads/2014/12/JUDICIARY-REPORT-FINAL.pdf (April 2002).

African Union. *Constitutive Act of the African Union*, https://au.int/sites/default/files/pages/34873-file-constitutiveact_en.pdf.

Africa Watch. *Somalia: A Government at War with Its Own People*, https://www.hrw.org/sites/default/files/reports/somalia_1990.pdf (1990).

Allison, Simon. "Somaliland: Losing Patience in the World's Most Unlikely Democracy", *Daily Maverick*, https://www.dailymaverick.co.za/article/2015-04-07-somaliland-losing-patience-in-the-worlds-most-unlikely-democracy/ (April 2015).

Anonymous. "Government Recognition in Somalia and Regional Political Stability in the Horn of Africa", *Journal of Modern African Studies* 40:2 (2002) 242–272.

Balthasar, Dominik. "State-Making in Somalia and Somaliland: Understanding War, Nationalism and State Trajectories as Process of Institutional and Socio-Cognitive Standardization" (Doctoral Dissertation, London School of Economics, 2012).

Balthasar, Dominik. "Somaliland's Best Kept Secret: Shrewd Politics and War Projects as Means of State-Making". *Journal of Eastern African Studies* 7:2 (2013) 218–238.

Balthasar, Dominik. "The Wars in the North and the Creation of Somaliland", *World Peace Foundation*, https://sites.tufts.edu/reinventingpeace/2013/10/28/the-wars-in-the-north-and-the-creation-of-somaliland/ (October 2013).

Balthasar, Dominik. "Thinking beyond Roadmaps in Somalia: Expanding Policy Options for State Building", A Report of the CSIS Africa Programme, *Centre for Strategic and International Studies*, https://www.csis.org/analysis/thinking-beyond-roadmaps-somalia (November 2014).

BBC News. "Who Are Somalia's al-Shabab?", https://www.bbc.com/news/world-africa-15336689 (22 December 2017).

Bradbury, Mark. *Becoming Somaliland* (London: Progression, 2008).

Bradbury, Mark, Abokor, Adan Yusuf and Yusuf, Haroon Ahmed. "Somaliland: Choosing Politics over Violence", *Review of African Political Economy* 30:97 (2003) 455–478.

Bryden, Matthew. "Somaliland: Fiercely Independent", *Africa Report* 35:5 (1994) 35–40.

Caspersen, Nina. "The Pursuit of International Recognition after Kosovo", *Global Governance* 21:1 (2015) 393–412.

Compagnon, Daniel. "Somali Armed Movements" in Christopher Clapham, ed., *African Guerrillas* (Oxford: James Currey, 1998) 73–90.

Economist, The. "Somaliland Sets 2016 Budget", *The Economist: Intelligence Unit*, http://country.eiu.com/article.aspx?articleid=1173782501&Country=Somalia&topic=Economy&subtopic=Forecast&subsubtopic=Fiscal+policy+outlook&u=1&pid=1076744091&oid=1076744091&uid=1 (17 December 2015).

European Commission. "Somaliland: EU Commissioner Andris Piebalgs Announces More Support for Stability and Regional Cooperation", *Press Release*, http://europa.eu/rapid/press-release_IP-11-837_en.htm (19 February 2018).

Gersony, Robert. "Why Somalis Flee: Synthesis of Accounts of Conflict Experience in Northern Somalia by Somali Refugees, Displaced Persons and Others", https://www.cja.org/downloads/Why%20Somalis%20Flee.pdf (August 1989).

Hansen, Stig Jarle, and Bradbury, Mark. "Somaliland: A New Democracy in the Horn of Africa?", *Review of African Political Economy* 34:13 (2007) 461–476.

Hoehne, Markus Virgil. "Limits of Hybrid Political Orders: The Case of Somaliland", *Journal of Eastern African Studies* 7:2 (2013) 199–217.

Huliaras, Asteris. "The Viability of Somaliland: Internal Constraints and Regional Geopolitics", *Journal of Contemporary African Studies* 20:2 (2002) 157–182.

Kaplan, Seth. "The Remarkable Story of Somaliland", *Journal of Democracy* 19:3 (2008) 143–157.

Ker-Lindsay, James. *The Foreign Policy of Counter-Secession: Preventing the Recognition of Contested States* (Oxford: Oxford University Press, 2012).

Lewis, Ioan. "The Politics of the 1969 Somali Coup", *Journal of Modern African Studies* 10:3 (1972) 383–408.

Mahmood, Omar, and Yusuf, Zakaria. "Somalia–Somaliland: A Halting Embrace of Dialogue", *International Crisis Group*, https://www.crisisgroup.org/africa/horn-africa/somalia/somalia-somaliland-halting-embrace-dialogue (August 2020).

Menkhaus, Ken. "State Failure, State Building, and Prospects for a 'Functional Failed State' in Somalia", *The Annals of the American Academy of Political and Social Science* 656:1 (2014), 154–172.

Messner, J.J. et al., *Fragile States Index 2017 Annual Report*, Fund for Peace, https://fragilestatesindex.org/2017/05/14/fragile-states-index-2017-annual-report/ (2017).

Messner, J.J. et al., *Fragile States Index 2018 Annual Report*, Fund for Peace, http://fundforpeace.org/fsi/2018/04/24/fragile-states-index-2018-annual-report/ (2018).

Pegg, Scott, and Kolstø, Pål. "Somaliland: Dynamics of Internal Legitimacy and (Lack of) External Sovereignty", *Geoforum* 66:1 (2015) 193–202.

Pegg, Scott, and Walls, Michael. "Back on Track? Somaliland after its 2017 Presidential Election", *African Affairs* 117:467 (2018) 326–337.

Phillips, Sarah. "Political Settlements and State Formation: The Case of Somaliland", DLP Research Paper 23, *Developmental Leadership Programme*, http://www.dlprog.org/news/political-settlements-and-state-formation-the-case-of-somaliland.php (2013).

Phillips, Sarah. "When Less Was More: External Assistance and the Political Settlement in Somaliland", *International Affairs* 92:3 (2016) 629–645.

Phillips, Sarah. *When There Was No Aid: War and Peace in Somaliland* (Ithaca, NY: Cornell University Press, 2020).

Poore, Brad. "Somaliland: Shackled to a Failed State", *Stanford Journal of International Law* 45 (2009) 117–150.

Posner, Daniel N., and Young, Daniel J. "The Institutionalization of Political Power in Africa", *Journal of Democracy* 18:3 (2007) 126–140.

Prunier, Gerard. "A Candid View of the Somali National Movement", *Horn of Africa* 13:3–4 (1990) 107–120.

Prunier, Gerard. "Somaliland Goes It Alone", *Current History* 97:619 (1998) 225–228.

Renders, Marleen. "Appropriate 'Governance Technology'? – Somali Clan Elders and Institutions in the Making of the 'Republic of Somaliland'", *Africa Spectrum* 42:3 (2007) 439–459.

Renders, Marleen. *Consider Somaliland: State-Building with Traditional Leaders and Institutions* (Leiden: Brill, 2012).

Richards, Rebecca. *Understanding Statebuilding: Traditional Governance and the Modern State in Somaliland* (Farnham, UK: Ashgate, 2014).

Somaliland Government. *Why Recognition: The Legal Case*, http://recognition.somalilandgov.com/legal/.

Somaliland Government. *Recognition of Somaliland*, http://recognition.somalilandgov.com/.

Spears, Ian S. *Civil War in African States: The Search for Security* (London: First Forum Press, 2010).

Verjee, Aly, et al. *The Economics of Elections in Somaliland: The Financing of Political Parties and Candidates"* (London: Rift Valley Institute, 2015).

Walls, Michael, and Kibble, Steve. "Beyond Polarity: Negotiating a Hybrid State in Somaliland", *Africa Spectrum* 45:1 (2010) 31–56.

Wan, James. "Otherwise We'll Have to Go to War: Somaliland Demands Recognition 26 Years on", *African Arguments*, http://africanarguments.org/2017/05/22/otherwise-well-have-to-go-to-war-somaliland-demands-recognition-26-years-on/ (22 May 2017).

World Bank. *Transitioning from State Building to Development*, The Somaliland Economic Conference, https://www.slministryofplanning.org/images/HHSurvey/Budget-Policy-2014.pdf (January 2014).

5 The Kurdistan Region of Iraq

The KRI is legally a region of Iraq, but the powers that the KRI holds according to the Iraqi Constitution give it the corporate body, territorial authority and social capacities of a de facto state. In fact, the unique empowerment under the Iraqi Constitution means that the KRI has some of the strongest diplomatic agency of all de facto states, resulting in a unique normative standing profile that can provide us with substantial comparative insight, especially given that it has not featured in the de facto state literature as frequently as, for example, the post-Soviet states of Abkhazia and South Ossetia.

The Formation of the KRI's Corporate Identity

In the fieldwork I conducted in the Kurdistan Region of Iraq, the most common narrative of the Kurdish nationalist project was uniformly described as having three distinct stages: the aftermath of the First World War, namely the 1920 Treaty of Sèvres and the 1923 Treaty of Lausanne; the al-Anfal campaign of the late 1980s and the implementation of the no-fly zones in Iraq in 1992 that provided the vacuum of power that the KRI filled; and then the post-2003 intervention by the United States and its allies. In interviews, diplomats emphasised the clear role that the Kurdish national narrative plays in strengthening the moral appeal of the KRI, and so the first section of this chapter has been structured to follow that Kurdish-generated narrative.

The Origins of Kurdish Nationalism in Iraq

The discourse of de facto states is rife with references to self-determination, a concept rooted in the milestone of Woodrow Wilson's 1919 'Fourteen Points' speech. That text's conceptualisation of self-determination was key to the first push for a Kurdish nation state. Kurdish representatives attended the 1919 peace conference, submitting a memorandum that requested an independent state for the Kurdish people. The request was persuasive and initially successful; in the 1920 Treaty of Sèvres, the Allied leaders responded to Kurdish claims and granted nominal autonomy to the Kurdish people. The inclusion came with a clause to the effect that, one year after the Treaty had been

DOI: 10.4324/9781003178521-6

officialised, the League of Nations would then consider the proposition of recognising complete Kurdish autonomy. The British, who were in control of the region after the First World War, recognised the Kurdish nation in the provisional 1921 Iraqi Constitution, providing some legal protections for both the nation and the Kurdish language, later ensuring Kurdish administration of much of the northern region of Iraq.[1] The practical administration of the region, combined with the prospect of full recognition being granted by the League of Nations, proved to be fertile ground for growing Kurdish nationalist aspirations, basing a call for independence on both the perceived historical right to the land, as well as the Ottoman-Turkish oppression of the Kurdish people,[2] and an appeal to the nascent conception of a right to self-determination. What followed in reality was nothing like those aspirations, or like the previously agreed treaty script, or like anything resembling autonomy.

After major Turkish victories in the Turkish War of Independence, Turkish leader Mustafa Kemal emphatically rejected the Ottoman-signed Treaty of Sèvres and destroyed the communal vision for an independent Kurdistan. The Great Powers negotiated with the successful Turkish nationalists, and this created not only the new Republic of Turkey, but also a complete reversal and abandonment of the almost-acquired independent status for the Kurds. It was in effect an externally enforced, politically expedient and legally sanctioned abortion of an embryonic state, in which the major powers morphed under pressure from visionary midwives to compliant vivisectionists.

The 1920 Treaty of Sèvres was replaced with the 1923 Treaty of Lausanne, which in the eyes of Kemal's forces formalised recognition of all Turkish claims and territorial liberation, and specifically did not include any of the conditions from the Treaty of Sèvres that had been intended to benefit the Kurds. Furthermore, the boundaries of the territory that the Kurds lay claim to were subsumed in land now split between the territorial units of Iran, Iraq, Syria and Turkey.[3] The impact of these externally imposed disempowering events, from near sovereignty to disaggregation and complete non-recognition, cannot be overestimated in the collective memory and political angst of the Kurdish struggle for independence.

The territory of Iraq became a British Mandate territory.[4] According to the League of Nations Covenant, this classified Iraq as one of the territories whose "existence as independent nations could be provisionally recognised, subject to administrative advice and assistance by a Mandatory until such time as they were able to stand alone".[5] Continuous rebellions across much of Iraq were one factor that contributed to the Mandate not being realised, and in 1922 the British negotiated the Anglo-Iraq Treaty, providing the opportunity for a local self-governorate.[6] Some stability was formed in the north with the signing of the Frontier Treaty in 1926, officialising the borders of the Mosul *vilayet*.[7] By this point, the disputes and resolutions led to the Kurdish population being concentrated into the northern regions of Iraq from Mosul in the west, to Sulaimaniyah in the east. The Kurdish nationalist cause continued to be pressed by Sheikh Mahmoud Barzanji, who inspired Sheikh

Ahmed Barzani to lead the Kurdish revolt of 1932 demanding Kurdish autonomy.[8] The British assisted Baghdad in quashing the Kurdish demands; Sheikh Ahmed Barzani was forced into exile, and the Iraqi state became independent.

In January 1946, the Kurdish Democratic Party (now Kurdistan Democratic Party, or KDP) was established, and with Qazi Muhammad at the helm it established the independent Mahabad Republic of the Kurds in Iran.[9] Qazi Muhammad gained the support of the Barzanis, who were led by Mullah Mustafa Barzani. The short-lived Mahabad Republic enjoyed some support from the Soviet Union; the extent of that support, however, is heavily debated.[10] Western influence forced the Soviet Union to withdraw its support, and in 1947 Iran's forces invaded, defeating the Mahabad Republic and retaking the land.[11] While short-lived, the Republic stoked the fire of Kurdish nationalist aspirations. Mullah Mustafa Barzani fled Iran to the Caucasus, returning to Iraq in 1958. In 1961, Mullah Mustafa led the KDP militia, known as the *peshmerga*, in an uprising against Baghdad, again demanding Kurdish autonomy from the Qassem regime. In 1963, Qassem was overthrown by the pan-Arab Socialist Ba'th Party, which briefly quelled the conflict with the Kurds as well. Mullah Mustafa pushed the new government harder for Kurdish autonomy, igniting intermittent conflict until 1970.[12]

In 1970, the new Ba'athist government, which had come to power in 1968, signed a peace agreement, indicating the first recognition of the argument for Kurdish autonomy in Iraq.[13] The accord, however, fell apart in 1974 when the Ba'th Party abandoned the implementation of the agreed measures specified under the Autonomy Law, re-inciting further violence between the Iraqi government and Barzani's KDP.[14] After the KDP lost the support of essential arms from Iran and the United States, its military position diminished rapidly and the KDP retreated from fighting in 1975.[15] Mullah Mustafa fled to Iran, from which he never returned.

Mullah Mustafa's once close friend, Jalal Talabani, led a secession from the KDP, inspiring followers of more leftist and Marxist orientations with whom he formed the Patriotic Union of Kurdistan (PUK).[16] There were significant tensions between the two parties, each varying its position, support and political direction throughout the Iran–Iraq War until 1987, when, facing increased anti-Kurdish aggression from Baghdad, the KDP and PUK united to form the Kurdistan Front.

The heightened aggression from Saddam Hussein culminated in the genocidal al-Anfal campaign that reportedly killed approximately 100,000 civilian Kurds.[17] Hussein's aims were clear: destroy the foundations of the Iraqi Kurdish rebellion and deter any future nationalist aspirations. The net effect, though, was to the contrary. After Hussein's invasion of Kuwait in August 1990, the international community was being made keenly aware of the atrocities committed by his regime. The liberation of Kuwait provided an opportunity for foreign intervention and eventually the establishment of a "safe-haven" for Iraq's Kurds.[18] This episode rather typified the sustained dilemma and official responses of the more powerful nations towards the Kurdish conundrum, which over time repeatedly produced ambivalence of attitude and vacillation in action: occasional flourishes of apparent sympathy and some protection for the people when absolutely necessary, but no cohesive willingness to confront other regional, already recognised and competing states in any formal process of differentiation and acknowledgement.

Forming the Foundation of the KRI's Corporate Identity

While the 1990–1991 Gulf War liberated Kuwait, it created fresh tumult in Iraq. With the Government of Iraq (GoI) forces kept pre-occupied suppressing the Shi'ite rebellion in southern Iraq, the *peshmerga* fuelled unrest in Kurdistan by leading attacks against the Iraqi Army.[19] By March 1991, the cities of Erbil, Sulaimaniyah, Dohuk and Zakho were in the hands of the Kurdistan Front.[20] After the rebellion briefly reclaimed Kirkuk, GoI forces retaliated violently and retook the city, killing up to 20,000 people and forcing 1.5 million refugees to flee into Turkey and Iran.[21] In response, the UN Security Council passed Resolution 688, prompting the Coalition led by the United States and the United Kingdom to implement a 'no-fly zone' in northern Iraq.[22] After more costly fighting and failed negotiations, Saddam Hussein's troops withdrew behind a defensive line and effectively put Kurdistan under economic and military blockade.[23] The power vacuum in Iraq's Kurdish areas established fertile conditions for a self-organising government to emerge.

The Kurdistan Front perceived Hussein's siege as an attempt to force them into accepting his terms of negotiation.[24] Yet it was also an opportunity for the Kurds to recompose and remap their own future. The Kurdistan Front set out to replace the Ba'thist-filled Legislative Assembly with an elected parliament and leader.[25] A democratic election was seen as the most effective way of forming an administration that could serve the needs of the Kurds in a manner conducive to settling the contest of power between Barzani's KDP and Talabani's PUK.[26] The Kurdistan Front undertook the rebuilding of Kurdish society using a democratic framework in order to align with perceived international norms, a measure likely to increase the perceived legitimacy of an autonomous government,[27] and a key consideration given the absence of past support for the Kurds from international powers. The KDP and PUK leadership deliberately avoided giving the title of 'Constitution' to the legal provisions established for the formation of government, in order to avoid provoking international criticism by appearing to be overtly seeking independence.[28]

Elections were held in May 1992, and, despite some accusations of fraud,[29] were deemed to be relatively free and fair with an estimated 90 per cent turnout.[30] Of the seven participating parties, only the KDP and PUK crossed the 7 per cent threshold of votes required to enter Parliament. The KDP won 51 seats to the PUK's 49 seats, but to avoid conflict arising from the fraud claims, they agreed to an even split.[31] Barzani won 48 per cent of votes for the leadership with Talabani claiming 45 per cent.[32] Again, in the interest of cooperation and political unity the result was set aside, and the leadership was allocated according to their home governorate. The first Kurdistan National Assembly convened on 4 June 1992, and within a month the Government of the KRI officially formed.

The decades-old KDP–PUK rift could not be bridged by the power-sharing arrangement that emerged from the 1992 elections and soon led to direct conflict between KDP and PUK *peshmerga* forces, specifically following a land dispute in May 1994. There were, however, multiple factors that contributed to armed conflict. The hasty implementation of a democratic administration, forcing a rushed transition from fighting in the hills to running a government and meeting civilian needs, was partly to blame.[33] A continuous disagreement over the distribution of tax revenue acquired at the Zakho border-crossing also contributed,[34] as did the ongoing political differences and rivalry that dated back to the formation of the PUK in 1975.

The civil war that resulted was more brutal than any prior intra-Kurdish conflict, exemplified by the turmoil in August 1996 when the GoI joined forces with the KDP to expel the PUK from Erbil and take Sulaimaniyah.[35] After the Iranian-backed PUK retook Sulaimaniyah, the Government of Kurdistan was divided geographically and politically. The KDP maintained control over Erbil and Dohuk, while the PUK administered Sulaimaniyah and its surrounding territory. After four years of debilitating atrocities, Talabani and Barzani agreed to a formal peace, signing the Washington Agreement on 17 September 1998.[36]

The civil war undoubtedly damaged the domestic legitimacy of the KRI and tainted its image abroad. Immediate prospects of a stable autonomous Kurdistan appeared remote. However, although the civil war deflated Kurdish nationalist consciousness in the short term, the conclusion of the war provided a platform on which the region's leaders could recommence state-building.[37] The 1996 geographic and political divisions resulted in the doubling of the number of civil servants and bureaucrats receiving the experience and training required to operate a substantial administration.[38] With the peace agreement in place, the consolidation of the KDP and PUK in their respective territories also allowed them in the final years of the 1990s and into the 2000s to focus on being "governments rather than parties".[39]

The UN Oil-for-Food Programme

The United Nations' Oil-for-Food Programme (OFFP) played a key role in consolidating the KRI's desired autonomy and in the formation of the KRI's corporate identity.[40] Its impact needs to be understood in the context of what immediately preceded it. In August 1990, the United Nations Security Council (UNSC) responded to Saddam Hussein's invasion of Kuwait by implementing Resolution 661, constituting a complete ban on all imports and exports to and from Iraq.[41] According to Gareth Stansfield, UNSCR 661 was "the most comprehensive and effective sanctions regime in history", crippling the Iraqi economy and stifling Hussein's ability to operate effectively.[42] Kurdistan's economic basis went from bad to worse in 1992, when Hussein additionally placed the region under siege. The GoI installed an economic and agricultural blockade in an attempt to force the Kurds to settle their dispute on Hussein's terms. In effect, this meant that Kurdistan was under a double embargo from 1992 until 1996. The price of kerosene soared to 200 times its 1990 price, and rice 80 times more.[43]

In 1996, the United Nations introduced the OFFP, allowing basic humanitarian necessities such as medicine and food to be imported in exchange for oil. Between 1996 and 2003, the OFFP resulted in US$64.2 billion worth of humanitarian goods being imported into Iraq, of which the KRI was entitled to 13 per cent.[44] Contrary to the rest of Iraq, where the programme was administered by the GoI, in Kurdistan the OFFP was administered directly by the UN Office of the Iraq Programme.[45] The United Nations' efficient administration maximised the benefits for the region. The OFFP not only hastened economic recovery by alleviating the effects of the double embargo, but the operations of the United Nations also provided invaluable state-building lessons. The United Nations "taught principles of good governance, negotiation, and administration", and the KRI representatives were given the opportunity to learn about best practices for liaising with international organisations.[46] Furthermore, the OFFP created the means for an entrepreneurial class to arise by generating millions of dollars' worth of contracts, contrasting previous short-term relief programmes that kept Kurdistan reliant entirely on aid and its black-market economy.[47] What first appeared to be an inevitably unstable aftermath of civil war had become a surprisingly firming foundation on which a KRI seeking autonomy could be constructed.

KRI Unification: Consolidation of the KRI Corporate Identity

The period from 2001 to 2006 was one of unprecedented unification for the KRI, despite the lingering effects of the Iraqi Kurds' civil war. Following the 11 September 2001 terrorist attacks (hereafter, '9/11') on the United States, the KRI realised the likelihood of an attempted regime change in Iraq and began cooperating as a more unified entity in order to best position itself to negotiate the establishment of a recognised Kurdistan region within Iraq.[48]

By 2003, the KRI had effectively administered its own internal security; organised the *peshmerga* into a collaborative force capable of defending the territory of Kurdistan; fostered and built an economic framework; and established organised institutions of political representation.[49] These strategic actions comprehensively strengthened the bargaining position of the KRI in negotiating the details of the Transitional Administrative Law (TAL), the legal framework that came into force after the removal of Hussein's regime in April 2003 and which provided juridical guidelines until an Iraqi constitution was created.[50]

148 *The Kurdistan Region of Iraq*

The partial autonomy of Kurdistan was officially recognised in the TAL, which allowed the Kurds to keep their system of government and *peshmerga* forces but denying them the right to manage natural resources.[51] The most valuable inclusion of the TAL was Article 61(C), which set the threshold for rejection of a draft constitution at three governorates.[52] Although it did not apply exclusively to the Kurds, it became known as the "Kurdish veto" because it allowed the three Kurdistan governorates of Dohuk, Erbil and Sulaimaniyah to band together to veto a constitution that was unfavourable to the Kurds.[53] Article 61(C) heavily influenced the development of the Iraqi Constitution, which was approved by referendum in October 2005.

The Kurds retained all the rights specified in the TAL with important beneficial additions, for it clearly distinguished between the right to administer existing oil fields and future oil fields. Article 112 indicated that existing oil fields fell to the federal government, while Article 115 indicated that future oil fields would fall to the regions; that the power of the regions in the Constitution could only be amended if the regions' governments gave consent and if the regions' people agreed through a referendum; and that state revenue from oil and gas was to be distributed according to population.[54] In 2005, the Iraqi Kurds held an informal referendum at the same time as national elections, in which 98 per cent of voters expressed a desire for independent statehood.[55] On 15 August 2005, Kurds took to the streets demanding the inclusion of an option for self-determination in the Constitution, essentially allowing the regional government to declare independence at will.[56] On 20 August 2005, the KRI retracted this demand, much to the Kurdish people's dismay.[57] In the historical context of Kurdish struggles, the composition of the Iraqi Constitution was nevertheless a momentous achievement.

Kurdistan was now protected under the federal Constitution and had achieved official recognition in Baghdad, allowing it shift its focus to finally mending the political fissures within its own territory. On 7 May 2006, Prime Minister Nechirvan Barzani announced the formation of a unified KRI.[58] Following the difficult lessons learnt in the aftermath of the 1992 elections, the KDP and PUK adopted a gradual merging process that extended until the full ministerial integration was completed in October 2008.[59] In parliamentary elections on 25 July 2009, the KDP and PUK ran together on the Kurdistan List ticket, claiming 59 seats in the 111-seat Parliament. The Goran Party, a reformist democratic splinter group from the PUK, whose name means 'change', won 25 seats. This signalled a new era of political pluralism,[60] jettisoning the image of two warring parties and recognising a representative regional government.

The Formation of KRI Type Identities and Role Identities

The most prosperous period in the KRI came after the adoption of the Iraqi Constitution in 2005 and lasted up until the rise of the Islamic State (IS) in 2014. The KRI began to market the federated region as a "democratic and economically vibrant region".[61] While some observers argued that the KRI was merely constructing a misleading image in an attempt to appear aligned with the norms of international society,[62] ministers of the KRI were prepared to admit that, although their democracy was flawed, the attempt to democratise was genuine.[63] This section will examine the claims to democratisation through this period. The attempt to establish a type identity that aligns with the preached praxis of international society is an informative opportunity to explore the utility of the international system's identity hierarchy as an analytical tool for better understanding the relationship between international society and de facto states.

State-Building and the Beginnings of Liberal Democracy

The state-building path that transitioned a politically divided region into a federated government is a crucial part in understanding the development of the KRI's type identity of an incipient democracy. Despite the civil war of the 1990s, Stansfield has argued that conflict was not inherent to Kurdistan's political culture: the division between the KDP and the PUK largely arose from socio-economic factors.[64] The territorial division of the KDP and PUK helped to facilitate some successful political developments of the post-Washington Agreement period: the 1990s conflict was, as Stansfield aptly describes, what happens when "two parties attempt to run before they can walk".[65] In fact, Stansfield suggests that the KDP–PUK unification in 2007 helped to construct the domestic legitimacy of the KRI within federal Iraq.[66] The strength of ethno-nationalist feeling amongst the Iraqi Kurds was arguably enforced, and unification resonated with the people. However, the combining of the two dominant parties created a fresh tension between government and society by creating an all-powerful, allegedly corrupt regime.[67] This is how unification actually had the unexpected effect of giving rise to a more pluralist political space: it did so simply by creating the perceived need. The first real competitor to the two major political parties emerged: the Goran Party. Goran seceded from the PUK in 2009, in time for the 2009 elections, in which it won nearly 25 per cent of the available seats. While the KDP–PUK dominance was still strong, the potential for a more sophisticated democratic dynamic through greater pluralism had formed.

The increasing socio-economic inequality within the KRI was an integral driver of the seemingly burgeoning pluralist political landscape. Denise Natali asserts that the "gross discrepancies in wealth" that emerged in the KRI motivated new swells of unrest and were key to the Goran movement gaining momentum.[68] In Natali's application of a developmental lens, she examines the social, economic and political development of the KRI with a specific focus on the influence of aid programmes in shaping the region.[69] According to Natali, post-2003 aid focussed on implementing effective state-building processes and democratic notions of good governance; however, the commitment to maintaining the "territorial integrity" of Iraq limited the development potential for the KRI by stunting its capacity to become self-sufficient with the continuing economic reliance on Baghdad.[70]

The US-led reconstruction of Iraq was guided by "democracy mission objectives", tying aid to the promotion of civil-society-building, decentralisation, protection of minority rights, and good governance.[71] The presence of civil society has become increasingly visible since then; however, its effectiveness is debateable. KRI Minister Bakir stated that although the prosperity of the region in this period was is in part the result of the "collective effort" of government, civil society and the growing business sector, civil society was certainly an area for growth.[72] The initial growth in civil society was predominantly with regard to NGOs, few of which were non-politicised.[73] This has changed since the establishment of the KRI NGO Directorate in 2013. Newer NGOs have been established under the procedures set out in the Law on Non-Governmental Organizations in the Iraqi Kurdistan Region (2011), the operation of which by the KRI up until 2013 was transparent.[74]

By 2014, the KRI had approved funding for a further 97 NGO projects in areas covering education, health, women's rights, children's rights and raising election awareness.[75] However, more critical perspectives perceived the increased NGO activity to offer minimal impact on the development of free and active civil society.[76] Although non-politicised NGOs were then flourishing and the KRI was funding human-rights-based projects, politically active NGOs advocating causes that were not aligned with KRI sympathies were few and poorly financed;[77] instead, the main voice for political change had become the Goran Party. Although growing in popularity, Goran was also limited in its ability to operate freely, with members suffering violent attacks in the lead up to the 2009 election.[78] These contrasting images of civil society in Kurdistan suggest that some demonstrable progress was made in this key field of democratic reform, but that pervasive political liberalisation was never achieved.

Improving the protection of women's rights is one area where NGOs had a clearly positive impact. While the quality of life for women in the rest of Iraq worsened after 2003,[79] significant steps were taken to protect and empower women in the Kurdistan region. In 2008, the KRI reformed the Personal Status Law, banning forced marriages. The Kurdistan Parliament passed a law in 2011 that brought the definitions of domestic violence in line with international norms and specifically outlawed female genital mutilation.[80] This followed KRI Prime Minister Barzani's decision to approach Kurdish mullahs in 2009 and prohibit them from mentioning disparaging issues about women in Friday prayers.[81] A 2012 International Rescue Committee report based on four years of research concludes that there had been "significant, if not historic, progress made to combat violence against women and girls in Kurdistan in recent years".[82] Similar progress has also been made in gender-balancing the workforce, which is a "top priority" for the KRI's public sector.[83] Women filled 36 of the 111 seats in the Kurdistan Parliament, reflecting a minimum quota of 30 per cent of the legislature.[84] Although the more traditional rural villages still need substantial progress to escape the current "medieval" practices directed towards women,[85] women's rights have progressed rapidly in the major cities of Kurdistan, and efforts to encourage and extend religious tolerance have been evident, strengthening the image of the KRI as democratically responsive.

Progression in women's rights was accompanied by the protection of minority rights, setting the Kurdistan region apart from an increasingly unstable, fractured Iraq.[86] The majority of Iraq's Christian population lived in Kurdistan at this time, a place described as a religious "safe haven" where "they are protected".[87] Kurdistan was (and still is) also the only place in Iraq and much of the Middle East where Yazidi religious holidays could be openly celebrated.[88]

The Beginnings of a More Liberal Economy

At the height of the KRI's prosperous period, the KRI's economy appeared as "two contrasting images".[89] The positive economic picture emphasised that 17 per cent of Iraq's annual budget was dedicated to the KRI, a thriving bilateral trade with Turkey valued at US$6 billion was estimated to grow further, and there was a steady yet increasing stream of foreign direct investment (FDI).[90] Furthermore, in moves to become more economically self-sufficient, the KRI implemented liberal investment laws that were reported to attract an influx of FDI.[91] Michael Gunter outlines the fruits of this approach, which was illustrated when *FDI Magazine* ranked the capital city of Erbil as the fifth most attractive Middle Eastern location for potential investors.[92]

However, even at the height of this prosperous period, the KRI still had all the hallmarks of a "classic rentier state": a bloated and inefficient public service that acted as a cost centre responsible for consuming approximately three-quarters of the region's budget, which was plagued by nepotism, corruption and an absence of transparency.[93] When I was conducting fieldwork in 2015 (after the negative impacts of the IS uprising had taken effect on the economy), a foreign diplomat working in Erbil described to me the government's efforts to diversify the economy as "farcical".[94] The official claimed that they did not make any sincere efforts, and that the liberal investment law, including "no capital gains tax", was misleading; the cost of securing the political support required to establish a business is, in effect, an equal or greater tax.[95]

A rentier 'mentality' impact is manifest in workforce data and practices. The rents streaming from the federal budget helped to construct an oversized, inefficient public service that employed around 30 per cent of the population.[96] The public payroll in total soaked up approximately 75 per cent of the KRI's budget.[97] Minister Bakir privately conceded that he wished the KRI "could import a Western work ethic or an Asian work ethic".[98] Minister Professor Baban confirmed this image, stating that in the public service "work practices are rotten. People go home by 1:30 pm".[99]

The public sector was used by the KDP and the PUK as a means of shoring up political support,[100] forming the patron–client networks typical of a rentier state. As the economy has developed, these patronage systems have increased the severity of emerging social cleavages, with a wealthy, politically connected elite emerging in parallel to a growing poor population.[101] Although small-scale development projects were conducted independently, bigger more lucrative projects have come to require the political backing of either major party, embedding KDP and PUK influence in the economy.[102] Corruption allegations have continued to plague the KRI as well. In 2013, the Minister of Natural Resources Ashti Hawrami was accused of secretly buying stock worth US$35 million in DNO International, an international oil company (IOC) with several KRI contracts.[103] The Goran Party has also accused the KDP and the PUK of skimming several millions of dollars a month from the revenue accrued from oil smuggled illegally into Iran.[104] The worsening of corruption, in combination with an entrenched patronage network and the absence of a robust work ethic, illustrates the problem of rentierism in the KRI.

The contrasting images of Kurdistan's political climate affirm Yaniv Voller's claim that "the KRG's portrayal of itself as a democratic oasis in a desert of tyranny has been mostly exaggerated".[105] De facto states often pursue the image of effectively governed democracies in an attempt to escape the connotations of violence, chaos and lawlessness often associated with ethnonational liberation movements.[106] The projection of a safe and secure democracy serves multiple instrumental functions, such as attracting FDI and appealing to the diplomatic practices of recognised states (explored in greater detail below). The KRI's adornment of a veil of democratisation served and still serves the long-term and ongoing aspiration of increasing international engagement.

Minister Professor Baban considered in mid-2013 that Kurdistan's democracy was "imperfect", but claimed that it was "improving".[107] Minister Bakir echoed this sentiment, emphasising the achievement of a peaceful and prosperous region run by leaders who were raised "fighting in the mountains".[108] Iraqi Kurds are traditionally tribal and agrarian, and under a repressive Ba'th regime they were brutally forced into being "sycophants of the Iraqi social welfare state".[109] That was before the genocidal al-Anfal campaign; the practices of dependence were more deeply engrained by a reliance on international aid; the 1994–1998 civil war; and the 2003 war. Iraqi Kurds are survivors of a tumultuous and devastating twentieth century, which was hardly conducive to a comprehensive, systematic and successful implementation of democracy. As an ex-KRI Minister for Higher Education colourfully described with a seemingly well-rehearsed depiction: "When you analyse the governance of the KRG, you must remember: we are in the Middle East. We are the Kurds. We went from cracking institutions, to building institutions".[110] In that vein, the KRI was only recognised in the Iraqi Constitution in 2005. To expect a rentier identity to be shed, and a model of liberal democracy to have taken root despite an increase in rentier imperatives, is unrealistic.

In the wake of the adoption of the 2005 Iraqi Constitution, Kurdistan was relatively unknown in much of the world. It suffered from the simplistic association made between Kurdistan and the rest of Iraq.[111] Hence, the KRI adopted an "open-door" foreign policy, inviting foreigners to "come and see for yourself".[112] This worked in tandem with the KRI actively diversifying its economy.[113] Economic well-being is an objective interest intrinsic to any state.[114] Attempting to economically diversify is a logical strategy for meeting this interest, especially for the KRI given the volatile relations with the GoI and subsequent disagreements with the latter over oil-field development and revenue distribution.[115] The image of a democratic KRI enhanced the image of Kurdistan as an attractive FDI destination. The need to escape connotations of violence, chaos and lawlessness in its international image was crucial.

KRI Role Identity: A De Facto State in the International System

The KRI has an international, alter-casted role identity that is crucial to understanding its recognition narrative. Since it constructed the Department of Foreign Relations in 2005, the KRI has been consistently and comprehensively assertive in building international relations with recognised states and international organisations. A process of increasing socialisation throughout the prosperous period of 2005–2014 was the result of successful strategies by the KRI, but it also conditioned a self-perception that contributed to the costly miscalculation of the 2017 independence referendum.

During the prosperous years after the establishment of the 2005 Iraqi Constitution, and before the rise of IS, the KRI utilised the constitutional freedom they had adeptly negotiated to cultivate an image of an international actor. Article 121 of the Constitution states that "offices for the regions and governorates shall be established in embassies and diplomatic missions in order to follow cultural, social, and developmental affairs".[116] The KRI capitalised on this provision, and by 2013 over 30 different countries had established diplomatic offices in Erbil. The majority of these offices are consulate generals, with a small minority operating as Commercial Offices.

The success of these efforts is evident in the remarks of one senior diplomat posted to Erbil, who claimed that the KRI "resembles a sovereign state".[117] While all diplomats interviewed in the course of this project's fieldwork were quick to confirm that the KRI was not sovereign, they also all agreed that the KRI is clearly an international actor with diplomatic agency. Another influential diplomat was forthright in confirming this perception:

> They have a Department of Foreign Relations which is resolute, competent and very active. They are direct recipients of international assistance. They have direct military liaisons. They are involved in capacity building with international partners.[118]

The impact of the alter-casting taking place in the KRI's international persona was most evident in an interview I had with one of the Consul Generals in Erbil in 2015. This official described the KRI as "certainly pushing boundaries for a 'region'; they push boundaries in everything they do". The official clearly outlined that "in all things" his consulate maintains a single Iraq policy because the Kurdistan Regional Government (KRG) is not sovereign, a fact that the consulate has in mind at all times. However, the official made clear that it had to be aware of how it is that its assistance, its stance, and its rhetoric may aid the KRI's future prospects, including independence aspirations. The official made clear that it must also be aware of where it would be placed, if the KRI were to become independent, and how its government's relationships could change.[119] The views expressed were a clear illustration of James Ker-Lindsay's argument that so long as recognised states articulate that they are not recognising a de facto state, the potential for diplomatic-like engagement is vast.[120]

There were two distinct views evident within the diplomatic community in Erbil about the KRI's legitimacy. Several diplomatic officials were asked about the impact of the KRI's comprehensive diplomatic relations, and how they might, or do, influence perceptions of the KRI as a legitimate international actor. All officials agreed that the KRI can be considered an international actor, and that comprehensive and systematic diplomatic relations increased its impact and its influence. However, three officials from different consulates referred to the pragmatic difference between influence and legitimacy, expressing the same judgement that one could not speak of international legitimacy because it is directly linked to being a subject of international law. Put succinctly by one diplomat: "Legitimacy is a delicate term because it pertains to legality. They are a legitimate Iraqi actor".[121] This view was echoed as well by several members of international organisations operating in the KRI.[122]

However, another diplomat from a separate consulate held a contrasting view, clearly stating that the diplomatic successes and interconnectedness of the KRI does legitimise it as an international actor. The difference in these views is significant in understanding that the diplomatic community held contrasting views about what constitutes legitimacy, more so than contrasting views about the *meaning* and *impact* of the KRI's diplomatic relations. The meaning and impact were clear: the KRI has agency and has increased its ability to influence recognised states through the successful conduct of diplomatic relations.

The successful fostering and maintaining of international relationships by the KRI, enabled by its corporate identity, was a distinct cognitive object of orientation for prominent members of the diplomatic community, demonstrating the role identity of a de facto state in the international system. As an entity that has achieved a degree of autonomy sufficient to be apparently free from direct external authority and control in key functions, but that has not been recognised as a sovereign state, the KRI is denied the rights of a fully confirmed state; rights that still only have meaning as a relational function within this social system. This evidence of the KRI operating as an agent in the international system also illustrates the impact that effectively adopting the practices of international society can have within that very society from which the KRI is legally excluded. Where the system and society may coalesce, as outlined in Chapter Two, the lens of normative standing demonstrates the manner in which the society shapes the practice of all entities in the international system.

The encouragement, establishment and growth of a diplomatic community in Erbil had a reinforcing effect. The European Union opened a liaison office in Erbil in August 2015, the head of which confirmed that one of the enablers for this development was the fact that many of the EU member states already had consulates in Erbil. The EU Liaison Office was opened with the specific aim of strengthening the relationship between the European Union and the KRI, an initiative driven by EU member states.[123] The first Counsellor of the EU Liaison Office reinforced the view of the KRI as an international actor, specifically citing the case of the KRI leading the submission to the International Criminal Court (ICC) on the recognition of the Yezidi Genocide as an example, highlighting the fact that it led the submission with the support of the European Union.[124] The KRI's international persona has become more than just a self-oriented image-building exercise; the de facto state is now capable of representing the interests of third parties and is being given international credibility in doing so.

It is important here to reiterate the way in which the KRI has operated within the confines of being a federated region of Iraq. The EU Liaison Office is in fact a liaison office to Iraq, but happens to be stationed in Erbil. The restriction of being a federated region in Iraq has obvious limitations for an aspiring international actor and prospective self-regulating organisation. A representative of the United Nations Assistance Mission in Iraq commented on the frustrations of its organisation being hamstrung at times because it is specifically for Iraq, which limits the impact that it can have in the Kurdish territories because Baghdad heavily influences the parameters of its operations.[125] While this reality must be acknowledged, as must the difference between the performative and substantive components of establishing a diplomatic circle in Erbil, it is also a testament to the ability of the KRI to establish, promote and pursue influence while operating within these confines.[126]

The image of investment potential in the KRI, as discussed above, played a key role in enabling the development of the KRI's comprehensive diplomatic relations. One diplomat described it as a mutually constituting relationship.[127] Business feels more confident investing if there is a strong diplomatic presence. Governments are more interested in coming to a place where they have recognisable and visible economic interest. All of the diplomatic sources that I interviewed agreed on the significance of this relationship. The Director of the Middle East Research Institute in Erbil described business and diplomacy in the KRI as going hand in hand.[128] He claims that the KRG saw the diplomatic engagement as a protection mechanism, and focussed on maximising the economic appeal of the KRI to attract the international community, stating that it "internationalised itself to protect themselves beyond the cage of the past".[129] Although Professor Dlawer al'Aldeen was referring to subordination by Baghdad, this strategy proved to be successful in the face of other threats as well. When questioned about the United States' airstrike intervention to stop the progression of IS' advance on Erbil in 2014 (discussed in detail in the following section), a US diplomatic source indicated the clear support of the United States for maintaining the stability of the KRG.[130]

An illustrative example of combining the effective exploitation of economic potential with expanding diplomatic relations is the KRI's management of its relationship with Turkey in the years prior to the rise of IS. The foundations of the seemingly unlikely partnership between the Turkish government and the KRI were laid from 2007/2008 onwards, evidenced by the extent of investment from Turkish businesses in Iraqi Kurdistan's developing economy.[131] Turkish trade with the KRI had grown to be greater than the combined total of Syria, Lebanon and Jordan by 2010.[132] Total Turkish investment in 2011 was US$12 billion.[133] The relationship quickly became fundamental to the perceived economic prospects of the KRI as Genel Energy Company began the construction of a pipeline from the oilfield of Taq Taq to the Iraq–Turkey pipeline.[134] When this development was denounced by the GoI in Baghdad, Turkish Prime Minister Recep Tayyip Erdogan declared that the agreement was deemed to be legal according to the Iraqi Constitution.[135] By the end of 2013, the KRI and the Turkish government had completed the pipeline, through which the KRI managed to begin oil exports which essentially subverted the GoI in Baghdad. The growing relationship was being built on more than just shared hydrocarbon interests' it was accompanied by the management of regional power dynamics as well.

The post-2011 conflict in Syria contributed significantly to the thawing of diplomatic relations between Turkey and the KRI. In the early stages of the Syrian Civil War, two significant Syrian-Kurdish opposition parties had become prominent in northern Syria. The first was the Democratic Union Party (PYD), which is perceived by many as a Syrian arm of the Kurdistan Workers' Party (PKK), the rebel Turk-Kurdish group that has been in conflict with the Turkish government since 1984 and is listed as a terrorist organisation by a number of powerful states such as the United States, the United Kingdom and Japan. The second party was the Kurdish National Council (KNC), incorporating 12 smaller Syrian-Kurdish parties that formed an alliance under the KNC within the sphere of influence of the KRI President Barzani in 2011.[136]

Barzani used his influence over the KNC to foster an accord between the KNC and the PYD with the aim of establishing a co-operative leadership within Syrian cities that were once the stronghold of the PYD.[137] Turkey perceived the PYD to be a cross-border PKK and was therefore alert to the increasingly powerful PYD in Syria, cautious of the potential for it to become a launch pad for the PKK.[138] Unsurprisingly, Barzani's efforts were agreeable to Turkey, as they attempted to diminish the power and influence of the PYD within Syria.[139] This relationship of unlikely but convenient co-operation across borders between the KRI and the Turkish government for economic and security gain was clear evidence of the sustained development of practicable diplomatic adeptness in the KRI, which continued to grow in that case until the existential threat of IS emerged.

The Road to Referendum

The sudden rise of the IS was a new challenge for the KRI; initially an existential threat that became a perceived opportunity for expansion and potential political consolidation. The first sign of a direct threat to the KRI was in 2013 when Abu Bakr Baghdadi established the IS as a single organisation spanning Syria and Iraq; an organisation comprising ex–al-Nusra Front members from Syria and ex–al-Qaeda fighters from Iraq. In December 2013, Baghdadi exploited simmering sectarian tensions and, with the help of Sunni ex-Hussein loyalists, the IS captured the city of Falluja and established a stronghold in Iraq.[140] In June 2014, the IS launched a major offensive on northern and central Iraq, capturing Mosul, Tikrit and much of the Ninawa Plains. As the IS swept across the north, it approached Kirkuk, where the *peshmerga* stepped in and taken control of the city after the Iraqi Army had fled.[141]

Securing Kirkuk seemed like an immediate strategic victory for the Iraqi Kurds; however, their forces were thinly stretched, and by August the IS had overrun the "totally unprepared"[142] Kurdish forces in Sinjar and Makhmour, and was within 15–20 miles of the capital of Erbil.[143] According to a diplomat who was posted in Erbil at the time, "most of the residents of Erbil were packed and ready to leave".[144] The KRI faced a truly existential threat. On 7 August 2014, US President Barack Obama authorised the official military intervention,[145] including airstrikes that were critical in stopping the IS advance towards Erbil.[146] Within days, allies of the KRI committed to further military support,[147] providing the *peshmerga* with the support that it needed to defend the KRI's territory.

The net effect of the IS insurgency was disastrous for the KRI. The government was already in a volatile fiscal position after Baghdad ceased to provide it with 17 per cent of the federal budget from February 2014 in retaliation for the KRI's unilateral agreements with international oil companies and oil export cooperation with Turkey.[148] These federal revenues were approximately 80 per cent of the KRI's budget.[149] The IS insurrection led to the capitulation of the private sector; some observers claim that over 5,000 investment projects were cancelled by September 2015.[150] By that time, the KRI had accumulated over $3 billion in new debt.[151] Fieldwork interviewees in September 2015 suggested that the oversized public service and the *peshmerga* had not been paid for three months.[152] Meanwhile, the KRI had experienced a 28 per cent population increase by February of 2015 due to the 1.5 million Syrian refugees and Iraqi internally displaced persons (IDPs) that were sheltering there.[153] The only positive development for the KRI was the fact that it had opportunistically taken control of Kirkuk and other disputed territories.

The significance of Kirkuk for the KRI needs to be emphatically underscored, as the representational importance of the city to the Iraqi Kurdish cause is deeper than the economic value of the potential hydrocarbon revenue. Kirkuk has great symbolic power stemming from its historical significance; some observers go so far as to claim that the drawcard of Kirkuk was one of the main reasons that the KRI was involved in rebuilding the Iraqi state after the 2003 invasion and not trying instead to seek independence.[154] The Iraqi Kurdish nationalist movement of the twentieth century laid claim to Kirkuk as part of Kurdistan, and this claim dates back to the shifting territorial boundaries in the wake of the First World War. From the end of the Ottoman Empire up until the 1960s, Kirkuk was administered by Kurds, Turcoman and Arabs; notably, Arabs were still a minority in the city at this time.[155] The heart of the Kirkuk issue was established with the Ba'thists' Arabisation campaign from 1968 onwards, which attempted to consolidate the Iraqi identity as an Arab identity. After the nationalisation of the petroleum industry in 1972, the Arabisation campaign increasingly focussed on Kirkuk.[156] The demography of northern Iraq shifted drastically as Turcoman and Kurds were forcibly removed and as Arabs from southern and central Iraq were relocated to Kirkuk. By the late 1980s, the Arabisation campaign had succeeded in establishing an Arab majority province, a fact that Natali argues galvanised the ethnicisation of Kurdish nationalism.[157] Ever since, Kirkuk has been a central focus for the Iraqi Kurds, sometimes even mawkishly referred to as the "Kurdish Jerusalem".[158] A key inclusion in the 2005 Iraqi Constitution is Article 140, which states that the Iraqi government has a responsibility to "perform a census and conclude through referendum in Kirkuk and other disputed territories the will of their citizens", the deadline for which was 31 December 2007.[159]

The management of Kirkuk and the disputed territories is central to understanding Iraqi Kurdish politics in the IS and post-IS years. While the KRG has been very vocal about the need to enact Article 140, a foreign diplomat based in Erbil stressed to me the importance of timing for this vote, suggesting that Barzani and the KDP may in fact have been in favour of the delay: "Democracy is all about who votes for you. Kirkuk is a strong PUK vote. The PUK *peshmerga* took Kirkuk and they still hold Kirkuk. Barzani is worried that if Kirkukis were allowed to vote, they would vote PUK".[160] Several sources claimed that similar inter-Kurdish politics were being played out in the disputed territories. The KDP and PUK were very strategic in who took control of which territories, with the central goal of shoring up their respective bases of political support.

President Masoud Barzani was quick to threaten an independence referendum soon after the IS battles began. Iraqi politics is full of grand rhetoric, and given the unstable security situation at the time, it was interpreted by many to be nothing more than just rhetoric. As the IS battles continued, and threats of an independence referendum also continued, the threat was widely perceived as a performative political manoeuvre lacking any substance beyond trying to strengthen the KRI's bargaining position with Baghdad.

As the impacts of the war against the IS intensified, domestic politics in the KRI became increasingly fraught. The general populace was concerned for the security and economic prospects of the region, with IS still approximately only 40 miles away and close to 1 million civil servant salaries not having been paid for months. In October 2015, protests broke out in Sulaimaniyah and local KDP offices were attacked. In retaliation, Prime Minister Nechirvan Barzani expelled five members of the Goran Party from his cabinet. As the tension between the KDP and the opposition parties grew, a significant issue stoked the fire: President Barzani's term as President had expired. Barzani had already received parliamentary approval to extend his presidential term by two years in 2013 when it was first due to expire, much to the dismay of Goran Party members. The extension ran out on 19 August 2015. The security situation prohibited an easy resolution to the question of Barzani's presidential term; however, much of the populace – whose salaries had not been paid – perceived the lack of a resolution as a betrayal of the democracy that they had been promised since the unification of the KRI.

As the political tensions simmered and began to escalate, so too did Barzani's rhetoric about holding an independence referendum; rhetoric that used to be a threat to Baghdad was increasingly becoming more a performance for his own domestic constituency.[161] The decision to continue to hold the independence referendum, in spite of the widespread international opposition and condemnation, is widely perceived to be an attempt by Barzani to win back much of the favour that he and the KDP had lost. Although the referendum was initially agreed to be non-binding, the KRI chose to include the disputed territories, including Kirkuk, in the vote for independence.

The voters in the KRI voted overwhelmingly in favour of independence, with 92.7 per cent voting 'yes'.[162] However voter turnout was low, and especially low in the regions that have traditionally been PUK strongholds; approximately 50 per cent of voters took part in Sulaimaniyah and 54 per cent voted in Halabja.[163] Such a poor voter turnout in PUK-favouring regions suggests that many of the Iraqi Kurds were not in favour of supporting a move that could strengthen Barzani's leadership and potentially help him to maintain his position as President years after his term had originally expired.

Barzani and KRI supporters of the independence referendum had made a costly miscalculation. In response to the referendum, the GoI retaliated by capturing the oil-rich province of Kirkuk. The referendum was held on 25 September, and by mid-October Kirkuk was in the hands of the Iraqi Army.[164] Recapturing Kirkuk was not only a strong reclamation of territory that sent a clear message to Erbil, it also severely reduced the KRI's economic prospects by reducing its daily oil production and exporting capacity from

160 *The Kurdistan Region of Iraq*

approximately 600,000 barrels per day to 280,000 per day, reducing the KRI's oil export revenue by 55 per cent.[165] The referendum was condemned internationally, including by perceived allies such as the United States.[166] In the wake of the referendum, Barzani declared that he would step down from the role of President. The economic, territorial and reputational costs due to the KRI independence referendum were severe. After years of building a strong role-identity-based international persona, the KRI had developed substantial international goodwill, but its focus on international relations was not accompanied by improving its relationship-building with the GoI, which ultimately had greater influence with, and the broader support of, the international community.

The KRI's Normative Standing

The KRI's Legal Standing

There are two main areas of practice that can be perceived as affecting the legal standing of the KRI: the signing of hydrocarbon agreements and the administration of the disputed territories. While Masoud Barzani may have miscalculated the consequences of conducting the 2017 independence referendum, resulting in territorial losses and deteriorating relationships with Baghdad, Tehran and Ankara, the legal status of the KRI as a federated region of Iraq has remained unchanged since the establishment of the 2005 Iraqi Constitution, as discussed at length in Chapter 1. The right of the KRI to power over "all administrative requirements of the region" is enshrined in the 2005 Iraqi Constitution.[167] The Constitution clearly states that regions have the power to amend the application of federal law on matters "outside the exclusive authority of the federal government",[168] and Article 110 delineates those exclusive authorities:

Article 110 of the Iraqi Constitution

> The federal government shall have the exclusive authorities in the following matters:

FIRST: Formulating foreign policy and diplomatic representation; negotiating, signing and ratifying international treaties and agreements; negotiating, signing, and ratifying debt policies and formulating foreign sovereign economic and trade policy.
SECOND: Formulating and executing national security policy, including establishment and managing armed forces to secure the protection and guarantee the security of Iraq's borders and to defend Iraq.
THIRD: Formulating fiscal and customs policy; issuing currency; regulating commercial policy across regional and governorate boundaries in Iraq;

drawing up the national budget of the State; formulating monetary policy; and establishing and administering a central bank.
FOURTH: Regulating standards, weights and measures.
FIFTH: Regulating issues of citizenship, naturalization, residency, and the right to apply for political asylum.
SIXTH: Regulating policies of broadcast frequencies and mail.
SEVENTH: Drawing up the general and investment budget bill.
EIGHTH: Planning policies relating to water sources from outside Iraq and guaranteeing the rate of water flow to Iraq and its just distribution inside Iraq in accordance with international laws and conventions.
NINTH: General population statistics and census.[169]

Article 110 outlines the GoI's supremacy over the KRI in administering foreign relations. The KRI's capability to conduct diplomacy and manage citizenship is limited, and these limitations show the GoI's legal authority over the KRI's relations with other states and international organisations. As demonstrated in the last section of this chapter, the KRI has been adept at operating within these legal confinements, building a strong international persona through the establishment of Consulate Generals and Commercial Offices, allowing them to maintain strong diplomatic relations without contravening international law.

The KRI's oil agreements have been one of the points of significant international legal contention. The KRG claims that the Iraqi Constitution makes a clear distinction between the right to manage existing oil fields and future oil fields. Managing existing oil fields is the exclusive zone of the federal government (Article 112), while the right to manage future oil fields is that of the regions (Article 115).[170] The KRI has managed to secure the investment of over 50 international oil companies, and, most controversially, with Iran and Turkey.[171] International constitutional law experts disagree on the legality of these contracts, suggesting that the KRI does have some grounds upon which to claim recourse to holding a legal position. While prevalent in the discourse about the KRI, the contention over oil contract legality is not a major sticking point for the KRI's normative standing; genuine legal ambiguity allows for states to pursue their own interests, and this is precisely what the KRI has done.

The KRI's Moral Standing

Moral appeal has been at the core of the KRI's recognition narrative. The moral appeal is built around two key interlinked components: a history of persecution and injustice, and, subsequently, the righteous transition from freedom fighters to an organised democratising de facto state. The history of persecution and injustice is built around two key historical turning points. The first turning point was the perceived betrayal in the establishment of the Treaty of Lausanne in 1923, abolishing the promises of Kurdish autonomy outlined in the Treaty of Sèvres of 1920. The second key turning point was the genocidal al-Anfal campaign that led to the loss of approximately 100,000 Kurdish civilians. The heinous nature of the al-Anfal campaign, and how recent the events were, has led to al-Anfal featuring in much of the contemporary discourse surrounding the Iraqi Kurds. However, interviews with the diplomatic community and international organisations in Erbil confirmed that both of these events are central to the moral appeal of the KRI.

A representative of the European Union Kurdish Friendship Group confirmed that the reason the Group was formed was predominantly for moral reasons.[172] The representative stated that many members of the Group (which at the time had 26 members in the European Parliament) believe that there is a moral debt dating back to the Treaty of Sèvres.[173] At the level of the Group's individual members' states, there have definitely been some trade and commercial opportunities as part of the engagement between the Group and the KRI. The European Parliament has certainly become more involved since the IS crisis, but the members of the European Union Kurdish Friendship Group do not have an "instrumental" motivation; rather, it is much more of an emotional and moral attachment.[174] This is a useful way in which they can have a strong voice and exert influence.[175]

For example, in the lead up the 2017 KRI independence referendum, the Group made an official pitch in the European Parliament in support of the referendum.[176] Charles Tannock, the Chair of the Group and a member of the European Parliament, even penned an opinion piece that was published in *The Telegraph* titled "The History of Kurdistan: Why Britain Owes a Debt to the Kurdish People", in which he declared: "I believe that the Kurds have a strong case for statehood in Iraq, and that the international community should contemplate carefully the result of the 25 September referendum".[177] Similar sentiments were expressed by a US Congressman[178] as well by former diplomats who served in Iraq.[179] Further to this, the type identity of an incipient democracy is also perceived by the KRI to strengthen its moral position because of the transition that it has undertaken from being a militia force in the mountains of northern Iraq, to an election-holding de facto state. While its democracy is imperfect and, from an electoral perspective, wavering, the state-building that has taken place, along with the establishment of a comparatively liberal society for the region, is perceived by the government to strengthen its moral pillar.

The KRI's Constitutional Standing

Contrasting the pre-referendum KRI to the post-referendum KRI illuminates the importance of the constitutional component of a de facto state's legitimation. In the prosperous period after the adoption of the 2005 Iraqi Constitution, the KRI's adoption – albeit gradual and uneven – of liberal democratic practices was crucial to developing strong international relations. They combined this with deft utilisation of the economic capability of the region to advance and exploit the possibilities of their constitutionally enshrined legal autonomy, developing the thriving diplomatic circuit in Erbil that enabled them to fully-realise the role identity of an international actor. While espousing liberal democratic principles, if exaggerating the success of their implementation, the growing formal diplomatic relations were indicative of the strong constitutional standing that the KRI enjoyed in 2013.

When the IS wreaked havoc throughout the north of Iraq, the United States was quick to intervene with airstrikes as soon as Erbil looked to be in genuine danger. In the words of a US diplomat: "There is no way the US will let the KRG fall".[180] In 2015, multiple members of the diplomatic community in Erbil confirmed that President Barzani, whose tenure as President had already been extended once and was due to expire, had crucial international support to remain as President, even though this would contravene the very democratic principles these countries claim to uphold.[181] The federated region had the type identity of an incipient democracy and the role identity of an international actor fighting to protect principles of freedom and human rights, which enabled the diplomatic community to gloss over the expiring presidential term. Two diplomats confirmed that their position in support of Barzani was to prioritise stability; this was war time, and democratic ideals were secondary to stability.

When this support for Barzani is juxtaposed with the strong international reaction against the non-binding 2017 independence referendum, it is logical to surmise that stability was consistently of paramount importance for these prominent members of international society. The KRI is an agent in the international system but is excluded from international society. An adverse reaction from the parent state and neighbouring states was likely to ensure that the result of the referendum was not going to alter the boundaries of any recognised members of international society. It is therefore reasonable to conclude that the overriding objective of international society to maintain order is in fact to maintain order in the international system. Order in the international system is interpreted and prioritised, *ipso facto*, as order in international society.

Conclusion

The KRI's deft political manoeuvring allowed it to develop a truly enabling legal status. The KRI utilised this legal status to great effect, establishing a comprehensive diplomatic presence in the federated region, upon which its role identity of a strong international persona has been alter-casted. Socially enabled more than other de facto states, the KRI has used this platform to ensure that its moral appeal is consistently voiced. Upon these pillars, the KRI developed a robust constitutional and normative standing, developing strong political ties within the region and across the globe. However, the KRI misjudged the support it received from those ties and learnt how rapidly constitutional standing can deteriorate. In the face of an ill-advised strategy with little external support for change, the status quo prevailed to the detriment and cost of the Iraqi Kurds' immediate hopes for independence. The KRI has been enabled by the fact that it can conduct comprehensive relations within the international system. The mere threat, however, of seeking to affect a substantive change in the conditions of legitimate membership evoked severe consequences that demonstrate international society's steadfast commitment to maintaining stability in that very system, and its cautious preference for a maintained and enduring equilibrium in the relationship between de facto states and international society.

Interviews Cited

Senior Diplomat (1), Interview with the author, Erbil, 18 September 2015.

Senior Diplomat (2), Interview with the author, Erbil, 24 September 2015.

Senior UN Official, Interview with the author, Erbil, 23 September 2015.

Falah Mustafah Bakir, KRG Minister and Head of Department of Foreign Relations (now Senior Foreign Policy Advisor), Interview with the author, Erbil, 7 July 2013.

Patrick Geysen, Counsellor in the Liaison Office of the Delegation of the European Union to the Republic of Iraq, Interview with the author, Erbil, 23 September 2015.

Independent Journalist, Interview with the author, Erbil, 1 July 2013.

Mohammed Rafiq, North Region Program Coordinator, Revenue Watch, Interview with the author, Erbil, 28 June 2013.

Dlawer al'Aldeen, Director of the Middle East Research Institute (MERI) and Former Kurdistan Regional Government Minister of Higher Education and Scientific Research, Interview with the author, Erbil, 28 September 2015.

Serwan Baban, KRG Minister of Agriculture and Water Resources (now former Minister), Interview with the author, Erbil, 27 June 2013.

Tawar Rasheed, Property Developer, Interview with the author, Erbil, 7 July 2013.

William Lavender, Assistant to the Minister of European Parliament Charles Tannock, Interview with the author, Erbil, 19 September 2015.

Notes

1 Denise Natali, *The Kurds and the State: Evolving National Identity in Iraq, Turkey and Iran* (Syracuse, NY: Syracuse University Press, 2005) 27–31.
2 Martin van Bruineissen, *Agha, Shaikh and State: The Social and Political Structure of Kurdistan* (London: Zed Books, 1992) 278–280.
3 David McDowall, *A Modern History of the Kurds* (New York: St Martin's Press, 2004) 179.
4 Toby Dodge, *Inventing Iraq: The Failure of Nation Building and a History Denied* (New York: Columbia University Press, 2003) 83–100.
5 *Covenant of the League of Nations,*http://avalon.law.yale.edu/20th_century/leagcov.asp.
6 *Treaty of Alliance between Great Britain and Iraq 1922*, held by The National Archives, Kew, UK.

7 Nevin Cosar and Sevtap Demirci, "The Mosul Question and the Turkish Republic: Before and After the Frontier Treaty, 1926", *Middle Eastern Studies* 42:1 (2006) 127.
8 McDowall, *A Modern History of the Kurds*, 179.
9 Ibid., 302–312.
10 Robert Rossow, Jr, "The Battle of Azerbaijan, 1946," *Middle East Journal* 10:1 (1956) 21.
11 McDowall, *A Modern History of the Kurds*, 296–297.
12 Ibid., 302–312.
13 Ibid., 327–328.
14 Ibid.
15 Ibid.
16 Ibid., 343.
17 Ibid., 359.
18 Sheri Laizer, *Martyrs, Traitors and Patriots: Kurdistan after the Gulf War* (London: Zed Books, 1996) 35.
19 McDowall, *A Modern History of the Kurds*, 371.
20 Ibid.
21 Ibid., 370–373.
22 Michael M. Gunter, "A De Facto Kurdish state in Northern Iraq", *Third World Quarterly* 14:2 (1993) 295.
23 Ibid.
24 McDowall, *A Modern History of the Kurds*, 379.
25 Ibid.
26 Ibid., 381.
27 Falaq al-Din Kakai, "The Kurdish Parliament", in Fran Hazelton, ed., *Iraq Since the Gulf War* (London: Zed Books, 1994) 120–121.
28 Gareth Stansfield, *Iraqi Kurdistan: Political Development and Emergent democracy* (London: Routledge, 2003) 124.
29 Jonathan Randal, "Kurds Declare Election a Draw", *Washington Post*, https://www.washingtonpost.com/archive/politics/1992/05/23/kurds-declare-election-a-draw/a53e9f77-fb64-490a-a519-fca605663a99/?utm_term=.b7af6ba025ae (23 May 1992).
30 Stansfield, *Iraqi Kurdistan*, 129.
31 There were 105 seats in total, 5 of which were reserved for Christians.
32 McDowall, *A Modern History of the Kurds*, 381.
33 Stansfield, *Iraqi Kurdistan*, 123–128.
34 Michael M. Gunter, "The KDP–PUK Conflict in Northern Iraq", *Middle East Journal* 50:2 (1996) 237.
35 Liam Anderson and Gareth Stansfield, *The Future of Iraq: Dictatorship, Democracy, or Division* (New York: Palgrave Macmillan, 2004) 175; Michael M. Gunter, *The Kurdish Predicament in Iraq: A Political Analysis* (New York: St Martin's Press, 1999) 86.
36 Anderson and Stansfield, *The Future of Iraq*, 177.
37 Gareth Stansfield, "Governing Kurdistan: The Strengths of Division", in Brendan O'Leary, John McGarry and Khaled Salih, eds., *The Future of Kurdistan in Iraq* (Philadelphia: University of Pennsylvania Press, 2005) 202–204.
38 Ibid.
39 Ibid., 202–203.
40 Michiel Leezenberg, "Iraqi Kurdistan: Contours of a Post-Civil War Society", *Third World Quarterly* 26:5 (2005) 631.
41 United Nations Security Council, "UNSCR 661", http://www.un.org/docs/scres/1990/scres90.htm (2 August 1990).
42 Stansfield, *Iraqi Kurdistan*, 48.

43　Ibid., 124.
44　Gareth Stansfield, *Iraq* (Cambridge: Polity Press, 2007) 148–149.
45　Stansfield, "Governing Kurdistan: The Strengths of Division", 209.
46　Natali, *The Kurdish Quasi-State: Development and Dependency in Post-Gulf-War Iraq* (Syracuse, NY: Syracuse University Press, 2010), 53.
47　Ibid., 56.
48　Raphael Israeli, *The Iraq War: Hidden Agendas and Babylonian Intrigue* (Brighton, UK: Sussex Academic Press, 2004) 82–83; Anderson and Stansfield, *The Future of Iraq*, 178.
49　Liam Anderson, "Internationalizing Iraq's Constitutional Dilemma", in Robert Lowe and Gareth Stansfield, eds., *The Kurdish Policy Imperative* (London: Royal Institute of International Affairs, 2010) 147.
50　Ibid.
51　Coalition Provisional Authority, "Law of Administration for the State of Iraq for the Transitional Period", http://www.iraqcoalition.org/government/TAL.html (8 March 2004).
52　Ibid.
53　Anderson, "Internationalizing Iraq's Constitutional Dilemma", 149.
54　Iraqi Constitution, http://www.wipo.int/wipolex/en/text.jsp?file_id=230000 (2005).
55　Peter Galbraith, *The End of Iraq: How American Incompetence Created a War without an End* (New York: Simon & Schuster, 2006) 171.
56　Mohammed M.A. Ahmed, *America Unravels Iraq: Kurds, Shiites, and Sunni Arabs Compete for Supremacy* (Costa Mesa, CA: Mazda, 2010) 126.
57　Ibid.
58　Kurdish Regional Government, "Members of the Fifth Cabinet, May 2006 to October 2009", http://www.krg.org/a/d.aspx?s=010000&l=12&a=10938 (7 May 2006).
59　Gareth Stansfield, "From Civil War to Calculated Compromise", in Robert Lowe and Gareth Stansfield, eds., *The Kurdish Policy Imperative* (London: Royal Institute of International Affairs, 2010) 139.
60　Discussed in greater detail in the following section.
61　Masoud Barzani, "Welcome to Kurdistan", in *Kurdistan: Invest in Democracy*, https://www.iraq-businessnews.com/pdf/Kurdistan_Investment_Guide_2011.pdf (April 2011) 12–16.
62　Yaniv Voller, "Kurdish Oil Politics in Iraq: Contested Sovereignty and Unilateralism", *Middle East Policy* 20:1 (2013) 77–79.
63　Falah Mustafah Bakir, KRG Minister and Head of Department of Foreign Relations (now Senior Foreign Policy Advisor), Interview with the author, Erbil, 7 July 2013; Professor Serwan Baban, KRG Minister of Agriculture and Water Resources (now Former Minister), Interview with the author, Erbil, 27 June 2013.
64　Stansfield, *Iraqi Kurdistan*, 152–153.
65　Stansfield, "Governing Kurdistan: The Strengths of Division", 214.
66　Stansfield, "From Civil War to Calculated Compromise", 143
67　Ibid.
68　Denise Natali, *The Kurdish Quasi-State*, 128.
69　Ibid.
70　Ibid., 130.
71　Ibid., 78.
72　Falah Mustafah Bakir, Interview with the author.
73　Mohammed Rafiq, North Region Program Coordinator, Revenue Watch, Interview with the author, Erbil, 28 June 2013; Natali, *The Kurdish Quasi-State*, 116–117.
74　Mohammed Rafiq, Interview with the author; International Center for Not-for-Profit Law, *Law on Non-Governmental Organizations in the Iraqi Kurdistan Region*, http://www.icnl.org/research/library/files/Iraq/krgngolaw-en.pdf.

75 NGO Coordination Committee for Iraq, "KRG NGO Directorate Approves Funding 97 Projects in the KRG", http://www.ncciraq.org/en/ngos/announcements/item/968-krg-ngo-directorate-approves-funding-97-projects-in-the-krg (4 June 2013).
76 Independent Journalist, Interview with the author, Erbil, 1 July 2013; Tawar Rasheed, Property Developer, Interview with the author, Erbil, 7 July 2013.
77 Natali, *The Kurdish Quasi-State*, 116.
78 Ibid., 117–119.
79 Nadje Al-Ali and Nicola Pratt, *What Kind of Liberation?* (Berkeley: University of California Press, 2009) 80–85.
80 Human Rights Watch, "Iraqi Kurdistan: Law Banning FGM a Positive Step", http://www.hrw.org/en/news/2011/07/25/iraqi-kurdistan-law-banning-fgm-positive-step (26 July 2011).
81 Natali, *The Kurdish Quasi-State*, 91–92.
82 International Rescue Committee, "Working Together to Address Violence against Women and Girls in Iraqi Kurdistan", *International Rescue Committee*, http://www.rescue.org/sites/default/files/resource-file/IRC%20Addressing%20Violence%20Against%20Women%20in%20Kurdistan%205-12.pdf.
83 Serwan Baban, Interview with the author.
84 Kurdistan Regional Government, "The Kurdistan Parliament", http://www.krg.org/p/p.aspx?l=12&s=030000&p=229.
85 Ibid.
86 Stratfor, "An Increasingly Unstable Iraq", *Stratfor*, http://www.stratfor.com/video/increasingly-unstable-iraq (23 January 2013).
87 Serwan Baban, Interview with the author.
88 Independent Journalist, Interview with the author; Mohammed Rafiq, Interview with the author.
89 Michael M. Gunter, "Iraqi Kurdistan's Two Contrasting Economic Images", *International Journal of Contemporary Iraqi Studies* 6:1 (2012) 90.
90 Ibid.
91 Kurdish Regional Government, *Kurdistan: Invest in Democracy* http://krg.org/uploads/documents/Kurdistan_Investment_Guide_2011.pdf (April 2011).
92 Iraq-Business News, "Erbil Ranked Fifth for Foreign Direct Investment", *Iraq-Business News*, http://www.iraq-businessnews.com/2011/03/16/erbil-ranked-5th-for-foreign-direct-investment/ (16 March 2011).
93 Gunter, "Iraqi Kurdistan's Two Contrasting Economic Images", 92; Michael M. Gunter, "Economic Opportunities in Iraqi Kurdistan", *Middle East Policy* 18:2 (2011) 104–106.
94 Senior Diplomat (2), Interview with the author, Erbil, 24 September 2015.
95 Ibid.
96 Gunter, "Iraqi Kurdistan's Two Contrasting Economic Images", 91.
97 Ibid.
98 Falah Mustafa Bakir, Interview with the author.
99 Serwan Baban, Interview with the author.
100 Gunter, "Iraqi Kurdistan's Two Contrasting Economic Images", 91.
101 Natali, *The Kurdish Quasi-State*, 114–115.
102 Ibid.
103 Gunter, "Economic Opportunities in Iraqi Kurdistan", 104.
104 Ibid.
105 Voller, "Kurdish Oil Politics in Iraq", 77.
106 See Nina Caspersen, *Unrecognized States: The Struggle for Sovereignty in the Modern International System* (Cambridge: Polity, 2012).
107 Serwan Baban, Interview with the author.
108 Falah Mustafa Bakir, Interview with the author.

109 Natali, *The Kurdish Quasi-State*, 25.
110 Professor Dlawer al'Aldeen, Director of MERI, Former Minister of Higher Education and Scientific Research, Interview with the author, Erbil, 28 September 2015.
111 Falah Mustafah Bakir, Interview with the author.
112 Ibid.
113 Ibid.
114 Alexander Wendt, *Social Theory of International Politics* (Cambridge: Cambridge University Press, 1999) 235.
115 Minister Bakir claimed that the KRG never received more than 10.8 per cent of the federal budget, even though it was owed 17 per cent. Falah Mustafah Bakir, Interview with the author.
116 "Article 121", in Iraqi Constitution, http://www.wipo.int/wipolex/en/text.jsp?file_id=230000 (2005).
117 Senior Diplomat (1), Interview with the author, Erbil, 18 September 2015.
118 Senior Diplomat (2), Interview with the author.
119 Senior Diplomat (1), Interview with the author.
120 James Ker-Lindsay, "Engagement without Recognition: The Limits of Diplomatic Interaction with Contested States", *International Affairs* 91:2 (2015) 284.
121 Senior Diplomat (1), Interview with the author.
122 Patrick Geysen, Counsellor in the Liaison Office of the Delegation of the European Union to the Republic of Iraq, Interview with the author, Erbil, 23 September 2015; William Lavender, Representative of Charles Tannock, EU Parliamentarian, Interview with the author, Erbil, 19 September 2015.
123 Patrick Geysen, Interview with the author.
124 Ibid.
125 Senior UN Official, Interview with the author, Erbil, 23 September 2015.
126 The effectiveness of the Department of Foreign Relations was acknowledged by multiple diplomatic sources.
127 Senior Diplomat (1), Interview with the author.
128 Professor Dlawer al'Aldeen, Interview with the author.
129 Ibid.
130 Senior Diplomat (2), Interview with the author.
131 Shwan Zulal, "Survival Strategies and Diplomatic Tools: The Kurdistan Region's Foreign Policy Outlook", *Insight Turkey* 14:3 (2012) 143.
132 Ibid.
133 Robin Mills, "Northern Iraq's Oil Chessboard: Energy, Politics and Power", *Insight Turkey* 15:1 (2013) 59.
134 Orhan Coskun, "Iraqi Kurdistan Poised to Pipe Oil to World via Turkey", *Reuters*, http://www.reuters.com/article/2013/04/17/iraq-kurdistan-oil-idUSL5N0D310920130417 (17 April 2013).
135 Mustafa Akyol, "Erdogan's Kurdish Policies Break from Kurdish Past", *Al-Monitor*, http://www.al-monitor.com/pulse/originals/2013/03/erdogan-kurdish-policy-shift-ocalan-speech.html (March 2013).
136 Gareth Stansfield, "The Unravelling of the Post-First World War State System? The Kurdistan Region of Iraq and the Transformation of the Middle East", *International Affairs* 89:2 (2013) 280.
137 Ben Gittleson, "Syria's Kurds look to Iraqi Minority for Support", *New York Times*http://www.nytimes.com/2013/01/31/world/middleeast/31iht-m31-kurds.html?_r=0 (31 January 2013).
138 International Crisis Group, "Syria's Kurds: A Struggle within a Struggle", *Middle East Report*, http://www.crisisgroup.org/en/regions/middle-east-north-africa/egypt-syria-lebanon/syria/136-syrias-kurds-a-struggle-within-a-struggle.aspx (22 January 2013).

139 Stansfield, "The Unravelling of the Post-First World War State System?", 280.
140 BBC News, "What Is 'Islamic State'?", https://www.bbc.com/news/world-middle-east-29052144(2 December 2015).
141 Tim Arango, et al., "Kurdish Fighters Take Key Oil City as Militants Advance on Baghdad", *New York Times*, https://www.nytimes.com/2014/06/13/world/middleeast/iraq.html (12 June 2014).
142 Najat Ali Saleh in Dexter Filkins, "The Fight of Their Lives", *The New Yorker*, https://www.newyorker.com/magazine/2014/09/29/fight-lives (29 September 2014).
143 Dexter Filkins in "The Fight of Their Lives" claims 15 miles, whereas the diplomatic source the author spoke to in September 2015 claimed 20 miles.
144 Senior Diplomat (2), Interview with the author.
145 Barack Obama, "Statement by the President", Transcript, https://obamawhitehouse.archives.gov/the-press-office/2014/08/07/statement-president (7 August 2014).
146 Senior Diplomat (2), Interview with the author.
147 Reuters, "Britain Ready to Supply Kurds with Arms", *UK Top News*, https://uk.reuters.com/article/uk-iraq-security-britain/britain-ready-to-supply-kurds-with-arms-idUKKBN0GF0L120140815;https://www.bbc.com/news/world-europe-29255711(15 August 2014).
148 BBC News, "Iraq Government Reaches Deal with Kurds on Oil Exports", https://www.bbc.com/news/world-middle-east-30289955 (2 December 2014).
149 Senior Diplomat (2), Interview with the author.
150 Ibid.; Senior UN official, Interview with author.
151 Senior diplomat (2), Interview with the author.
152 Ibid.; Senior Diplomat (1), Interview with the author.
153 Ibid.
154 Aram Rafaat. "Kirkuk: The Central Issue of Kurdish Politics and Iraq's Knotty Problem", *Journal of Muslim Minority Affairs* 28:2 (2008) 252.
155 Denise Natali, "The Kirkuk Conundrum", *Ethnopolitics* 7:4 (2008) 435.
156 Ibid.
157 Natali, *The Kurds and the State*, 48–64.
158 The Economist, "Iraq and the Kurds: The Other Jerusalem", *The Economist*, https://www.economist.com/middle-east-and-africa/2007/04/04/the-other-jerusalem (7 April 2007) 45–46.
159 Iraqi Constitution.
160 Senior Diplomat (2), Interview with the author.
161 Ibid.
162 Bethanen McKernan, "Kurdistan Referendum Results: 93% of Iraqi Kurds Vote for Independence, say reports", *Independent*, https://www.independent.co.uk/news/world/middle-east/kurdistan-referendum-results-vote-yes-iraqi-kurds-independence-iran-syria-a7970241.html (27 September 2017).
163 Nicole Watts, "Most Kurds in Iraq Support Independence: So Why Did Some Voters Stay Home during Last Week's Referendum?", *Washington Post*, https://www.washingtonpost.com/news/monkey-cage/wp/2017/10/06/most-kurds-in-iraq-support-independence-so-why-did-some-voters-stay-home-during-last-weeks-referendum/?utm_term=.c12cfbdd15fa (6 October 2017).
164 Erika Solomon, "Iraqi Forces Seize Control of Kirkuk from Kurdish Fighters", *Financial Times*, https://www.ft.com/content/18abfba0-b1ff-11e7-a398-73d59db9e399 (17 October 2017).
165 Denise Natali, "Iraqi Kurdistan Was Never Ready for Statehood", *Foreign Policy*, https://foreignpolicy.com/2017/10/31/iraqi-kurdistan-was-never-ready-for-statehood/ (31 October 2017).
166 Marina Ottaway, "United States Policy and the Kurdistan Referendum: Compounding the Problem", Wilson Center, https://www.wilsoncenter.org/publica

tion/united-states-policy-and-the-kurdistan-referendum-compounding-the-problem (28 September 2017).
167 Anderson, "Internationalizing Iraq's Constitutional Dilemma", 150.
168 Ibid.
169 Iraqi Constitution.
170 Ibid.
171 Rudaw, "Iran-Erbil Agree on Energy Deals and Boosting Trade", *Rudaw*, http://www.rudaw.net/english/kurdistan/29042014 (29 April 2014).
172 William Lavender, Interview with the author.
173 Ibid.
174 William Lavender, Interview with the author.
175 Patrick Geysen, Interview with the author.
176 Sadar Sattar, "MEPS Support the Independence Referendum Plan in Kurdistan Region", *Basnews*, http://www.basnews.com/index.php/en/news/kurdistan/260716 (24 February 2016).
177 Charles Tannock, "The History of Kurdistan: Why Britain Owes a Debt to the Kurdish People", *The Telegraph*, https://www.telegraph.co.uk/news/world/kurdistan-independence-referendum/history-of-britain-and-the-kurdish-people/ (21 September 2017).
178 Rudaw, "US Congressman Introduces Bill Backing Kurdistan Right to Self-Determination", *Rudaw*, http://www.rudaw.net/english/world/260920171 (26 September 2017).
179 Laurie Mylroie, "Criticism Grows of US Opposition to Kurdistan Referendum", *Kurdistan 24*, http://www.kurdistan24.net/en/Analysis/a6e9f8cb-8ba7-4a56-a34e-7b1074ba35a8 (29 September 2017).
180 Senior US Diplomat, Interview with the author, Erbil, 24 September 2015.
181 Senior Diplomat (1), Interview with the author; Senior Diplomat (2), Interview with the author; Senior UN Official, Interview with the author.

Bibliography

Ahmed, Mohammed M.A. *America Unravels Iraq: Kurds, Shiites, and Sunni Arabs Compete for Supremacy* (Costa Mesa, CA: Mazda, 2010).
Al-Ali, Nadie, and Pratt, Nicola. *What Kind of Liberation?* (Berkeley: University of California Press, 2009).
Al-Din Kakai, Falaq. "The Kurdish Parliament", in Fran Hazelton, ed., *Iraq Since the Gulf War* (London: Zed Books, 1994).
Akyol, Mustafa. "Erdogan's Kurdish Policies Break from Kurdish Past", *Al-Monitor* http://www.al-monitor.com/pulse/originals/2013/03/erdogan-kurdish-policy-shift-ocalan-speech.html (March 2013).
Anderson, Liam. "Internationalizing Iraq's Constitutional Dilemma", in Robert Lowe and Gareth Stansfield, eds., *The Kurdish Policy Imperative* (London: Royal Institute of International Affairs, 2010).
Anderson, Liam, and Stansfield, Gareth. *The Future of Iraq: Dictatorship, Democracy, or Division* (New York: Palgrave Macmillan, 2004).
Arango, Tim, *et al.* "Kurdish Fighters Take Key Oil City as Militants Advance on Bagdad", *New York Times*, https://www.nytimes.com/2014/06/13/world/middleeast/iraq.html (13 June 2014).
BBC News. "Iraq Government Reaches Deal with Kurds on Oil Exports", https://www.bbc.com/news/world-middle-east-30289955 (2 December 2014).

BBC News. "What Is 'Islamic State'?", https://www.bbc.com/news/world-middle-east-29052144 (2 December 2015).
Barzani, Masoud. "Welcome to Kurdistan", in *Kurdistan: Invest in Democracy*, https://www.iraq-businessnews.com/pdf/Kurdistan_Investment_Guide_2011.pdf (April 2011) 12–16. Bruineissen, Martin van. *Agha, Shaikh and State: The Social and Political Structure of Kurdistan* (London: Zed Books, 1992).
Caspersen, Nina. *Unrecognized States: The Struggle for Sovereignty in the Modern International System* (Cambridge: Polity, 2012).
Coalition Provisional Authority. "Law of Administration for the State of Iraq for the Transitional Period", http://www.iraqcoalition.org/government/TAL.html (8 March 2004).
Cosar, Nevin, and Demirci, Sevtap. "The Mosul Question and the Turkish Republic: Before and After the Frontier Treaty, 1926", *Middle Eastern Studies* 42:1 (2006) 123–132.
Coskun, Orhan. "Iraqi Kurdistan Poised to Pipe Oil to World via Turkey", *Reuters*, http://www.reuters.com/article/2013/04/17/iraq-kurdistan-oil-idUSL5N0D310920130417 (17 April 2013).
Covenant of the League of Nations, http://avalon.law.yale.edu/20th_century/leagcov.asp.
Dodge, Toby. *Inventing Iraq: The Failure of Nation Building and a History Denied* (New York: Columbia University Press, 2003).
Economist, The. "Iraq and the Kurds: The Other Jerusalem", *The Economist*, https://www.economist.com/middle-east-and-africa/2007/04/04/the-other-jerusalem (7 April 2007) 45–46.
Filkins, Dexter. "The Fight of Their Lives", *The New Yorker*, https://www.newyorker.com/magazine/2014/09/29/fight-lives (29 September 2014).
Galbraith, Peter. *The End of Iraq: How American Incompetence Created a War without an End* (New York: Simon & Schuster, 2006).
Gittleson, Ben. "Syria's Kurds Look to Iraqi Minority for Support", *New York Times*http://www.nytimes.com/2013/01/31/world/middleeast/31iht-m31-kurds.html?_r=0 (31 January 2013).
Gunter, Michael M. "A De Facto Kurdish State in Northern Iraq", *Third World Quarterly* 14:2 (1993) 259–319.
Gunter, Michael M. "The KDP-PUK Conflict in Northern Iraq", *Middle East Journal* 50:2 (1996) 225–251.
Gunter, Michael M. *The Kurdish Predicament in Iraq: A Political Analysis* (New York: St Martin's Press, 1999).
Gunter, Michael M. "Economic Opportunities in Iraqi Kurdistan", *Middle East Policy* 18:2 (2011) 102–109.
Gunter, Michael M. "Iraqi Kurdistan's Two Contrasting Economic Images", *International Journal of Contemporary Iraqi Studies* 6:1 (2012) 89–95.
Human Rights Watch. "Iraqi Kurdistan: Law Banning FGM a Positive Step", http://www.hrw.org/en/news/2011/07/25/iraqi-kurdistan-law-banning-fgm-positive-step (26 July 2011).
International Center for Not-for-Profit Law. *Law on Non-Governmental Organizations in the Iraqi Kurdistan Region*, http://www.icnl.org/research/library/files/Iraq/krgngolaw-en.pdf.
International Crisis Group. "Syria's Kurds: A Struggle within a Struggle", *Middle East Report No. 136*, http://www.crisisgroup.org/en/regions/middle-east-north-africa/

egypt-syria-lebanon/syria/136-syrias-kurds-a-struggle-within-a-struggle.aspx (22 Jan 2013).
International Rescue Committee. "Working Together to Address Violence against Women and Girls in Iraqi Kurdistan", *International Rescue Committee*, http://www.rescue.org/sites/default/files/resource-file/IRC%20Addressing%20Violence%20Against%20Women%20in%20Kurdistan%205-12.pdf.
Iraq-Business News. "Erbil Ranked Fifth for Foreign Direct Investment", *Iraq-Business News* http://www.iraq-businessnews.com/2011/03/16/erbil-ranked-5th-for-foreign-direct-investment/ (16 March 2011).
Iraqi Constitution. http://www.wipo.int/wipolex/en/text.jsp?file_id=230000 (2005).
Israeli, Raphael. *The Iraq War: Hidden Agendas and Babylonian Intrigue* (Brighton, UK: Sussex Academic Press, 2004).
Ker-Lindsay, James. "Engagement without Recognition: The Limits of Diplomatic Interaction with Contested States", *International Affairs* 91:2 (2015) 1–16.
Kurdistan Regional Government. "The Kurdistan Parliament", http://www.KRI.org/p/p.aspx?l=12&s=030000&r=319&p=229.
Kurdish Regional Government. "Members of the Fifth Cabinet, May 2006 to October 2009", http://www.krg.org/a/d.aspx?s=010000&l=12&a=10938 (7 May 2006).
Kurdish Regional Government. *Kurdistan: Invest in Democracy*, http://krg.org/uploads/documents/Kurdistan_Investment_Guide_2011.pdf (April 2011).
Laizer, Sheri. *Martyrs, Traitors and Patriots: Kurdistan after the Gulf War* (London: Zed Books, 1996).
Leezenberg, Michiel. "Iraqi Kurdistan: Contours of a Post-Civil War Society", *Third World Quarterly* 26:5 (2005) 631–647.
McDowall, David. *A Modern History of the Kurds* (New York: St Martin's Press, 2004).
McKernan, Bethanen. "Kurdistan Referendum Results: 93% of Iraqi Kurds Vote for Independence, Say Reports", *Independent*, https://www.independent.co.uk/news/world/middle-east/kurdistan-referendum-results-vote-yes-iraqi-kurds-independence-iran-syria-a7970241.html (27 September 2017).
Mills, Robin. "Northern Iraq's Oil Chessboard: Energy, Politics and Power", *Insight Turkey* 15:1 (2013) 51–62.
Mylroie, Laurie. "Criticism Grows of US Opposition to Kurdistan Referendum", *Kurdistan 24*, https://www.kurdistan24.net/en/story/12861-Criticism-grows-of-US-opposition-to-Kurdistan-Referendum (29 September 2017).
Natali, Denise. *The Kurds and the State: Evolving National Identity in Iraq, Turkey and Iran* (Syracuse, NY:Syracuse University Press, 2005).
Natali, Denise. "The Kirkuk Conundrum", *Ethnopolitics* 7:4 (2008) 433–443. Natali, Denise. *The Kurdish Quasi-State: Development and Dependency in Post-Gulf War Iraq* (Syracuse, NY:Syracuse University Press, 2010).
Natali, Denise. "Iraqi Kurdistan Was Never Ready for Statehood", *Foreign Policy*, https://foreignpolicy.com/2017/10/31/iraqi-kurdistan-was-never-ready-for-statehood/ (31 October 2017).
NGO Coordination Committee for Iraq. "KRG NGO Directorate Approves Funding 97 Projects in the KRG", http://www.ncciraq.org/en/ngos/announcements/item/968-krg-ngo-directorate-approves-funding-97-projects-in-the-krg (4 June 2013).
Obama, Barack. "Statement by the President", Transcript, https://obamawhitehouse.archives.gov/the-press-office/2014/08/07/statement-president (7 August 2014).
Ottaway, Marina. "*United States Policy and the Kurdistan Referendum: Compounding the Problem*", Wilson Center, https://www.wilsoncenter.org/publication/united-sta

tes-policy-and-the-kurdistan-referendum-compounding-the-problem (28 September 2017).
Rafaat, Aram. "Kirkuk: The Central Issue of Kurdish Politics and Iraq's Knotty Problem", *Journal of Muslim Minority Affairs* 28:2 (2008) 251–266.
Randal, Jonathan. "Kurds Declare Election a Draw", *Washington Post*, https://www.washingtonpost.com/archive/politics/1992/05/23/kurds-declare-election-a-draw/a53e9f77-fb64-490a-a519-fca605663a99/?utm_term=.b7af6ba025ae (23 May 1992).
Reuters. "Britain Ready to Supply Kurds with Arms", *UK Top News*, https://uk.reuters.com/article/uk-iraq-security-britain/britain-ready-to-supply-kurds-with-arms-idUKKBN0GF0L120140815;https://www.bbc.com/news/world-europe-29255711 (15 August 2014).
Rossow, Robert Jr. "*The Battle of Azerbaijan, 1946,*" *Middle East Journal* 10:1 (1956) 17–32.
Rudaw. "Iran-Erbil Agree on Energy Deals and Boosting Trade", *Rudaw*, http://www.rudaw.net/english/kurdistan/29042014 (29 April 2014).
Rudaw. "US Congressman Introduces Bill Backing Kurdistan Right to Self-Determination", *Rudaw*, http://www.rudaw.net/english/world/260920171 (26 September 2017).
Sattar, Sadar. "MEPS Support the Independence Referendum Plan in Kurdistan Region", *Basnews*, http://www.basnews.com/index.php/en/news/kurdistan/260716 (24 February 2016).
Solomon, Erika. "Iraqi Forces Seize Control of Kirkuk from Kurdish Fighters", *Financial Times*, https://www.ft.com/content/18abfba0-b1ff-11e7-a398-73d59db9e399 (17 October 2017).
Stansfield, Gareth. *Iraqi Kurdistan: Political Development and Emergent Democracy* (London: Routledge, 2003).
Stansfield, Gareth. "Governing Kurdistan: The Strengths of Division", in Brendan O'Leary, John McGarry and Khaled Salih, eds, *The Future of Kurdistan in Iraq* (Philadelphia: University of Pennsylvania Press, 2005) 195–218.
Stansfield, Gareth. *Iraq* (Cambridge: Polity Press, 2007).
Stansfield, Gareth. "From Civil War to Calculated Compromise", in Robert Lowe and Gareth Stansfield, eds., *The Kurdish Policy Imperative* (London: Royal Institute of International Affairs, 2010) 130–144.
Stansfield, Gareth. "The Unravelling of the Post-First World War State System? The Kurdistan Region of Iraq and the Transformation of the Middle East," *International Affairs* 89:2 (2013) 259–282.
Stratfor. "An Increasingly Unstable Iraq", *Stratfor*, http://www.stratfor.com/video/increasingly-unstable-iraq (23 January 2013).
Tannock, Charles. "The History of Kurdistan: Why Britain Owes a Debt to the Kurdish People", *The Telegraph*, https://www.telegraph.co.uk/news/world/kurdistan-independence-referendum/history-of-britain-and-the-kurdish-people/ (21 September 2017).
Treaty of Alliance between Great Britain and Iraq of 1922, held by The National Archives, Kew, UK.
United Nation Security Council. "UNSCR 661", http://www.un.org/docs/scres/1990/scres90.htm (2 August 1990).
Voller, Yaniv. "Kurdish Oil Politics in Iraq: Contested Sovereignty and Unilateralism", *Middle East Policy* 20:1 (2013) 68–82.
Watts, Nicole. "Most Kurds in Iraq Support Independence: So Why Did Some Voters Stay Home during Last Week's Referendum?", *Washing Post*, https://www.washing

tonpost.com/news/monkey-cage/wp/2017/10/06/most-kurds-in-iraq-support-indep
endence-so-why-did-some-voters-stay-home-during-last-weeks-referendum/?utm_
term=.c12cfbdd15fa (6 October 2017).

Wendt, Alexander. *Social Theory of International Politics* (Cambridge: Cambridge University Press, 1999).

Zulal, Shwan. "Survival Strategies and Diplomatic Tools: The Kurdistan Region's Foreign Policy Outlook", *Insight Turkey* 14:3 (2012) 141–158.

Conclusion

The gateway to international society, no matter how narrow, distant, fortified or treacherous, remains open for de facto states in the foreseeable future, but it is more of a portcullis than a welcoming arch or a set of swinging doors. De facto states and secessionist entities continue to be drawn to that entrance by the sirens of formal recognition, self-focussed but externally supported economic growth, perceived independence and the legal protections offered by membership. Those excluded entities outside the gates have proven to be much more resilient and persistent than initially predicted, and some have become key players in regional power balances, a fact acknowledged by major international club members. Developing a clearer theoretically based understanding of the conceptual space that such de facto states occupy is a step forwards for both IR theorists and empirical researchers.

A Framework of Normative Standing and Its Implications

The first contribution I hope to have achieved is providing clarity in the conceptualisation of the relationship between de facto states and international society by applying the lens of identity and synthesising existing IR theories to construct a framework of normative standing. De facto states are corporate entities in the international system. Recognised states are accepted and acknowledged members of international society. The international system has ontological priority over international society; the society cannot exist without the system, but, once together, the system and the society coalesce. The distinction between system and society provides the clarification required to better conceptualise the inclusion of recognised states and the exclusion of de facto states.

In this instance, the explanatory utility of the framework was enhanced by examining state identity as a conceptual lens with which to analyse the relationship between recognised states, the international society that they inhabit and the existence and functioning of de facto states in the international system. De facto and de jure states have comparable corporate identities, each of which constitutes its presence as an entity in the international system. Type identities are an illuminating lens because they have social meaning for

DOI: 10.4324/9781003178521-7

recognised and de facto states. Role identities provide explanatory power because they are formed between two or more states in the system, regardless of the divide created by recognition; recognition constitutes a role identity in itself and denotes rights within international society.

Constructing this conceptual framework brings to light de facto statehood as the basis of international, alter-casted role identities. These role identities are crucial to understanding recognition narratives. Recognition itself confers a certain kind of identity, but so too does non-recognition. The social sanctioning of a state as accepted into international society confers rights upon that polity that have meaning in relation to the other constituents of the system. Similarly, an entity that has achieved a degree of autonomy sufficient to be free from external authority but that has not been recognised as a sovereign state is denied those same rights, rights that still only have meaning as a relational function within that social system. De facto statehood is therefore a role identity in the international system.

The significance of this relational identity cannot be understood separately from the corporate apparatus that underpins it. De facto states are not perceived by the international community as non-state actors per se because of their corporate identity. Although members of the international community do not refer to them specifically as de facto states, they act towards them as prospective members of international society, alter-casting this role identity by creating an inter-subjective understanding about their position in the system. The effects of this social conditioning were demonstrated by foreign diplomats in the KRI and by the Head of the KRI's Foreign Relations Department. Powerful members of international society have explicitly stated that the question of Somaliland's recognition lies in the hands of the African Union. Nagorno Karabakh is the one case study where there are no formal diplomatic communications to demonstrate this conditioning, indicating that there is a spectrum of alter-casting that exists. The priority for international order within international society has contributed to the social isolation of Nagorno Karabakh. Isolation sits at one end of de facto states' socialisation spectrum; engagement without recognition is at the other. The empirical exploration of de facto state identity in the case study chapters illustrates this spectrum of socialisation, shining a more powerful light on the processes that contribute to the formation of the "qualitatively different" kinds of statehood that Nina Caspersen espouses.[1]

The role identity of de facto statehood underpins the social conditioning of de facto states in the system; this is the foundation upon which their system-level identity formation is constructed and defines their position on this spectrum. This in turn has great influence on the formation of their recognition narrative. The severe isolation of the NKR and the alter-casted reality spawned a shift in its approach to recognition and its shedding of recognition as a primary imperative. This in turn reinforced the perceived role identity of 'victor' for many years. Conversely, the strong international persona of the KRI strengthened its normative standing, emboldening the leadership to a point where it miscalculated its social currency and held an independence referendum which may have garnered symbolic internal support but which brought swift and resolute negative reaction externally to detrimental effect. Somaliland's position relative to the failed parent state reinforces its perception of the right to self-determination as a normative obligation.

State identity is an insightful lens through which to understand the basis of how de facto states relate to international society, an understanding that is deepened by discerning its constitution. The first order principle of that society is legitimacy. The second order principles form a framework that has been used to interpret the recognition narratives of de facto states and articulate their legitimation. Legitimation is a continuous process that de facto states are engaged with. De facto states do not have membership in international society, so they cannot be deemed to have legitimacy. Normative standing is the extent to which de facto states' behaviours relate to international society's norms of morality, legality and constitutionality, and it is a concept which provides a deeper understanding of the condition of constant legitimation that exists between de facto states and international society. De facto state literature has studied the reasoning that de facto states pursue as justification for their inclusion in international society; normative standing provides a clearer conceptualisation of why these cases have been constructed. Furthermore, it considers how closely the conduct of de facto states aligns with international society's norms of conduct in accordance with the society's second order principles. The application of the morality, legality and constitutionality triad as a framework for interpreting processes that are intrinsic to the relationship between de facto states and international society provides the deeper, more explanatory and defensible account of this relationship which this book has set out to establish.

The framework of normative standing has implications for how the concept of legitimacy is currently used by scholars in the field of de facto state studies. The interpretation of international legitimacy that I have proposed argues against the possibility of de facto states having degrees of legitimacy. Normative standing conceives of de facto states' international relations as conducting practices deemed legitimate within international society, which may increase the normative standing of de facto states but which does not increase their legitimacy within international society, because they are not rightful members. One also cannot say that it increases their legitimacy in the international system, because the system does not constitute a community. An entity with the corporate identity of a state in the system does not have to be socially sanctioned. A state's existence in the system is marked by the formation of the corporate identity that maps to the definition of the de facto state that this book employs. Increased diplomatic relations, therefore, may increase a de facto state's normative standing, but they do not confer upon it a greater or lesser degree of legitimacy.

Developing diplomatic relations clearly facilitates and enables a de facto state more than it empowers it. The social sanctioning of recognised states as legal entities with rights within the society empowers them, so that they can directly contribute to shaping the institutions and norms of international society. Engagement without recognition can enable a de facto state to develop economically or strengthen its defence platform, but it does not allow it to shape the constitution of the society it seeks to join. An empowered state, through membership, contributes to the political and normative contours of the society to which it belongs. This is where, regardless of their respective engagement level or kind, de facto states, without explicit legal recognition, do not have the social status required to influence the constitutionality of their social structure, and therefore do not have international legitimacy.

A complexity that arises from this notion of legitimacy is the difficulty of differentiating the behaviours and practices that are purely instrumental adaptations aimed at gaining recognition or increasing one's normative standing from those which are underpinned by other motivations but align with the normative preferences of international society. The framework of state identity has utility when it comes to such differentiation, as is demonstrated by the unpacking of the NKR's democratic type identity that is in accordance with international society's normative preferences that is also crucial for securing economic means for its survival. Discerning state-identity formation and maintenance can develop deeper, more comprehensive understandings of the motivations behind specific actions, but its limitations must be acknowledged. As a tool of interpretation, it can facilitate richer understandings, but these understandings may not be complete or absolute. While the parallel motivations spurred by NKR's type identity can be identified, this does not mean that it will be discernible if or when one motivation is stronger or dominant over the other. To develop the identity complex further in order to clearly distinguish between competing motivations could be a beneficial area for future research.

State identities and normative standing do not fit together like adjoining pieces of a puzzle; rather, they are interwoven like fibres that form a distinctive fabric. Identity formation can contribute to key components of recognition narratives, yet it can also constitute them. Contrasting the case studies' respective pillars of normative standing has helped to illustrate the complexity of this relationship.

The legal standing of the three case studies differs greatly. Somaliland's claims to have dissolved a union that has legal precedence underpins other core components of its recognition narrative. The KRI's shrewd negotiation of a federal arrangement has enabled it to operate with diplomatic reach while maintaining respect for international legal parameters, which is fundamental to the strong constitutional standing it developed prior to the independence referendum. The KRI's hydrocarbon dealings have caused some legal questions to be raised, but these are questions of genuine legal debate, over which constitutional experts are divided. The NKR's legal claims are based on a framework established in a country that no longer exists, preventing a definitive ruling and contributing to the conditions of stalemate that it currently endures and that have been pivotal in shaping its recognition narrative. Contrasting the legal standing of these case studies brings an important note to light: the importance of having and sustaining a legal argument.

All three case studies have positioned their democratic credentials as forming part of their moral standing. In the NKR, the democratic credentials serve a subjective interest of engaging the diaspora. This type identity has also enabled it to perceive itself as morally superior to Azerbaijan because of the legitimate practice espoused by society, a perspective that has been reinforced by the symbolic recognition of their right to self-determination. While the KRI also perceives its moral standing to be strengthened by its democratic credentials, the KRI's moral appeal is extended to focus on the history of the Kurdish struggle. The moral appeal of both an incipient democracy and historic victim has been a central part of the diplomatic platform it has built, from which it has been able to propagate its recognition narrative to an empowered audience. Similarly, Somaliland's type identity as a unique democracy underpins Somaliland's moral appeal to international society for being the prisoner of a failed state. The shared perspective that democratic credentials qualify an entity to some degree of moral obligation from international society highlights a telling discordance between the subjective perspective of a de facto state's moral standing and international society's inter-subjective agreement about that which is deemed to be a moral imperative. Although the 'standards before status' discourse was once prevalent in discussions about the future recognition of states, standards alone have never been a defining criterion of successful recognition.

Where the importance of having a legal argument is especially notable, a crucial insight to be drawn from the morality pillar is the fact that moral arguments *can* and *do* matter. The empirical findings here suggest that the sphere of morality is one in which there will be dissonance between the subjective perspectives of de facto states and the moral reasoning of international society. But the fact that international society can form inter-subjective agreement on moral grounds allows for the contestation over what constitutes moral reasoning and justification. So long as there is a perception that international society will take into account the moral implications of an action, or indeed inaction, even if it is rarely the driving force, it will enable the development of subjective, moral components of de facto states' recognition narratives and the associated perceptions of legitimation.

Constitutionality is inherently the most specific to each case study. For instance, the KRI's current constitutional standing has been severely diminished by the 2017 independence referendum. Over the ten years before the referendum, the KRI's shrewd political manoeuvring and utilisation of its unique legal status gave it diplomatic access to build strong international relations and a subsequent arsenal of political capital. The drastic change in the KRIs constitutional standing illustrates how dynamic this pillar of normative standing can be.

There is one element of constitutional commonality across the three case studies: international society's status quo bias. The three case studies have all claimed to be democratising, albeit at different speeds and with strengths and weaknesses specific to each. Where effective state-building and adopting democratic practices has been perceived as an unofficial pre-requisite for admission into international society, the unintended consequence is an apparent removal of incentives for external actors to resolve the question of recognition. International society's fundamental goal of maintaining order in the international system means that the demonstration of effective, democratic statehood can in fact incentivise members of the international community to default to the status quo. This is creating a dilemma for de facto states. Whereas, prior to the Second Nagorno Karabakh War, the NKR evolved its recognition narrative to accommodate the reality that non-recognition could be a permanent condition, Somaliland's leaders did for a time begin using increasingly aggressive rhetoric. This dilemma could prove to be the catalyst for a paradigmatic shift in the approach that de facto states take towards international society. Time will tell.

The empirical research clearly shows that the legal components are the most clearly understood by de facto states. The amorphous political dynamics that constitutionality encompasses are the hardest to interpret, and, I argue, are where de facto states are likely to have the biggest blind spots. The conceivable humiliation of Somalia as a by-product of Somaliland's quest for independence and the international efforts to stabilise Somalia demonstrate this. The KRG's decision to push ahead with the referendum was a gross miscalculation of international society's investment in the stability of the system. Constitutionality is not clearly defined, it does not have official precedents and, as has been demonstrated, its contours are continuously being refined.

The capability and potential of the theoretical approach that I propose in this book derive from its conceptualisation of great power politics and the normative element of international society in one framework. The creation and fate of de facto states can so rarely be reduced to one or the other. The utility of this framework is that it can be used to discern the principles upon which de facto states relate to international society. This provides a more objective platform upon which to assess their claims; it recognises that the 'ought' is defined by international society at any point in time without giving undue priority to precedents. Precedents, of course, do matter, but stability in the system matters more.

The Stasis of the Relationship

The conceptual contribution of this book provides a foundation upon which many of the more commonly accepted reasons for the stasis in the relationship between de facto states and international society can be better understood. For de facto states which do not have the support of the parent state to secede, recognition is not about proving one is an eligible member; it is about making an argument for why international society should evolve as a community. It is simplistic to suggest that recognition is a matter of international law or great power politics. Legitimacy is the first order principle of international society, and it is composed of both legitimate membership and legitimate conduct. A change in the rules that govern legitimate membership in a society is a change in the constitution of the society itself. Once a de facto state is deemed to be ineligible based on the current rules, to then admit it as a legitimate member would require the acceptance of a previously unacceptable trait. For de facto states in the current era, this trait is the lack of agreement from the parent state. While de facto states can make compelling arguments based on an array of different grounds as to why they are not breaking this rule, or why there should be an exception to the rule, once deemed to be ineligible in the eyes of international society they are arguing for international society itself to evolve.

De facto states do not desire sovereign statehood for the sake of sovereign statehood. There is the legal protection of security and access to resources for economic development. But there is more than that contributing to the stasis of the present relationship between these states and international society. The mere existence of NKR has been a significant win for the Armenian people. Every day that it exists, it defies Azerbaijan and is a success for the Armenian nation worldwide. For the KRI, the threat of independence had proven to be a most powerful bargaining tool in its relationship with Baghdad up until the 2017 referendum. Articulating the identity of each de facto state is crucial to understanding this stasis because it helps us avoid reductionist interpretations based on assumed motivations. The NKR's international engagement efforts are as much about serving its role and type identities as they are about international legitimation. Contrary to some assumptions in the literature, until recently Somaliland fundamentally lacked a coherent legitimation strategy. Somaliland's rhetoric had been in response to the discourse within international society, but its strategy had not. The recent push to develop a strategy has been driven by popular demand, a sign of the strength of its democracy. In the KRI, the government has been enabled significantly through international engagement; however, the sense of empowerment that came with their international persona and increased normative standing partially contributed to their miscalculation of the likely reaction of international society to their independence referendum. This is not to suggest that de facto states do not attempt to interpret the discourse in international society. Rather, this suggests that the multi-layered state identity complex contributes to their international engagement strategies, or lack thereof, and internal state-building efforts. Understanding their identity and their interests, illuminated through the fresh conception of their relationship with international society, allows us to more accurately understand the stasis of this relationship, and how that in turn partially constitutes the identity of these socially excluded polities.

One important caveat must be made about generalising findings based on the discussion of corporate identities. This is not a full analysis of the formation of de facto states' corporate identity; rather, this is an analysis of how the key components of their corporate-identity formation shape type and role identities that in turn influence their recognition narratives, and, centrally, their normative standing with international society. There is a wealth of literature on state formation that can further enrich and inform understandings of de facto states, and indeed could prove to be a fruitful avenue for further research.

Where to From Here?

The vastly different relationships between nationalist narratives and state formation are an interesting find in the case study analyses. Nagorno Karabakh became the beating heart of Armenian nationalism so late in the narrative of Armenian nationalism, whereas Kurdish nationalism and the quest for a state have gone hand in hand for almost the entire length of the twentieth century. In Somaliland, the quest for statehood has been tethered to a component of shared identity; however, the idea of a Somalilander identity has been powered by the establishment of the state. There is a breadth of scholarship analysing the relationship between nation and state, but the question that this finding compels is the following: are there any unique elements of the relationship between nation and state in de facto states, as compared to the relationship between nation and state in recognised states? A cognate question is: how have de facto statehood and the condition of non-recognition shaped different nationalisms? Further examination and more detailed analyses of the relationship between structural corporate identity and associated role identities and of the ideological influences that have contributed to the formation of said identity could generate powerful insights that can inform the understanding and development of future de facto states.

Employing my proposed framework in the three case studies has provided insights into how the formation and maintenance of state identity can impact the disposition of a de facto state's populace. In this case, a useful insight that can be observed across all three case studies is the impact of having generations that have grown up in de facto states, whose binding community and state administration is that of their respective de facto state. Now that this generation has grown into young adults, their nationalism is strong and their ability to perceive their de facto state as merely a secessionist entity could be diminished. Statehood is a perceived reality for them. As such, research contrasting the perspectives of different generations, especially comparing those who were adults at the time the de facto state formed with those who were born after its formation, could prove to be useful source of data that scholars can use to understand the likely domestic political trends and trajectories within de facto states.

The proposal that international system and society are coalescing social structures, the former having ontological priority and the latter developing institutions that shape the actions of both entities, is a position congruent with existing theory but one that has not been previously explored in depth.

That precept has been instructive in informing a deeper understanding of the relationship between de facto states and international society. It would be of wider benefit to the field of International Relations, and more specifically to systems theory, constructivism and the English School, to perform a deeper study that analyses the historical relationship of society and system coalescing. Articulating points in history where this relationship has been most dissonant, compared to times when it has been completely congruent, and revealing the drivers behind those disparate contexts would be valuable to all scholars who seek to understand the major systems that are fundamental subjects of International Relations.

Finally, this book has tried to provide a richer conceptual lens with which to deepen our understanding of de facto states. The framework presented in this book to examine the complex enduring situations of de facto states will hopefully help to create enhanced awareness and heightened discussion between more theoretically grounded approaches to International Relations and the rigorous, policy-minded empirical researchers who specialise in de facto states. Bridging these two adjoining spheres of influence will hopefully strengthen the discussion in a manner that enables the knowledge-based analytical world of the scholar, with its explanatory theories and illuminating constructs, to have a greater impact on the action-based pragmatic world of the practitioner in its many forums, be it the rules- and precedent-based chambers of the lawmaker, the political theatres of national leadership or the decision-based and colourful, if not kaleidoscopic, assemblies of the international community.

Note

1 Caspersen, *Unrecognized States: The Struggle for Sovereignty in the Modern International System* (Cambridge: Polity, 2012), 74.

Bibliography

Caspersen, Nina. *Unrecognized States: The Struggle for Sovereignty in the Modern International System* (Cambridge: Polity, 2012).

Index

Abdi, Musa Bihi 123
Abkhazia 8, 38, 65, 96
Abulof, Uriel 39
Africa, non-settler colonies of 36
African Union 126, 176
agent-structure framework 57
Ahmed, Abiy 133
al'Aldeen, Dlawer 156
Alan As 118, 119, 121
al-Shabaab 130
Anglo-Iraq Treaty 143
Aristotle 53
Armenian Revolutionary Federation (Dashnaktsutiun, Dashnaks) 80, 90, 91
Armenian Soviet Socialist Republic (SSR) 83, 84
Asia, non-settler colonies of 36
Ataturk, Mustafa Kemal 82
Australia 96; democratic type identity 30; Legislative Council of the state of New South Wales 98
authority: domestic 21; exclusive 20, 27, 160; external 26, 27, 154, 176; formal 21; GoI's 28, 161; and legitimacy 51; political 51; primacy of 22
autonomy 26, 37, 124, 143–144, 148, 154, 176
Autonomy Law 144
Azerbaijan 9

Baban, Serwan 151, 152
Babayan, Samvel 90
Badinter Arbitration Commission 37
Baghdadi, Abu Bakr 157
Bahcheli, Tozun 3
Bakir, Falah Mustafah 150–152
Balasanyan, Vitaly 92
Balthasar, Dominik 118, 119

Bangladesh, recognition of 37, 38
Barre, Mohammed Siyad 115–117, 121
Barzani, Masoud 156, 158
Barzani, Mullah Mustafa 144
Barzani, Nechirvan 159, 160, 163
Barzani, Sheikh Ahmed 143–144
Barzanji, Sheikh Mahmoud 143–144
Ba'thists, 1968 Arabisation campaign 158
Beetham, David: critique of Weberian empiricism 52; on legitimacy 51–53, 56, 57, 63
Berg, Eiki 22, 66
Bihi, Muse 133
Bishkek Ceasefire 86, 88, 89, 102
Blakkisrud, Helge 92
Bradbury, Mark 115, 118, 122
Broers, Laurence 89
Buchanan, Allen 54–55, 61
Bull, Hedley 25, 32

Caspersen, Nina 3, 4, 23, 38, 39; degrees of legitimacy 64; on sovereignty 21; *Unrecognized States in the International System* 5–6; *Unrecognized States: The Struggle for Sovereignty in the Modern International System* 5
Caucasian Bureau of the Communist Party 83
Centre for Policy Analysis (CPA), in Hargeisa 125
Chayes, Abram 56
Chayes, Antonia 56
China 36
Chorev, Matan 6
civilisation, standard of 36
Clark, Ian 12, 22, 27, 60–62, 66, 67
Claude, Inis 54
Closson, Stacy 6

Cold War, state recognition after 37–39
collective identity 29
Communist and Post-Communist Studies 63
consensus, and legitimacy 53, 63
constitutionality 12, 61–62, 67–68, 103, 130, 177–180
Constitutive Act of the African Union, Article 4(b) 127
constitutive approach to statehood 33, 60
constructivism 10, 11, 13, 183
contested state 7, 23
Cornago, Noé 64
corporate identity 29, 30, 177, 182
Council of NGOs 94
Crawford, James 37

Dashnak Party 90
declaratory approach to statehood 33
de facto states: definition of 4, 22–24; identity, in international system 28–32; in international law 33–34; and international legitimacy 63–66; in international system 24–28; normative standing of 49–69; perceived limbo of 1–2; recognition narratives of 11; resilience of 2, 3, 5, 7, 22, 39; and sovereignty 20–22
Democratic Party of Artsakh 91
Democratic Union Party (PYD) 156, 157
determinacy 67
DNO International 152
domestic sovereignty 21, 22
Dudwick, Nora 84

earned sovereignty 89
Egal, Muhummad Haji Ibrahim 118–122
empirical sovereignty 21
empowerment, and legitimacy 59
English School 2, 4, 11, 13, 22, 68, 183
Eritrea 68
Ethiopia 124, 133
EU *see* European Union (EU)
European Friends of Armenia 96
European Union (EU) 96, 133; Kurdish Friendship Group 162; Liaison Office 155
external authority 26, 27, 154, 176
external legitimacy 63–65
external sovereignty 21, 26

Fabry, Mikulas 34
Fairbanks, Charles 3
fairness, and legitimacy 56

Farmajo, Abdullahi Mohamed 133
foreign direct investment (FDI) 151, 152
'Four-Day War' of 2016 88, 102
France 96
Franck, Thomas: on determinacy 67; on legitimacy 53–57, 61–63
Free Motherland Party 91
Frontier Treaty (1926) 143

Gasparyan, Onik 88
Geertz, Clifford 9
Geldenhuys, Deon 3, 21, 23
genocidal al-Anfal campaign 162
Georgia 38
Germany 96
Ghukasyan, Arkadi 90–92
Godane, Ahmed Abdi 130
Goran Party 150, 152, 159
Gorbachev, Mikhail 84
Greece 36
Gulf War (1990–1991) 145

Hamidian Massacres of 1895–1896 79
Harutyunyan, Arayik 88, 92
Harvey, James 6, 23, 39
Hirsi, Mohamed Saeed 116
historical institutionalism 10
historicisation 11–12
Hitler, Adolf 81
Hoehne, Markus 121
Holsti, Kalevi 20, 22
Hurd, Ian 56–58, 63, 65
Hussein, Saddam 144, 146, 147

identity: collective 29; corporate 29, 30, 58, 177, 182; definition of 28; power of 30; role 29, 148–160; state 58, 177, 178; type 29, 148–153, 178, 179
IICK *see* Independent International Commission on Kosovo (IICK)
Independent International Commission on Kosovo (IICK) 61, 62
institutionalism, constructivist/historical 10
interdependence sovereignty 21
internalisation thesis, Hurd's 57, 58
internal legitimacy 3, 63, 64
internal sovereignty 21, 26
international community 8, 22
international law, de facto states in 33–34
international-legal sovereignty 21, 22
international legitimacy: de facto states and 63–66; definition of 60
International Relations Theory 2

186 *Index*

International Rescue Committee report (2012) 150
international society 7, 22, 25, 56; constitution of 60; de facto states and 2, 7, 11, 22, 24, 26, 68, 78, 102, 103, 149, 164, 175, 177; distinguished from international system 67–68; fundamental principle of 102; interests of 130, 134; legitimacy in 60–61, 63, 66, 177; norms of 27, 67, 69, 95, 101, 103, 149, 178; and politics of recognition 33–39; status quo bias 132, 134, 180; *see also* international system
International Society and the De Facto State (Pegg) 3–5
international system 22; de facto state identity in 28–32; de facto states in 24–28; distinguished from international society 67–68; proposition of status quo bias in 103
Iran–Iraq War 144
Iraq: United Nations Assistance Mission in 155; US-led invasion of 61, 62; US-led reconstruction of 150; *see also* Kurdistan Region of Iraq (KRI)
Iraqi Constitution 2005 152, 162; Article 110 27–28, 160–161; Article 112 161; Article 115 27, 161; Article 121 153; Article 140 158

Jackson, Robert 20, 26, 36
juridical sovereignty 21

Kemal, Mustafa 143
Ker-Lindsay, James 3, 39, 64, 129, 154
Kingston, Paul 3, 23
Klosko, George 51
KNC *see* Kurdish National Council (KNC)
Knudsen, Rita 35
Kocharyan, Robert 87, 90
Kolstø, Pål 3, 23, 63–64, 92, 129
Kosovo: as de facto state 24; population of 61; recognition of 37, 38; UN mission in 37
Krasner, Stephen 21, 22
Kratochwil, Friedrich 30
KRG *see* Kurdistan Regional Government (KRG)
KRI *see* Kurdistan Region of Iraq (KRI)
Kurdish Democratic Party (now Kurdistan Democratic Party, or KDP) 144

Kurdish National Council (KNC) 156
Kurdistan Front 145
Kurdistan Regional Government (KRG) 8, 12, 27–28
Kurdistan Region of Iraq (KRI) 7–9, 11, 12, 20, 28, 96, 142–164; Autonomy Law 144; constitutional standing 162–163; corporate identity, formation of 142–148; foreign direct investment 151, 152; Foreign Relations Department 176; internal sovereignty of 27; legal standing 160–161; liberal democracy 149–151; liberal economy 151–153; moral standing 161–162; nationalism, origins of 142–145; normative standing 160–163, 176–180; road to referendum 157–160; role identities 148–160; role in UN Oil-for-Food Programme 146–147; stasis of the relationship 181; state-building 149–151; threat of independence 181; type identities 148–153; unification 147–148; *see also* Iraq
Kurdistan Workers' Party (PKK) 156
Kuusk, Ene 22, 66

Law on Non-Governmental Organizations in the Iraqi Kurdistan Region (2011) 150
League of Nations 35, 143
Lebanon 96
legality 9, 61
Legislative Council of Somaliland 114
legitimacy 2, 3, 9, 12, 13; authority and 51; Beetham on 51–53, 56, 57, 63; Caspersen on 64; Clark on 60–62, 66, 67; consensus and 53, 63; definition of 49; degrees of 64; empirical–normative divide, bridging 50–52; empowerment and 59; external 63–65; fairness and 56; Franck on 53–57, 61–63; group level *versus* individual level 50; incorporating sources of 52–54; internal 3, 63, 64; international 49–69; obligation and 51; power and 58, 59; procedural 52, 53; relationship with legality 9; Reus-Smit on 56, 58, 63, 65; rightful conduct 59–66; rightful membership 59–66; substantive 52–53
Lewis, Ioan 8
liberal democracy 149–151
liberal economy 151–153
Lipset, Seymour 53

Locke, John 51, 53
Lynch, Dov 3, 23

Mayilian, Masis 92
Ministry of Foreign Affairs and International Cooperation (MFAIC) 125–127, 132, 133
Mogadishu 124
Montevideo Convention on the Rights and Duties of States (1933) 12, 26, 33
morality 12, 54–56, 61, 62, 67, 68, 129, 130, 177, 179
Movement 88 91
Mulaj, Kledja 6
Muse, Iisa 118

Nagorno Karabakh Autonomous Oblast (NKAO) 85
Nagorno Karabakh Republic (NKR) 7, 8, 78–104, 122, 182; Armenian–Azerbaijani enmity, origins of 79–81; civil society, role of 93; conflict in 81–86; constitutional standing 101–103; democratic credentials 89–95; democratic type identity 178–179; international legitimation 99–103; legal standing 100; moral standing 100–101; normative standing 176; para-diplomatic relations 95–99; Second Nagorno Karabakh War 180; stasis of the relationship 181; state-building process 93; symbolic recognition 95–99; victim 86–89; victor 86–89
narrative construction 10
Natali, Denise 149–150
National Charter, Somaliland Republic 119
National Security Service (NSS) 115
NATO see North Atlantic Treaty Organisation (NATO)
negative sovereignty 21
New Zealand: corporate identity 30; type identity 29
NK Helsinki Initiative-92 93
NKR see Nagorno Karabakh Republic (NKR)
North Atlantic Treaty Organisation (NATO) 61

Obama, Barack 157
objective interests 30
OFFP see Oil-for-Food Programme (OFFP)

Ogaden War 124
Oil-for-Food Programme (OFFP) 146–147
ontological status of the state 30–32
OSCE Minsk Group 96, 102
Ottoman Empire 36
Owtram, Francis 6

Pakistan 37, 129
pan-Arab Socialist Ba'th Party 144
Pan-Turkism 79
para-diplomacy: definition of 64; Nagorno Karabakh Republic 95–99
Paris Peace Conference 82
Parsons, Talcott 53
Patriotic Union of Kurdistan (PUK) 144–146, 149, 152, 158
patron state 8
peace-building 117–120
Peace, Unity and Development Party (Kulmiye) 122, 126
Pegg, Scott 39, 63–64, 123–124, 129; de facto state, definition of 23; distinction of internal and external legitimacy 63; *International Society and the De Facto State* 3–5; on sovereignty 21
Phillips, Sarah 123
Piebalgs, Andris 131
pirate states 3
PKK see Kurdistan Workers' Party (PKK)
political obligation 51
positive sovereignty 21
Posner, Daniel 124
Pouliot, Vincent 9
power, and legitimacy 58, 59
PUK see Patriotic Union of Kurdistan (PUK)
PYD see Democratic Union Party (PYD)

Qazi Muhammad 144
quasi-state 7, 20, 23

Rawls, John 51, 53
remedial secession 37
Renders, Marleen 121
Reus-Smit, Christian 25, 32, 39, 56, 58, 63, 65
Richards, Rebecca 121
rightful conduct 59–66
rightful membership 59–66, 68
Riyale Kahin, Dahir 122–124
Robertson, Geoffrey 81
role identity 29, 148–160, 176

Rousseau, Jean-Jacques 53
Russia/USSR 96; Abkhazia and South Ossetia, recognition of and support for 38, 65; *Law on Procedure for Resolving Questions Connected with a Union Republic's Secession from the USSR* 100; Russian Revolution of 1905 79

Sahakyan, Bako 92
Salafism 130
Sargsyan, Serzh 87
Scharpf, Fritz 52
self-determination 1, 11, 39, 67, 89, 98, 142, 148, 178; right to 36–38, 101, 130, 177, 179; Wilsonian re-conceptualisation of 35
Sénégambia Confederation 127
senior diplomat 11
Serbia 37
Sharmake, Abdirashid Ali 115
Silanyo, Ahmed Mohamoud 122, 123
sobjectivism 9, 10
social conditioning 9, 176
social constituency 6, 22, 53, 57, 59, 65
social reality 10, 33
Social Theory of International Politics (Wendt) 31
Somaliland Republic 3, 7–9, 12, 38, 68, 96, 113–134; Centre for Policy Analysis (CPA) 125; civil war 115–116; clans 113–114; constitutional standing 130–133; corporate identity, formation of 113–120; democratic responsiveness strengthening nationalism 124–125; internal legitimacy 64; international legitimation 125–133; legal standing of 126–127; Legislative Council of Somaliland 114; Ministry of Foreign Affairs and International Cooperation (MFAIC) 125–127, 132, 133; moral standing 128–130; National Charter 119; National Security Service (NSS) 115; normative standing 178; peace-building 117–120; Somaliland Council of Elders 114; Somaliland National Electoral Commission 123; Somaliland Youth Development Association (SOYDA) 124–125; Somali National Movement (SNM) 115–118, 121; state-building 117–124; type identity 179; Union of Somalia 114–115, 124, 127

South Ossetia 38, 65, 96
sovereignty 2–4; and de facto states 20–22; domestic 21, 22; earned 89; empirical 21; external 21, 26; interdependence 21; internal 21, 26; international-legal 21, 22; juridical 21; in modern international system, struggle for 5; negative 21; positive 21; Westphalian 21, 22
Sovereignty: Organized Hypocrisy (Krasner) 21, 22
Soviet Union, dissolving of 37; *see also* Russia/USSR
Spears, Ian S. 3, 23
SSR *see* Armenian Soviet Socialist Republic (SSR)
Stansfield, Gareth 5–6, 23, 39, 149
state: agency 10, 57; as cogito 31, 32; contested 7, 23; criteria of 25; identity 58, 177, 178; ontological status of 30–32; patron 8; as persona 32; pirate 3; recognition 34–39; unrecognised 5, 7, 23
state-building 93, 117–124, 149–151
Stepanakert Press Club 93, 94
subjective interests 30, 95
Suchman, Mark 65
Supreme Council of the Azerbaijani SSR 85
system–society distinction 25

Taiwan 24, 96
Talabani, Jalal 144
Tannock, Charles 96, 162
Ter-Petrosyan, Levon 87, 90
Transdniestria 8
Treaty of Batum *see* Treaty of Peace and Friendship between the Imperial Ottoman Government and the Republic of Armenia
Treaty of Kars 83
Treaty of Lausanne (1923) 161–162
Treaty of Peace and Friendship between the Imperial Ottoman Government and the Republic of Armenia 81
Treaty of Sèvres (1920) 142, 143, 162
Tur, Abdirahman Ahmed Ali 117, 119, 121
Turkey 133, 156
type identity 29, 148–153, 178, 179

UAE *see* United Arab Emirates (UAE)
UDUB *see* United People's Democratic Party (UDUB)
UN *see* United Nations (UN)

'Unheard Voice' 93–94
Union of Somalia 114–115, 124, 127
United Arab Emirates (UAE) 132
United Kingdom 29
United Nations (UN) 1, 24, 36–38, 54; General Assembly 38; Oil-for-Food Programme 146–147; Resolution 1514 36
United Nations Security Council (UNSC) 61, 85, 146; Resolution 661 146–147; Resolution 688 145
United People's Democratic Party (UDUB) 122
United States 61, 62, 96, 133, 150
unrecognised state 5, 7, 23
Unrecognized States in the International System (Caspersen and Stansfield) 5–6
Unrecognized States: The Struggle for Sovereignty in the Modern International System (Caspersen) 5
UNSC *see* United Nations Security Council (UNSC)
USSR *see* Russia/USSR
uti possidetis juris, principle of 34–38, 67

Verjee, Aly 123

Walls, Michael 124
Waltz, Kenneth 25
war on terror 62
Weber, Max 50, 57, 59, 67
Wendt, Alexander 10, 26–27; on identity 28, 30; *Social Theory of International Politics* 31; theory of state identity 58
Westphalian sovereignty 21, 22
Wight, Martin 59–60
Williams, John 56
Wilson, Woodrow 35, 142
World Bank 128

Yezidi Genocide 155
Young, Daniel 124
Young Turk Revolution (1908) 80
Yugoslavia, dissolution of 37
Yunis, Habar 118

Zaum, Dominik 26
Zelditch, Morris 50

Taylor & Francis eBooks

www.taylorfrancis.com

A single destination for eBooks from Taylor & Francis with increased functionality and an improved user experience to meet the needs of our customers.

90,000+ eBooks of award-winning academic content in Humanities, Social Science, Science, Technology, Engineering, and Medical written by a global network of editors and authors.

TAYLOR & FRANCIS EBOOKS OFFERS:

- A streamlined experience for our library customers
- A single point of discovery for all of our eBook content
- Improved search and discovery of content at both book and chapter level

REQUEST A FREE TRIAL
support@taylorfrancis.com